Center for Jewish Studies
Harvard Judaic Monographs
6

HARVARD UNIVERSITY
CENTER FOR JEWISH STUDIES

The Jewish Sermon in 14th Century Spain: The Derashot of R. Joshua ibn Shu'eib

by

Carmi Horowitz

Distributed by
HARVARD UNIVERSITY PRESS
Cambridge, Massachusetts and London, England
1989

Library of Congress Cataloging in Publication Data

Horowitz, Carmi, 1943-
The Jewish sermon in 14th century Spain : the derashot of R. Joshua ibn Shu'eib / Carmi Horowitz.
p. cm. -- (Harvard Judaic monographs : 6)
Bibliography: p.
Includes index.
ISBN 0-674-47455-4. ISBN 0-674-47456-2 (pbk.)
1. Ibn Shu'eib, Joshua, 14th cent. Derashot 'al ha-Torah. 2. Jewish sermons--Spain--History and criticism. I. Harvard University. Center for Jewish Studies. II. Title. III. Series.
BM740.I263H67 1989
296.4'2--dc19 88-24601
CIP

Publication of this book was made possible by funds from the William Landau Lecture and Publication Fund and from the Martin D. and Helen B. Schwartz Lecture Fund, Harvard University Center for Jewish Studies.

For the memory of my father

Dr. Edward Horowitz

רבי אפרים בר׳ שמואל יצחק הלוי איש הורוביץ ז״ל

חלוץ השפה העברית, מחנך בחסד עליון

For my mother תבל״א

Silvia Horowitz

שיינדל בת ר׳ אברהם שלמה הכהן ז״ל לבית סולומון

A woman of rare talent, sensitivity and insight

פיה פתחה בחכמה

ותורת חסד על לשונה...

רבות בנות עשו חיל

ואת עלית על כולנה...

תנו לה מפרי ידיה

ויהללוה בשערים מעשיה

TABLE OF CONTENTS

ABBREVIATIONS

Abramson, Introduction	S. Abramson's introduction to the reprint of the Cracow 1573 edition of the *Derashot 'al Hatorah.* Jerusalem 1969
B.R.	*Bereshit Rabbah,* Genesis Rabbah
EJ	*Encyclopedia Judaica*
HUCA	*Hebrew Union College Annual*
JJS	*Journal of Jewish Studies*
K.S.	*Kirya Sefer*
MGWJ	*Monatsschrift für Geschichte und Wissenschaft des Judentums*
M.H.	Isaiah Tishby, *Mishnat Hazohar*, 2 vols. (Jerusalem, 1957-1961)
M.T.	*Mishneh Torah* of Maimonides
PAAJR	*Proceedings of the American Association for Jewish Research*

Proper Names

Rambam	Maimonides, R. Moses b. Maimon
Ramban	Naḥmanides, R. Moses b. Naḥman
Rashba	R. Solomon b. Abraham ibn Adret
Ritva	R. Yom Tov b. Abraham of Seville
Rosh	R. Asher b. Yeḥiel

Note on References

I refer to the *Derashot 'al Hatorah* as the Derashot. A specific sermon is referred to as a *derashah* (pl. *derashot*). This study is based on the Cracow 1573 edition. I have consulted the Constantinople 1523 edition and various manuscripts in order to check problematic readings.

Page references are by folio, column and third of page. Thus 93Cb would refer to folio 93, column 3, middle third of the page. If no lower case letter appears, then the reference is to the entire column or to more than one-third of it. Page references to the Derashot are not prefaced by any title unless necessary for clarity.

References to the Mishnah are by chapter and mishnah; references to the Babylonian Talmud are by tractate, folio and page of the standard edition.

PREFACE

"The new ideas of a handful of men in one generation become the fashionable thoughts of the upper class in the next, and the common beliefs of the common man in the third" (Jacques Barzun). For the study of the dissemination of ideas and their penetration to wider levels of the population, there is perhaps no genre of medieval literature more important than the sermon literature. In it we see the ideas that preachers of different countries and different eras tried to communicate to a popular audience. The *derashah* literature served medieval Jewry as a vehicle for the expression of a variety of ideological stances, through the use of interpretation, exegesis, and associative thought. Also, one can sometimes see in the sermons, if read carefully and interpreted with caution, the outline of the underlying social realities of the preacher's society.

The *derashah* literature is an enormous one, one of the largest branches of Hebrew literature; yet it has been little considered in Jewish historiography. The *Derashot 'al Hatorah* of Rabbi Joshua ibn Shu'eib is an appropriate point of departure for a study of the *derashah* literature. It opens an era of homiletic works highly developed in form and comprehensive in their range and scope. The Derashot are important too for a balanced picture of the Jews in Spain and in particular Navarre, ibn Shu'eib's home, at the beginning of the fourteenth century.

An early version of the present work was written as a doctoral dissertation at Harvard University. During my years of graduate study I incurred a debt of gratitude to teachers, scholars, friends and family, who taught, enlightened, guided, inspired and comforted me.

To Professor Isadore Twersky I owe a deep and profound intellectual and personal debt of gratitude. From the beginning of my stay at Harvard he guided and inspired me and helped me in ways too numerous to count. His genuine concern for my welfare, his generosity and sensitivity greatly eased the inherent difficulties of graduate study, particularly those incurred while raising a family. I have learned much from him as a scholar, as a *talmid ḥakham* and as a person, and he has had a profound effect on my thinking and my life. He has helped me immeasurably both directly and indirectly during the writing of the dissertation and during its transformation into book form. Many ideas, approaches, generalizations and interpretations in this book originated in or are outgrowths of Professor Twersky's lectures, seminars, *shi'urim* or private conversations; I have not always explicitly acknowledged them in their place, so I wish to express at the outset profound gratitude for letting me draw on his vast learning. Of course I take full responsibility for any errors.

To Professor Yosef H. Yerushalmi I am indebted for the guidance he provided in critical thinking and scholarly methods. His sense of history and historical method widened my horizons and sharpened my thinking.

To Rabbi David G. Shapiro I owe a debt of gratitude for much more than a close friendship—he has been a model of humanity, a conscience, a guide and a support.

To my wife Sara, *sheli v'shelakhem, shelah hu*, she literally made my years of graduate study possible by incredible devotion and self-sacrifice. Her love, support and wisdom carried us through many difficult years. This work is truly hers.

My children—Orli, Atara Shira, Hananel Yizhak, Amitai Shlomo, and now Elisha Moshe—loaned their father many hours that belonged to them while I was working on this book. I am deeply grateful.

During my years of study at Harvard University I made my home within the Brookline-Brighton Jewish community. The friendship and hospitality that was extended, and particularly the warmth, inspiration, learning and piety of the Talner Beth Hamidrash, provided support and spiritual nourishment for me and my family.

Early parts of this work were supported by grants from the Memorial Foundation for Jewish Culture and The National Foundation for Jewish Culture. My deep thanks for their support.

Professors Gerald Blidstein, Moshe Idel, Daniel Lasker and Bernard Septimus read all or parts of the manuscript and offered valuable suggestions which proved very useful in my work. My deepest thanks to all of them.

I am grateful to Joseph Davis for his copy-editing work on the typescript and to Carolyn Cross for skillfully preparing the photocopy of this volume for publication.

For the privilege of being the son of Dr. Edward Horowitz ז״ל and תבדל לחיים ארוכים Silvia Horowitz, for being able to grow up in a home rich in Judaism, in *hakhanasat orḥim*, the Hebrew language and Ereẓ Yisrael, a home of warmth and adventure, for that privilege, I dedicate this book to them—to the memory of my father who passed away on 29 Marheshvan 5747 and in honor of my mother—as a very small token of my love and appreciation.*

Jerusalem 1989-5749

*The manuscript was completed and submitted in 1984.

Chapter I

Ibn Shu'eib and Rabbinic Culture in Fourteenth-Century Spain

1. Time and Place

> In the year 5088 [= 1328] God's wrath fell upon His nation. The king of France, who ruled over Navarre, died and the populace arose and decided to destroy, murder and devastate all the Jews in their realm. Then a new king arose over Navarre and the children of those slain complained to him of the oppression, asking him to avenge the spilt blood of our fathers—but to no avail.
>
> In those days I studied for about two years with my master, Rabbi Joshua ibn Shu'eib, may his soul rest in Eden. Then I came to this land [Castile] in '91 [= 1331] and was convinced to stay in Alcale.[1]

This passage, from the autobiographical introduction to *Ẓedah Laderekh* by R. Menaḥem ben Zeraḥ, is the only direct testimony we possess about the life of the preacher R. Joshua ibn Shu'eib. The passage tells us that R. Menaḥem ben Zeraḥ studied with ibn Shu'eib in Navarre from 1329 to 1331. Ibn Shu'eib's career as a preacher started much earlier, however. In his

[1]R. Menaḥem b. Zeraḥ, *Ẓedah Laderekh* (Warsaw 1889), p. 4a. See English translation in Leo Schwarz, *Memoirs of My People* (New York 1963), pp. 37-38. Concerning R. Menaḥem ben Zeraḥ, see Alfredo Freimann, "Menaḥem b. Zeraḥ," *Annuario Di Studi Ebraici* 1 (1934) 147-167. M. Kayserling in *Die Juden in Navarra* (Berlin 1861), p. 84, connects this passage with R. Menaḥem's statement that (!) קבלתי עלי ללמוד תורה לטוליטולה and implies that he studied with ibn Shu'eib in Toledo. The narrative, however, clearly reverts back to the years spent in Navarre and the oath to study in Toledo is fulfilled later. Kayserling says (p. 85) that the ibn Shu'eib family did not arrive in Navarre until late in the fourteenth century. The documents in F. (Y.) Baer, *Die Juden im Christlichen Spanien* (Berlin 1936) show that they were an established and leading family in Tudela in the thirteenth century (see below, n.9).

Derashot 'al Hatorah, his teacher R. Solomon ibn Adret (Rashba) is sometimes referred to as living.[2] This implies that ibn Shu'eib was delivering sermons *(derashot)* before 1310, the approximate date of Rashba's death.[3] We may learn by implication that ibn Shu'eib was a mature scholar before Rashba's death from another source as well. R. Meir b. Solomon ibn Sahula at the end of *Or Haganuz*, his commentary to *Sefer Habahir*, writes that his teachers were R. Joshua ibn Shu'eib and R. Solomon ibn Adret—in that order.[4]

From an examination of ibn Shu'eib's literary sources it can be established, however, that the Derashot themselves were written no earlier than the turn of the fourteenth century. We find many quotations in the Derashot from the Zohar, which was first circulated in the 1280's.[5] Further, there are many homiletical motifs which seem to have their source in the writings of R. Baḥya b. Asher written around 1291.[6] Finally, two passages in the Derashot have

[2]נר״ו (= נטריה רחמנא ופרקיה) appears on pp. 27Ab and 94Db. From the use of ז״ל little can be concluded for later scribes frequently changed the reference.

[3]See J. Perles, *R. Salomo b. Abraham b. Adereth, sein Leben und seine Schriften* (Breslau 1863), p. 57.

[4]*Sefer Habahir*, ed. R. Margaliyot (Jerusalem 1951), p. 94:
ולכן שמתי אני את לבי לגלות כבוד ה׳ כפי מה שקבלתי והבנתי מפי רבותי הרב ר׳ יהושע אבן שועיב ומפי הרב ר׳ שלמה מברצילונה שקבל מהרמב״ן והוא קבל מן ר׳ יצחק סגי נהור בנו של הראב״ד והוא קבל מאליהו הנביא במהרה יבוא אלינו
See below, Ch. V, n.91, where I have noted passages in the Derashot which appear to have been derived from Meir Aldabi's *Shevilei Emunah* (Warsaw 1887). If indeed that is the case, the Derashot were not written until as late as 1360. More probable, however, is a common source for both.

[5]Some of the places where he cites the Zohar, which he calls *Midrash R. Shim'on ben Yoḥai*, are: 11Ba, 18Aa, 33Cb, 60Aa, 67Cb (see Zohar III, 176a), 69Ac, 71Ac (see Zohar III 210a), 73Cb. In addition, some passages in the Derashot which may have their source in the Zohar are: 24Ca (Zohar II 85a), 27Bc (Zohar II 90a), 45Bc (Zohar I 169a).

[6]See E. Gottlieb, *The Kabbalah in the Writings of R. Baḥya ben Asher* (Tel Aviv 1970), p. 148. For parallels which I believe can be shown to have their source in R. Baḥya and borrowed by ibn Shu'eib, compare ibn Shu'eib 26Bb and R. Baḥya Exodus 17:12 (ed. C. Chavel [Jerusalem 1967], p. 155); ibn Shu'eib 36Db and R. Baḥya Lev 23:24 (p. 550); ibn Shu'eib 47Da and R. Baḥya Lev 12:2 (p. 472); ibn Shu'eib 52AB and R. Baḥya Deut 8:10 (p. 300); ibn Shu'eib 69Db and R. Baḥya's Commentary to *Pirkei Avot (Kitvei Rabbenu Baḥya*, ed. C. Chavel [Jerusalem 1969]), p. 594; ibn Shu'eib 89Dc and R. Baḥya, *Kad Hakemaḥ*, s.v. *ẓiẓit*, in *Kitvei Rabbenu Baḥya*, p. 347; and other places as well.

According to Gottlieb (p. 225), Meir ibn Sahula, to whom he attributes the *Be'ur Sodot Haramban* (see below, Ch. VIII, n.7 and Appendix, n.12), did not see R. Baḥya's commentary to the Torah. If, however, ibn Shu'eib is the author of the *Be'ur*, then perhaps it was written before the composition of the Derashot.

their source in *Sefer Hazikaron* by R. Yom Tov b. Abraham of Seville (Ritva).[7] We have no way of dating *Sefer Hazikaron* precisely, but it could hardly have been written before the end of the thirteenth century.[8] Ibn Shu'eib belongs, thus, to the last decades of the thirteenth century and the first decades of the fourteenth.

R. Menaḥem ben Zeraḥ says that he studied with ibn Shu'eib in Navarre, but he does not tell us in which city in Navarre. Most likely, however, it was in Tudela, where the ibn Shu'eib family was a well-established family. A Saul ben R. Samuel ben Shu'eib was one of the signatories to several ordinances *(taḳḳanot)* of the Tudelan community in 1288. One ordinance decreed excommunication for informers; another dealt with taxation; the third established that any ordinance adopted by the Tudelan community must have the approval of representatives of eight prominent families, one of which was the ibn Shu'eib family itself.[9] A Joshua b. Samuel (no family name mentioned) whose signature appears on several *takkanot* in 1305 might be a brother of the above-mentioned Saul and might actually be R. Joshua ibn Shu'eib himself.[10] Below I shall show that certain passages in the Derashot in all probability reflect ibn Shu'eib's response to situations referred to in *takkanot* of Tudela from the beginning of the fourteenth century.[11]

[7]69Ac and *Sefer Hazikaron, parashat Ḥukkat*. See Abramson, Introduction, p. 26. The passage is cited in the name of "one who answers Naḥmanides' questions on Maimonides."

[8]Ritva was born c. 1250. See E. Kupfer, *EJ* 16, pp. 846-848.

[9]Baer, *Die Juden*, pp. 953 and 957. Cf. M. Kayserling, *Die Juden in Navarra*, pp. 56, 84, 85. Concerning the name Shu'eib, one would speculate that it is derived from Shu'eib, a prophet who is mentioned in the Koran. A. Geiger in *Judaism and Islam* (repr. New York 1970), p. 137, suggests that Shu'aib (his transcription) is identical with Jethro. Dr. Hadassah Shy informs me that in *Al-Munjit, Fi A'lam* (Beirut 1973), p. 389, s.v. *shu'aib*, he is identified as a prophet from Midian mentioned in several Suras. Concerning the correct pronunciation, Dr. Shy informs me that, based on the Arabic spelling, the proper pronunciation should have a long diphthong—Shu'*ai*b. However, the spoken language usually contracts the diphthong to something closer to Shu'eb. In the documents in Baer's *Die Juden* (see also below nn.10 and 13), the Hebrew spelling is שעיב, whereas the transcription into Latin letters is Xoep, Enxoep and Enssoeb (see Baer, p. 995, n.2) indicating that the diphthong was contracted in actual use.

[10]Saul's signature is listed as שאול בר׳ שמואל זלה״ה בן שעיב; few of the other signatories have זלה״ה (=זכרנו לחיי העולם הבא) following their father's names—they are usually followed by ז״ל (זכרונו לברכה). Joshua signs his name יהושע בר׳ שמואל זלה״ה; if it is the same Samuel as Saul's father, then the Joshua is Joshua ibn Shu'eib and perhaps the author of the Derashot.

[11]See below, pp. 43-44.

Additional evidence that R. Joshua lived in Tudela is a responsum sent by Rashba to "Tudela for R. Joshua."[12] In light of the fact that ibn Shu'eib possessed substantial halakhic knowledge it is certainly likely that he was called on for decisions in halakhic matters. Furthermore, since he faithfully recorded many of Rashba's customs and decisions, it is likely that he corresponded with him on halakhic matters.[13]

Members of the ibn Shu'eib family remained prominent in Tudela in the fourteenth and fifteenth centuries: a David b. Isaac Shu'eib[14] is mentioned as a *mukkadam* (councilman) in a Tudelan *takkanah* which Y. Baer dates to after 1391[15] and Joel ibn Shu'eib, a fifteenth-century preacher, author of a book of *derashot*, called *'Olat Shabbat*, was likewise a resident of Tudela.[16]

Further on, we shall examine ibn Shu'eib's training and his wide erudition in Hebrew literature. Let us note here his linguistic abilities. As S. Abramson has shown, ibn Shu'eib knew Arabic well enough to provide original

[12]See the heading to responsum 185 in part 3 of Rashba's Responsa (Bnei Brak 1965) טודילה לר׳ יהושע.

[13]Two more possible references to ibn Shu'eib may be added. In Baer, *Die Juden*, p. 273, a "Jucef fillo de Ossua Xoep" in Tudela 1290 is listed. If this Jucef who, to be listed in tax rolls in 1290, one would assume to be at least twenty years old is ibn Shu'eib's son, that would make the father about forty at the time and close to eighty when he taught R. Menaḥem b. Zeraḥ. While this is chronologically possible, it would seem that ben Zeraḥ would have mentioned his teacher's advanced age in his reference.

A second possible allusion to ibn Shu'eib is in an anonymous poem published by Y. Baer in *Minḥah Ledavid* (Jerusalem 1935), p. 200, in which the author says: ועשיתי בזמן שהיה הויכוח לר׳ יהושע עם ר׳ אבנר כי באותו הזמן גדלו הצרות ורבה העבודה בקרב הארץ וכמעט הצר אכלנו לולי ה׳ שהיה לנו. Naftali Hacohen, author of *Shem Hagedolim Alufei Ya'akov* (Haifa 1967) suggests (s.v. R. Joshua ibn Shu'eib) that the ר׳ יהושע is ibn Shu'eib and Abner is Abner of Burgos. Since he is referred to in the poem as ר׳ אבנר, one would imagine that the poem was written and the debate took place prior to his apostacy. While it is a chronological possibility, we have no other evidence that such a debate indeed took place. See below, however, Ch. IV, p. 76. One more geographical fact may be ascertained from a reference of ibn Shu'eib's to a custom in Catalonia which differs from his own. The custom deals with the question as to whether one sits or stands during the recital of the blessing, *leisheiv basukkah* (to sit in the *sukkah*).

[14]Could he be the same R. David b. Shu'eib of Calatayud mentioned in the responsa of Rivash #508?

[15]Baer, *Die Juden*, p. 984.

[16]See the conclusion to R. Joel's commentary to Lamentations (Venice 1611, photocopy Israel 1971), p. 105b: והיתה ההשלמה בחדש אב בשנת חמשת אלפי׳ ומאתים וארבעים וחמשה למנינו בתטילא יע״א. In the Spanish-Jewish diaspora of Saloniki, the name ibn Shu'eib appears occasionally. Dr. Bernard Cooperman brought my attention to I. S. Emmanuel's book, *Maẓevot Saloniki* (Jerusalem 1963) where on p. 27 the tombstone of a young member of the ibn Shu'eib family is noted.

translations of Jewish philosophical texts written in Arabic and to sprinkle the Derashot with Arabic words.[17] He also refers to Latin—or to be precise *leshon romi*[18]—and to the local Navarre vernacular.[19] He was aware of the different Romance languages and the resultant difficulties in communication between local populations.

> The punishment [of the builders of the Tower of Babel] was to separate them by language and country....For originally they had had only one language and a unity of expression. There are nations who have a common language *(safah aḥat)* [Gen 11:1] but do not use the same words *(devarim aḥadim)* [ibid.] as is the case in Spain and France who have the same language *(la'az eḥad)* but do not speak the same way *(einan medabrim lashon eḥad)* for they understand each other only with great difficulty. The same is the case with other nations in Lombardia.[20]

The languages now spoken by the nations of the world, he continues, contain words derived from Hebrew. It is with this presumption that ibn Shu'eib justifies *derashot* in the Talmud which explain the meaning of Hebrew words on the basis of foreign languages. The Sages, he says, knew which Hebrew words had become part of other languages and were able to recover them.[21]

[17]On p. 85Aa he refers to the Arabic original of the *Guide of the Perplexed*. See Abramson, Introduction, pp. 24b, 28b. Arabic words may be found on pp. 16Ba, 22Da, 23Ab, 37Cb, 64Cc, 72Cc, 82Cb, 84Cb, 84Da, 85Bb. On the use of Arabic in fourteenth-century Spain, see A. A. Neuman, *The Jews in Spain* (Philadelphia 1942), vol. II, pp. 11 and 278, n.29; Y. Baer, *Toldot Hayehudim Bisfarad Hanoẓrit*, second edition (Tel Aviv 1959), p. 141. Even a kabbalistic work—by Joseph ibn Waqar—was written in Arabic in the middle of the fourteenth century.

[18]72Cc.

[19]82Cb. On the language of the Derashot see below Ch. II, pp. 32-33.

[20]5Ba. See A. D. Deyermond, *A Literary History of Spain: The Middle Ages* (London 1971), p. 1. See too A. Terry, *A Literary History of Spain—Catalan Literature* (London 1972), p. 4, who says, "Often dialects developed with much in common but were still distinct languages such as Provencal and Catalan."

[21]The notion that Hebrew was the first tongue out of which other tongues developed is old. For immediate medieval precedents see *Cuzari*, II, 68; Ibn Ezra Gen 11:1. For the history of this idea, see the discussion by A. S. Halkin, "The Medieval Attitude Toward Hebrew" in A. Altmann, ed., *Biblical and Other Studies* (Cambridge MA 1963), p. 241; H. A. Wolfson, "The Veracity of Scripture from Philo to Spinoza," in *Religious Philosophy. A Group of Essays* (Cambridge MA 1961); and Louis Ginzberg, *Legends of the Jews*, vol. 5 (Philadelphia 1928), p. 205-206.

2. Rashba and the Tradition of Esotericism

Ibn Shu'eib was a student of R. Solomon b. Abraham ibn Adret, known as Rashba, the most prominent leader of Spanish Jewry during the second half of the thirteenth century and the first decade of the fourteenth. There are almost two dozen references to Rashba in the Derashot[22]—as "my teacher" or "my teacher Rashba"—in all areas: Scriptural exegesis, aggadic interpretation, and halakhic practice. His intellectual debt to Rashba was great, and his opinions and attitudes in many areas can be traced back to his teacher.

The quotations of Rashba's interpretations of aggadic passages include a long verbatim quotation from Rashba's responsa discussing the possibility of prophecy among the non-philosophically trained[23] and quotations from unknown responsa on aggadic themes. For example, ibn Shu'eib quotes Rashba's explanation of the aggadah (Shabbat 9a) that when God wanted to give the Torah to Israel "He held the mountain over their heads like an inverted cask and said: either accept the Torah or you will be buried here."[24] Ibn Shu'eib also quotes from Rashba's commentary to the aggadot[25] and from aggadic interpretations which ibn Shu'eib heard personally. An example of an important idea which he attributes to Rashba but which we do not know from elsewhere is Rashba's explanation of the superiority of the non-rational *mizvot* over the rational. Rashba says that the more hidden the *mizvot* are, the more closely they reflect the essence of the Godhead who is a *Deus Absconditur.*[26] When ibn Shu'eib quotes Rashba in aggadic matters, his opinion is often the only opinion presented[27] or the last and hence the final opinion on the matter. Such is the case, for example, in his explanation of Jacob's blessing to Esau.[28]

Ibn Shu'eib also reports a number of halakhic opinions which he ascribes to Rashba. Once again, the Derashot is our only source for some. Some of the

[22]See Derashot 10Dc, 25Db, 26Cc, 27Ab, 36Da, 40Ac, 40Bc, 40Ca, 40Cb, 41C, 59Bc, 71Ac, 72Ab, 79Bc, 81Ab, 86A, 89Da, 90Ac, 93Cb, 94D.

[23]See Derashot 25Df and the Responsa of Rashba part 4, #234. Some of Rashba's responsa were circulated in book form even during his lifetime. See, e.g., his comment in Responsa part 4, #161.

[24]8A.

[25]See, e.g., Derashot 41C taken from Rashba's *Ḥidushei Aggadot*, ed. S. M. Weinberger (Jerusalem 1966), p. 30. The same text appears in Joseph Perles' *R. Salomon b. Abraham b. Adereth*, Hebrew section, p. 38.

[26]36Da. His source is *Cuzari* II, 48 and III, 7. Cf. R. Baḥya b. Asher, *Kad Hakemaḥ*, s.v. *ẓiẓit*. See E. Gottlieb's discussion in his *The Kabbalah in the Writings*, p. 244, and below Ch. V, nn.53 and 55.

[27]36Da.

[28]10Dc.

opinions are on subjects of dispute, such as his report that Rashba would recite the Rosh Hashanah prayers completely bowed[29] and his description of the manner in which Rashba arranged the *mazot* before the blessing at the Passover seder.[30] His description of how Rashba would shake the *lulav*[31] is confirmed by Rashba's own account in a responsum.[32]

What ibn Shu'eib adds—and this is not found in the responsum—is a kabbalistic reason. The 72 wavings of the *lulav* symbolize the 72-letter name of God, and the 12 wavings in each direction symbolize the 12 zodiacal constellations *(mazalot)* "that sustain the world" and the 12 *gevulei alakhsonim* ("diagonal borders") referred to in *Sefer Yeẓirah.*[33] This kind of explanation is not forthcoming in Rashba's writings, and herein lies one of the most important differences betwen Rashba and his students such as ibn Shu'eib.

Rashba's attitude towards Kabbalah is firmly within the esoteric tradition that preceded Ramban. Like Rabad of Posquières,[34] although not so consistently, Rashba declines public, literary discussion of kabbalistic matters. That he was a kabbalist there is no doubt. His responsa and his commentary to the aggadot contain scattered kabbalistic explanations.[35] In

[29]90Ac. היה נוהג בכל תפלה לשחות. Another student, R. Ḥayyim b. Samuel b. David of Tudela, mentions in his *Ẓeror Haḥayyim* (ed. Samuel Ḥagai Yerushalmi [Jerusalem 1966], p. 22) this same custom without, however, mentioning the Rashba by name. In several cases, ibn Shu'eib advocates his teacher's position in opposition to the school of the Rosh and the Tur. Ibn Shu'eib does occasionally decide against Rashba, either expressly or by omitting his differing opinion, e.g., 40Aa on the purging of vessels (see Rashba, Responsa, vol. I, # 233); again 40Ac on salt in maẓah (see *Ẓeror Haḥayyim*, p. 127).

[30]40Ca. Both blessings should be made while holding both, one whole maẓah and one broken maẓah; so in *Ẓeror Haḥayyim* (p. 28) without attribution. Ibn Shu'eib himself differed with his teacher and held that the first blessing, *Hamoẓi*, should be made on two whole maẓot. The entire halakhic part of the *derashah* for *Shabbat Hagadol* is dotted with references to Rashba's customs.

[31]94Db ומורי נר"ו היה נוהג.

[32]Part I #437 (= 776).

[33]94Db. Concerning the meaning of *gevulei alakhsonim* see *Sefer Yeẓirah*, ch. 5, mishnah 2; *Sefer Habahir* (ed. R. Margoliyot), par. 95; Ramban, Torah Commentary, Deut 33:6 and *Derush Leḥatunah* in *Kitvei Haramban* I (Jerusalem 1964), p. 135.

[34]See I. Twersky, *Rabad of Posquières* (Cambridge MA 1962), pp. 286-300; cf. G. Scholem, *Reshit Hakaballah* (Jerusalem 1948), pp. 70ff.

[35]A substantial portion of the aggadot commented upon (in the printed edition) are the same aggadot that R. Azriel discusses in his commentary to the aggadot, but Rashba usually avoids the kabbalistic explanation. That kabbalists had a tradition of "problematic" aggadot which served as a vehicle for kabbalistic exposition has been pointed out by I. Tishby. See his "Aggadah Vekabbalah Beferushei Ha'agadot shel R.

addition, some of his students, many of whom were kabbalists, quote kabbalistic traditions in their teacher's name.[36] But his kabbalistic comments are few, and they are terse and elusive. Usually the furthest he will go is to say "there is a *sod*, a mystery, in this aggadah"[37] In his responsa he is even more consistent in his avoidance of any kabbalistic explanation. Again there are brief statements such as: "Even though there is a profound meaning for this, I have attempted to present to you as rational an explanation as I can,"[38] or "I already said we have no business with hidden matters but we may examine their plain explanation."[39]

These may sound like the standard disclaimers that we find throughout early kabbalistic literature, but the following is more explicit and more forceful:

> With respect to the other item in your letter, the kabbalistic meaning of the *mizvah* of *Shiluah Haken* [sending away the mother bird; see Deut. 22:6], about which you hinted that there are two approaches in the Torah, you should know that except for certain exceptional individuals it is impossible to reveal the explanation that the kabbalists have given, for two reasons: one due to the deficiency in the teacher and the other due to the student. For those who know the kabbalistic explanation of the *mizvot*[40] have declined in numbers. I would be amazed if there is anyone in this generation who can discuss these matters because of the grandeur of the matter and because of the decline of its knowledge. It is very rare to find people with whom one could discuss these matters because of the difficulty and the subtlety of the material.[41]

Rashba is going beyond the standard disclaimer of kabbalists by claiming an actual decline in contemporary knowledge of kabbalistic matters. His statement is strange because he is writing during the period of intense kabbalistic activity after Naḥmanides, just before and just after the appearance of the Zohar. There were certainly many competent and learned kabbalists, such as R. Joseph ibn Gikitilia, R. Moses de Leon and Todros

Ezra ve R. Azriel Migeronah," *Minḥah Liyehudah* (Jerusalem 1950), pp. 170-174. See now my article in *Da'at* 18 (1987-88) 15-25.

[36]E.g., the author of *Ma'arekhet Ha'elohut* (Mantua 1558) quotes Rashba on pp. 66B and 192B.

[37]E.g., his commentary to Berakhot p. 7a (p. 14); 8a (p. 26).

[38]Responsa, part V #50: ואפ׳ אם יש בענין סוד עמוק, כבר קרבתי לך בענין הזה במה שאפשר אצלי לקרב לפי ק״ד (קוצר דעתי)

[39]Ibid. #55.

[40]חן עדך המצוות.

[41]Ibid. part I #94. A little earlier, R. Isaac Hacohen said something similar. "In our generation there are but a few here and there who have received tradition from ancients...or have been vouchsafed the grace of Divine inspiration" (G. Scholem, *Major Trends in Jewish Mysticism* [New York 1961], p. 120).

Abulafia. The responsum, it seems, should be read as a critique of some contemporary kabbalists who, rather than retain the esotericism of earlier kabbalists, were actively involved in propagating and disseminating kabbalistic studies. It is thus perhaps ironic that his own students such as R. Shem Tov ibn Gaon, R. Baḥya ibn Asher, R. Meir ibn Sahula, and R. Joshua ibn Shu'eib became major disseminators of Kabbalah in the next generation.[42]

3. Halakhah, Kabbalah and Philosophy

The beginning of the fourteenth century was a spiritually intense, intellectually creative, culturally vital moment in the history of the Jews in Spain. The thirteenth century saw the Jews in the Spanish kingdoms achieve a relatively secure political and economic position; culturally, there were significant achievements in halakhah, philosophy, Kabbalah, and Bible study. Some of these advances achieved overwhelming approval and were quickly adopted by the Jews in Spain; others resulted in rifts and polarization but also in continued and perhaps more intense creativity.

In halakhic studies, thirteenth-century Spain inherited the twelfth-century revolution in Talmudic analysis, the method of the Tosafot and Provencal scholars. This method, which emphasized the definition of fundamental Talmudic concepts and which has been characterized as a "critico-conceptual approach"[43] was brought to Spain by Ramban, who studied with students of the Tosafists. He passed the tradition on to his students, such as Rashba, who in turn disseminated and popularized the Tosafistic method. Ramban's Talmud commentary filled the same need for Spanish students of Talmud as the Tosafot did for Ashkenazic students, and his commentary was studied in Spain alongside Rashi's commentary.[44]

Rashba was the outstanding halakhic authority in Spain in the second half of the thirteenth century and the leader of Spanish Jewry. His yeshivah in Barcelona attracted large numbers of students, and through his large following he exerted considerable influence on Jewish life and thought in

[42]One can only speculate as to whether this reticence was affected by the incident surrounding Abraham Abulafia, or the publication of the Zohar. Cf. Moshe Idel, "We Have No Kabbalistic Tradition on This," in I. Twersky, ed., *Rabbi Moses Nahmanides: Explorations in His Religious and Literary Virtuosity* (Cambridge MA 1983), p. 64.

[43]I. Twersky, *Rabad*, pp. 62-63.

[44]See A. Zacuto, *Sefer Yuḥasin Hashalem*, ed. Z. Filipowski (Frankfort 1857), p. 221: ואחר הרמב״ן בארגון ובקשטיליא קורין התלמוד עד הגירוש בישיבות ברש״י וחדושי הרמב״ן ומעט מזעיר מי שהיה קורא תוספות ולא היו נחשבין. R. Isaac Kanfanton, one of the most important halakhic scholars in fifteenth-century Spain, emphasizes the care with which one should study Ramban's Talmudic commentaries. See *Darkhei Hagemara* (Petaḥ Tikvah, n.d.). See now A. David in *Kiryat Sefer* 51 (1976) 324-326, concerning Kanfanton's life and writings.

Spain.[45] His literary activity covered many different areas. His Novellae *(Ḥidushim)* to the Talmud combine commentary with the keen dialectical analytic method of the Tosafot. Rashba, who shows an exquisite sensitivity to all the nuances of Talmudic logic, integrates his analyses of the Talmudic text with discussion of the opinions of Sefardic Rishonim and of the Tosafists. In his *ḥidushim* he is primarily analytic and commentatorial; he was also concerned, however, with the practical side of the halakhah, as evidenced by the special code of law he wrote—*Torat Habayit*, which deals with *issur veheter*, particularly the laws of kashrut. He displays the Maimonidean talent for gathering disparate sources and molding them into a single unit. However, the style of the book is very different from Maimonides' *Mishneh Torah.* Unwilling to eliminate the dicussion of sources, and yet wishing to provide a usable, concise summary of the halakhah, Rashba composed two versions of the *Torat Habayit*: one was *Torat Habayit He'arokh* which integrates a discussion and analysis of the sources with the final decision and a second, *Torat Habayit Hakaẓar*, which provides a crisp summary of the law.

As a *posek*, a rabbinic authority on halakhah, Rashba's responsa are as significant as his code. He authored many thousands of responsa, preserved them, and published them during his lifetime.[46] In Spain, it should be kept in mind, responsa was considered an important genre of halakhic literature. The geographical scope of the inquiries and the types of questions asked both testify to Rashba's prominence. Questions reached him from all parts of Spain and from outside Spain as well, and the topics covered include virtually every area of practical halakhah: marriage, divorce, inheritance taxes, buying

[45]See *Beit Habeḥirah on Avot* by R. Menahem Hame'iri (Jerusalem 1964), p. 57, "הרחיב גבול התלמידים". Meiri was a contemporary of Rashba and corresponded with him. See "Ḥoshen Mishpat," *Tif'eret Seivah (Zunz Jubelschrift*, Berlin 1884), Hebrew section, pp. 142-174. See also David Estillia, "Kiryat Sefer," in A. Neubauer, ed., *Medieval Jewish Chronicles* (Oxford 1887; Jerusalem 1967), vol. II, p. 232. For Rashba's activities and impact as communal leader see Y. Baer, *Toldot*, pp. 167-178 (History, vol. I, pp. 281-305); I. Epstein, *The Responsa of Rabbi Solomon ben Adereth of Barcelona* (repr. New York 1968).

[46]For Sefardic Jews, it should be kept in mind, responsa was considered an important genre of halakhic literature. Prof. Haym Soloveitchik pointed out to me that we have very few responsa from the Rosh before he came to Spain. From after that period we have one of the most outstanding collections of responsa in rabbinic literature. Perhaps it was the Spanish tradition of keeping records and preserving them that encouraged the preservation of responsa by their authors in Spain. See now H. Soloveitchik, *Pawnbroking, A Study in the Interrelationship between Halakhah, Economic Activity and Communal Self-Image* (Hebrew) (Jerusalem 1985), p. 83.

and selling, interest, torts, customs and rituals, as well as theological problems.[47]

Halakhic studies in Spain received a very important infusion of talent and also an important challenge with the arrival of the Rosh, R. Asher b. Yehiel, from Germany in 1304. Already an accomplished and recognized scholar upon his arrival, the Rosh quickly assumed a position of major influence among halakhic scholars in Spain. His *Halakhot*, structured like the *Halakhot* of R. Isaac Alfasi (Rif), brought the accumulated traditions of Ashkenazic Jewry within the Sefardic cultural sphere. His responsa contain many important halakhic essays, and his *Tosafot* are in the style of the classical *Tosafot.*

R. Yom Tov b. Abraham of Seville (Ritva), ibn Shu'eib's contemporary, continued the tradition of Rashba, who was one of his teachers, and successfully adapted and developed his teacher's style of Talmudic commentary. His *ḥidushim* have become classics of the genre. In addition, Ritva wrote short halakhic manuals, such as *Hilkhot Berakhot*, obviously intended for a wider, more popular audience, in which he stated only the practical halakhah, omitting any theoretical discussions.[48]

Many popular works, particularly popular halakhic works, made their appearance at the beginning of the fourteenth century, and many of them came from the school of Rashba. Popular works may be characterized as those whose scope is limited to very specific areas and whose authors take little for granted on the part of the reader. The concise halakhic codes of Ritva mentioned above would fit into this category, as would the *Shulḥan shel Arba'*[49] of R. Baḥya ben Asher, another student of Rashba, who was primarily an exegete and a preacher. *Shulḥan shel Arba'*, which is concerned with the laws connected with meals, is interspersed with midrashic explanations for some of the laws.

Another student of Rashba, R. Ḥayyim b. Samuel b. David, wrote *Ẓeror Haḥayyim*, a code of law concentrating on ritual laws such as prayer, the meal, Sabbath, Festivals, Fast Days, circumcision, and marriage. The style is not so terse as that of Ritva's manuals for the author does quote sources for proof and discusses alternate opinions. He quotes Rashba's opinions on many practical matters, and indeed he considered his work to be an attempt to continue the codificatory work of Rashba. The popular nature of this work is indicated by the rather brief halakhic discussions aimed at practical

[47]For the geographical range of Rashba's responsa see the list in Kayserling, *Die Juden*, pp. 11-12. For the range of topics in his responsa, see, e.g., I. Epstein, *The Responsa of Rabbi Solomon ben Adereth.*

[48]See his *Hilkhot Berakhot* in M. Blau , ed., *Kitvei Haritva* (New York 1963).

[49]The most recent edition is in C. Chavel's *Kitvei Rabbenu Baḥya* (Jerusalem 1969).

conclusions as well as by the occasional fragments of *derashot*, probably derived from his book of *derashot* to which he once alludes.[50]

Ẓedah Laderekh, by ibn Shu'eib's student, R. Menaḥem b. Zeraḥ, is the best example of this type of popular halakhic literature. Written explicitly for Jewish courtiers and diplomats, it goes beyond *Ẓeror Haḥayyim* in scope and in the use of non-halakhic material within the code.[51] In addition to the laws treated by R. Ḥayyim, R. Menaḥem includes *issur veheter*, laws of idolatry, oaths and vows, laws of the *niddah*, mourning, and a concluding essay on eschatology. In addition, *Ẓedah Laderekh* makes a sustained effort to provide an axiological framework of rationales for *miẓvot* in order to inspire their performance.

Sefer Haḥinukh, whose author was another student of Rashba's, is another excellent example of popular halakhic literature. Written "to awaken an awareness of the *miẓvot* each week in the heart of my young son and his friends, to get them accustomed to them and to engrave in their minds pure thought and important matters...," the anonymous Barcelonan author[52] reviews the important details of all 613 commandments and provides reasons and explanations for most of them.

What brought about this spate of popular works? Perhaps it was the contemporary feeling of decline in learning, a common notion frequently encountered in Jewish history and yet reflecting historical reality.[53] From the responsa of two early fourteenth-century personages, Ritva and R. Judah b. Asher of Toledo, we hear complaints of decline in Torah studies. Says Ritva: "Because of our sins, there are many ignoramuses *(amei ha'areẓ)* who do not know the last paragraph or indeed even the first verse of the *Shema.*"[54] Similarly, in a query to R. Judah, the Toledan rabbi is told: "...because of our

[50]R. Hayyim b. Samuel b. David of Tudela, *Ẓeror Haḥayyim*, p. 1 of text. על כן יעצוני כליותי לחבר ספר אחד מהדברים אשר ראיתי מרבותי מהם בכתב מהם בע״פ...; ibid. והדרך השלישי משפטי השבת והמילה מה שלא כתב מורי הרב ר׳ שלמה זלה״ה בספרו עבודת הקודש. For examples of *derashot*, see pp. 85-88, 92-94, 112-114, 118-121, 131-134. On p. 133 he refers to his book of *derashot* ובספר הדרש הארכתי בזה. See Kayserling, *Navarre*, p. 83 and n.3

[51]On the problem of extra-halakhic material in a code of law, see I. Twersky, "The Shulhan 'Aruk," *Judaism* 16 (1967) 153-156 (repr. *The Jewish Expression*, ed. J. Goldin [New York 1970], pp. 330-333).

[52]See *Sefer Haḥinukh*, ed. C. Chavel (4th printing, Jerusalem 1960), introduction, pp. 5-6; Gerson Appel, *A Philosophy of Miẓvot* (New York 1975), pp. 191-193; Y. Tashmu, "Meḥabro Haamiti shel Sefer Hahinukh," *Kiryat Sefer* 55 (1980) 787-790.

[53]See the penetrating analysis of the notion of the decline of learning and its effects on literary creativity in I. Twersky, "Mishneh Torah. Magamato Vetafkido," *Proceedings of the Israel Academy of Sciences and Humanities* 5 (Jerusalem 1972) 8-15.

[54]Ritva, *She'elot Uteshuvot*, ed. J. Kafaḥ (Jerusalem 1959) #97, p. 117.

sins, the Torah has been forgotten and no one understands the Talmud properly."[55]

In other kinds of works as well, we find allusions to this decline. The passage quoted just above from the *Sefer Haḥinukh* reflects this feeling as does the following passage from *Meshal Hakadmoni* by Isaac b. Solomon ibn Sahula.[56] "They said with a bitter soul and lack of wisdom that it is enough to recite the *Shema* in its proper time and say prayers properly, for events have constrained us and pressures have imposed upon us hardships and suffering."[57]

Professor Twersky has suggested also that the rise of popular literature at this time may be a result of a feeling of post-classicism that arises after a period of intense creativity. The beginning of the fourteenth century perhaps is an example of such a post-classical period, following Ramban and Rashba. At such a time, the notion that it is necessary to solidify and popularize, perhaps to flesh out and develop somewhat but not to imitate the previous generation, would motivate the writing of works intended to disseminate their ideas and conclusions. That is not to say that such a period is lacking in creativity. Creativity may be channeled into the form of presentation and exegetical substantiation as well; just as in ibn Shu'eib's Derashot, there is much creativity in the assemblage and molding of the diverse materials of midrash, philosophy, halakhah, and kabbalah into one unit.

Another factor which may have spurred the writing of popular works, particularly halakhic manuals, was the prominence of a courtier class whose knowledge of Judaism was shallow and whose motivation to observe those *halakhot* was weak. As R. Menaḥem b. Zeraḥ puts it:

> ...for I have seen those who walk in the court of our master the king, who shield and protect His nation according to their stature and place. However, because of the unsettled time and because of their desire for luxuries and other unnecessary items, they have declined in their observance of *miẓvot*, particularly those who travel, the servants and those who sit before the king. They abandon prayer and blessings; they ignore the laws of permitted and prohibited food, Shabbat and holidays, laws concerning women and laws of wines, even completely abandoning those laws.[58]

[55]R. Judah b. Asher, *Zikhron Yehudah*, ed. J. Rosenberg (Berlin 1846; repr. Jerusalem 1968) #56, p. 9B.

[56]Dr. Moshe Idel, in a private communication, was somewhat doubtful that Isaac was the brother of R. Meir b. Solomon ibn Sahula since their kabbalistic traditions are different.

[57]*Meshal Hakadmoni*, ed. I. Zamora (Tel Aviv 1953), introduction, p. 5.

[58]See, e.g., *Ẓedah Laderekh*, p. 4a.

It was this situation which motivated R. Menaḥem to write the kind of book which he did.

A final factor that may have motivated these kinds of works was the feeling among philosophers or students of philosophy that the minute study of halakhah was less important than the study of philosophy. Hence there may have been a demand for halakhic handbooks which could serve as a guide to halakhic practice and provide freedom for philosophic study.[59] It is not clear, however, if the authors of these halakhic manuals shared this point of view.

The emergence of Kabbalah onto the scene of literary history is the most novel feature of the cultural history of the thirteenth century. With the inclusion of kabbalistic allusions in Naḥmanides' commentary to the Torah, the veil of esotericism which covered Jewish mystical expression was partially lifted, a trend which intensified with the writing of commentaries on his kabbalistic allusions a generation after his death.[60]

The wealth of kabbalistic literature can be measured not only in the sheer number of kabbalistic works that appeared but in their variety of forms as well. The Zohar, a kabbalistic midrash to the Torah, appeared in the 1280's. Though it is not systematic in its presentation, we find in it a fully developed kabbalistic world of ideas which elaborate explicitly and in great detail upon the world of the *Sefirot*, the *miẓvot*, and the place of the Jew in this world. Its immediate impact was not great—it was not extensively quoted by contemporaries[61]—but its appearance was a factor in the rapid production of new kabbalistic works.

The students of Rashba, for example, do occasionally quote the Zohar, but they concentrated their efforts on examining the Kabbalah of Ramban.[62] *Keter Shem Tov* of R. Shem Tov b. Abraham ibn Gaon,[63] *Be'ur Sodot Haramban* attributed to ibn Shu'eib's student R. Meir ibn Sahula but which

[59]See, e.g., Joseph Caspi's will in I. Abrahams, ed., *Hebrew Ethical Wills*, p. 138.

[60]See G. Scholem, *Kabbalah* (Jerusalem 1974), p. 61, and E. Gottlieb, *Meḥkarim Besifrut Hakabbalah*, ed. J. Hacker (Tel Aviv 1976), pp. 569-670.

[61]The early use and quotation from the Zohar was often anonymous, as is the case with R. Isaac ibn Sahula; sometimes the Zohar is cited as *Midrash R. Shim'on bar Yoḥai*, and it is in this manner that ibn Shu'eib himself cites the Zohar. See above n.5.

[62]See E. Gottlieb, *Meḥkarim*, pp. 569-570.

[63]Printed in the collection *Ma'or Vashemesh* by R. Judah Coriat (Livorno 1839). The book was written during the lifetime of Rashba according to G. Scholem, "Leḥeker Kabbalat R. Yiẓhak Hakohen," p. 46. On R. Shem Tov see G. Scholem, "Seridei Sifro shel R. Shem Tov ibn Gaon 'al Yesodot Torat Hasefirot," *Kiryat Sefer* 8 (1931) 397-408, 534-542; 9 (1932) 126-133; D. S Loewinger, "R. Shem Tov b. Abraham b. Gaon," *Sefunot* 7 (1963) 9-29.

may have been written by ibn Shu'eib himself,[64] and *Me'irat Einayim* of R. Isaac of Acco,[65] all are commentaries to Ramban's *sodot*. R. Baḥya b. Asher's commentary to the Torah is likewise heavily indebted to Ramban, although he also draws heavily on the Zohar and other kabbalists as well.[66]

Systematic manuals of Kabbalah were also composed at this time. *Ma'areket Ha'elohut*, whose (anonymous) author quotes Rashba, deals in a systematic fashion with many of the same ideas we find in the Zohar. Beginning with a non-kabbalistic introduction concerning Providence and the unity of God, he uses *Sefer Yeẓirah* as the basis for a description of the Sefirot and their various names and interrelationships. He includes discussion of basic problems in Kabbalah such as the essential character of *Sefirot*, mystical sins, the problem of evil, and more.[67] R. Joseph ibn Gikitilia's *Sha'arei Orah* is another systematic introduction to Kabbalah, with ten chapters, each discussing one of the ten *Sefirot*, explaining the different symbols for each *Sefirah*. Both of these books may have been accessible to ibn Shu'eib.[68]

Kabbalists produced works of Biblical and aggadic exegesis as well. R. Baḥya b. Asher's commentary to the Torah, which later achieved tremendous popularity, was the first to systematically incorporate kabbalistic explanations in a commentary that included other methods of exegesis. *Peshat*, that is, the simple explanations, and also midrashic and philosophic explanations stand alongside kabbalistic explanations in R. Baḥya's work.

Todros Abulafia's *Oẓar Hakavod*[69] is a kabbalistic commentary to the aggadot in the tradition of earlier kabbalistic aggadic exegesis such as that of R. Ezra and R. Azriel. As we shall discuss in Ch. VII, aggadic exegesis was important for both kabbalists and philosophers, for both saw the aggadah as the bearer of esoteric kabbalistic or philosophic doctrine.[70]

Kabbalistic interpretations of the *miẓvot* was another important area of kabbalistic activity. (We shall discuss the topic at greater length below in Ch.

[64]See above, n.6.

[65]Extant in many manuscripts, e.g., Harvard University MS Heb. #59.

[66]R. Baḥya says בדרך הזה אטיף ואזה מרמזי משה מופת הזמן See the introduction of C. Chavel to his edition of *Rabbenu Baḥya, Be'ur 'al Hatorah*, vol. 1, p. 5. See also the index to *Kitvei R. Baḥya*, s.v. Ramban. Cf. E. Gottlieb, *The Kabbalah in the Writings of R. Baḥya b. Asher*, pp. 167ff., and his critique of Chavel, pp. 214ff.

[67]See now Gottlieb, *Meḥkarim*, pp. 289-343.

[68]See below ch. VIII on his Kabbalah.

[69]Warsaw 1879 (repr. Jerusalem 1970). See now Leon Feldman, "Otzar He-Kabod Completum on Tractate Ketubot by Rabbi Todros ha-Levi Abulafia of Toledo" in *Salo Baron Jubilee Volume* (Jerusalem 1974), Hebrew section, pp. 297-317.

[70]See I. Tishby, "Aggadah Vekaballah Beferushei Ha'agadot," pp. 170-174.

V.) For kabbalists, the *miẓvah* became a profound symbolic act with Divine repercussions. Thirteenth-century kabbalists invested a great deal of effort in trying to understand the secret mysteries of the *miẓvot*. The *Ra'ya Mehemna*, R. Moses de Leon's *Shekel Hakodesh*, R. Menaḥem Recanati in his *Ta'amei Hamiẓvot* and Joseph Meshushan Habirah in his *Sefer Ta'amei Hamiẓvot,*[71] all contributed to the literature on the subject.

By the end of the thirteenth century, Kabbalah had come of age. A look at the map of Spain shows it dotted with cities that were important centers of Kabbalah. Gerona, Barcelona, Toledo, Saragossa, Burgos, Guadalajara and Soria were all connected with major kabbalistic figures.[72] By incorporating Kabbalah into the major genres of Jewish literature, kabbalists demonstrated that it was indigenous to Judaism. Only the *derashah* was not utilized as a medium for kabbalistic expression, and ibn Shu'eib filled this lacuna with skill. Kabbalah, like philosophy before it, had been woven into the texture of Jewish expression.

Jewish philosophy in the thirteenth century stands in the shadow of Maimonidean thought. Whether they agreed with Maimonides or not, all thirteenth-century Jewish philosophers responded in some manner to him. Few systematic works were written in the thirteenth century; much of the work of Jewish philosophers was channeled into works of popularization. R. David Kimḥi incorporated into his Biblical commentary many Maimonidean ideas and doctrines and made extensive use of Maimonides' method of allegorical interpretation.[73] The *derashot* of R. Jacob Anatoli are models of philosophic sermons intended to propagate and encourage a philosophic understanding of Judaism. In the area of commentaries to aggadah, the recently identified and analyzed massive volume of R. Isaac b. Yedaiah[74] illustrates the importance Jewish philosophers attached to aggadah and the extent to which they were eager to read aggadah through their philosophic glasses. Another vehicle for the dissemination of philosophic knowledge was through commentaries to Maimonide' Guide, such as Shem Tov Falaqera's commentary or those of Joseph ibn Caspi and Moses Narboni a few years later.

[71]See A. Altmann, *Kiryat Sefer* 40 (1965), p. 405; M. Meier, "A Critical Edition of Sefer Ta'amei ha-Miẓvot" (unpublished Ph.D. thesis, Brandeis University, 1974).

[72]For Gerona, Burgos, Guadalajara and Soria, see the entries in *EJ*. Rashba lived in Barcelona and many of his students were kabbalists. Toledo was the home of the kabbalist R. Joseph ibn Wakkar, and R. Baḥya ben Asher lived in Saragossa.

[73]See Frank Talmage, "David Kimhi and the Rationalist Tradition," *HUCA* 39 (1968) 177-218.

[74]See Marc Saperstein, *Decoding the Rabbis* (Cambridge MA 1980).

Vigorous advocacy of philosophy appears in popular works such as Falaqera's *Sefer Hamevakesh*. In addition, a great deal of energy was invested in translation and commentary upon Arabic philosophical texts; the works of Alfarabi, Avicenna, Al-Ghazzali and Averroes were translated by Jews into both Hebrew and Latin.

It is this attempt to popularize philosophy which is one of the distinguishing aspects of Jewish philosophical studies in Christian Spain.[75] Maimonides designed the Guide for an intellectual elite and stressed the esoteric character of philosophical knowledge; yet he was eager to have philosophic knowledge spread. Anatoli, Falaqera and Caspi and others fulfilled this desire by spreading their message to as wide an audience as possible, using preaching, exegesis and philosophic-belletristic writing as their major modes of expression.

The blatant exotericism of these students of philosophy had two results. It created a climate of antagonism towards philosophy among those who felt that philosophy was both unnecessary and dangerous. The dangers to which antagonists pointed were many; one of their major objections was to the excessive use of allegory—a method which, they feared, might undermine belief in the historical veracity of Scripture and ultimately the halakhic validity of the entire Torah.

Second, kabbalists could no longer ignore philosophy but had to respond explicitly to the problems it raised. As Joseph Dan has pointed out, they responded in several different ways.[76] There were firm antagonists, such as some of the Gerona kabbalists who opposed philosophy as a method and rejected the presuppositions and most of the results of the various philosophic systems. Others, such as R. Moses of Burgos, rejected philosophy as a method but accepted many of the conclusions of the philosophers. They saw kabbalists as standing on the shoulders of the philosophers, so to speak, and going beyond them.[77] Finally, there were the few who attempted to correlate or synthesize philosophic and kabbalistic concepts, such as R. Isaac ibn Latif

[75]The same is true of Provence; see I. Twersky, "Aspects of the Social and Cultural History of Provencal Jewry," *Journal of World History* 11, no. 1-2 (1968) 195-207.

[76]See his review of G. Vajda, *Recherches sur la philosophie et la kabbale* in *Kiryat Sefer* 39 (1963) 341-344.

[77]See G. Scholem, *Major Trends*, pp. 24 and 354 n.22. The statement is R. Moses of Burgos': הפילוסופים שאתם משבחים חכמתם, דעו באמת כי מקום מעמד ראשם מעמד רגלינו. Scholem is equivocal in interpreting this passage as referring to the aphorism of standing on the shoulders of giants. See Robert K. Merton, *On the Shoulder of Giants* (New York 1965). (I thank R. Jeffrey Woolf for directing me to this source.) See particularly the citation on p. 242 from *Shibbolei Haleket* (Vilna 1886), p. 18a (correct footnote in Merton).

and R. Joseph b. Shalom Ashkenazi.[78] Those in the second category felt comfortable with certain elements of philosophic thought and picked and chose ideas from the world of philosophers at will. It is this second approach which is characteristic of ibn Shu'eib's outlook.

In summary, we see ibn Shu'eib operating in a cultural setting dominated on the one hand by Rashba and his legacy as a halakhist; we shall see below in greater detail how *halakhah* and *minhag* play an important role in the Derashot. Kabbalah as a systematic explanation of Torah and reality also emerged as a dominant force during this time and, along with fellow students of Rashba, ibn Shu'eib became one of the important figures in the spread of Kabbalah in the fourteenth century. On the other hand, the Maimonidean school wielded important influence in thirteenth- and fourteenth-century intellectual life, and the Derashot with its frequent use of Jewish philosophic sources reflects the extent to which philosophic ideas and language had become an essential and integral part of Jewish thought and expression.

[78]Concerning ibn Latif, see S. O. Heller-Wilensky, "Isaac ibn Latif—Philosopher or Kabbalist" in A. Altmann, ed., *Jewish Medieval and Renaissance Studies* (Cambridge MA 1967), pp. 185-223. Concerning Ashkenazi, see G. Vajda, "Un chapitre de l'histoire du conflit, entre la Kabbale et la Philosophie," in *Archives d'Histoire Doctrinale et Littéraire du Moyen Age* (1956) pp. 45-144.

Chapter II

The Derashot

The *Derashot 'al Hatorah* consists of sermons for each *parashah* (weekly reading) and each holiday. In them ibn Shu'eib displays an encyclopaedic knowledge of Talmudic and midrashic works, including many lost midrashim which are unknown to us otherwise;[1] works of Biblical exegesis such as the commentaries of R. Sa'adia Gaon, R. Ḥananel, R. Isaiah of Trani, R. Abraham ibn Ezra, Ramban and R. Baḥya ben Asher (although the latter is not mentioned by name); major works of Jewish philosophy, such as *Ḥovot Halevavot, Cuzari* and *Moreh Nevukhim*; works of Kabbalah, such as *Sefer Yeẓirah* and *Sefer Habahir*, the works of the Gerona kabbalists and Ramban, the Zohar, and works of ibn Shu'eib's contemporaries who explained the *sodot*, the kabbalistic portions of Ramban's commentary to the Torah; halakhic literature, Geonic, Sefardic and Tosafistic; the literature of *minhagim* and their reasons; *piyyutim*; and many passages and epigrams from the wisdom literature of the Middle Ages such as *Musarei Hapilosophim.*[2]

Of particular significance is ibn Shu'eib's extensive use of Kabbalah in the Derashot. His use of Kabbalah is important because the Derashot are the first important examples we have of extensive popularizing of Kabbalah in *derashot*, comparable to Naḥmanides' and R. Baḥya b. Asher's popularization of Kabbalah in their Biblical commentaries. The fact that ibn Shu'eib's *derashot* were committed to writing in their *derashah* form further attests to the desire to make them accessible in a popular style.[3]

[1]See below, p. 185.

[2]On ibn Shu'eib's sources, see S. Abramson's introduction to the reprint of the Derashot.

[3]In addition we may see an attempt to provide *darshanim* with models of *derashot*. It is not for another century that we find explicit directions for delivering sermons in

But to assess better the significance of the Derashot in the history of the *derashah* literature, let us now review that history from its beginnings and through the fourteenth century.

1. The *Derashah* Literature

The sermon or *derashah* was an integral part of Jewish life from antiquity. Rabbinic literature has preserved many early sermons in the two Talmuds and the midrashim, although in forms that have been changed by various kinds of editing, such as abbreviation, or connecting several sermons together, or adding additional material.[4] The focal point of the *derashah* was Scriptural interpretation—the word *darash* means to expound—and the *derashah* served as a vehicle for religious education by explaining Scripture and deriving ethical and moral instruction from the sacred text.

The *derashot* of Rabbinic times vary greatly in their content and style, from short compact homilies to long extended ones in which the Rabbinic disposition towards associative thought is displayed. The Rabbinic sermon often combined halakhic matters, presented in a simple and popular style, with its aggadic content. There are two primary forms of Midrashim—the exegetical and the homiletical.[5] The exegetical, such as *Bereshit Rabbah*, follows the order of the Biblical verses and comments on individual verses or individual phrases. Homiletical midrashim, such as the *Tanḥuma* and the *Pesiktot*, select certain verses of the *parashah* for homiletical development. While both contain material that originated in oral sermons, it is difficult to reconstruct that underlying oral basis.[6]

Although some of the aggadic Midrashim were edited during Talmudic times, and others as late as the twelfth century, most were redacted during the Geonic period. Do these Midrashim reflect the type of *derashah* which was

Hebrew works. *'Ein Hakore* of R. Joseph ibn Shem Tov is the first Hebrew *ars praedicandi*. It has never been printed, except for a small selection in A. Jellinek's *Kuntres Hamafteaḥ* (Wien, 1881), p. 30; but it exists in many manuscripts. R. Joel ibn Shu'eib gives recommendations for preachers in his *'Olat Shabbat* (Venice 1577), p. 1b. (The author may very well have been a descendant of ibn Shu'eib.) In contemporary Christian preaching the *ars praedicandi* was a well-developed branch of literature; see, e.g., James J. Murphy, *Rhetoric in the Middle Ages* (Berkeley 1974) and his *Medieval Rhetoric. A Select Bibliography* (Toronto 1971).

[4]See I. Bettan, *Studies in Jewish Preaching, Middle Ages* (Cincinnati, 1939), p. 46; J. Heinemann, *Derashot Beẓibbur Bitkufat Hatalmud* (Jerusalem 1970), p. 11; A. Shinan, "The Aggadic Literature: Written Tradition and Oral Transmission" (Hebrew), in *Jerusalem Studies in Jewish Folklore* I (1980) 44-60, and the literature referred to there.

[5]J. Elbaum has suggested recently that *Tana Devei Eliyahu* occupies a unique position in this respect and does not fit into either category. See his "Bein Midrash Lesefer Musar" in *Jerusalem Studies in Hebrew Literature* I (1981) 144-154.

[6]See A. Shinan, above n.4.

being delivered at that time as well? One may assume a certain congruence between literary production and oral activity, but it is difficult to establish their actual correlation in the absence of corroborating evidence. There is, however, one book that does certainly reflect one type of Geonic *derashah*—the *She'iltot* of R. Aḥai of Shabḥa. Although the *She'iltot* combine both halakhic and aggadic material, the halakhic is dominant. Scholars have debated, however, whether the primary function of the *She'iltot* was to deal with halakhah or whether there is a purposeful interweaving of halakhah and aggadah.[7]

What the delivery of an actual *derashah* was like in Geonic times is reported by Nathan Habavli of the tenth century. In *Seder Olam Zuta* we have a report of a *derashah* in which he describes the formalities of the oration as well as the charged atmosphere when the sermon was delivered.

> When the Exilarch would preach, he would preach with awe, close his eyes, enwrap himself in his prayer-shawl until it covered his forehead. The congregation would not dare utter a sound at that time. If he should feel that someone was talking, he would open his eyes and a great fear and trembling would fall on the congregation.[8]

The content of the sermon is not reported, but, since it was followed with an halakhic discourse, it must have been aggadic.

In early medieval Europe, there is ample evidence that the *derashah* was an established part of Jewish life throughout the continent,[9] although actual sermons or sermon books do not appear until later. We have reports of sermons and preachers from *Megillat Ahima'az,*[10] R. Baḥya ibn Pakuda,[11] Rashi,[12] Benjamin of Tudela,[13] R. Eleazar of Worms,[14] Judah Alharizi,[15] R.

[7]On the *She'iltot* see the article in *EJ* and the bibliography there. Add to it Abraham Weiss, *Studies in the Literature of the Amora'im* (Hebrew; New York 1962), pp. 154ff.

[8]Ed. A. Neubauer, *Medieval Jewish Chronicles*, II (Oxford 1895; repr. Jerusalem 1967), p. 84. See entry in *EJ* and bibliography there.

[9]See L. Zunz, *Haderashot Beyisrael*, ed. H. Albeck (Jerusalem 1954), ch. 22.

[10]Ed. B. Klar (Jerusalem 1944). See I. Zinberg, *A History of Jewish Literature*, trans. B. Martin, vol. II (Cleveland 1972), p. 164.

[11]*Duties of the Heart*, part 10, ch. 6.

[12]Commentary to *Sotah* 49a.

[13]*Mas'ot Binyamin* (London 1907), p. 11.

[14]*Sefer Rokeaḥ* (Jerusalem 1960), *Hilkhot Shabbat*, ch. 56.

[15]*Taḥkemoni* (Warsaw 1899), *Sha'ar* 24, p. 221; see Dinur, *Yisrael Bagolah* II, 2, p. 287 and notes.

Judah Halevi,[16] Maimonides,[17] R. Moses of Coucy,[18] R. Jonah of Gerona[19] and others.

We have, however, virtually no *derashah* literature per se from the Jews in Moslem Spain. (Joseph Dan has pointed out one exception: the essays of R. Abraham bar Hiyya in his *Higayon Hanefesh* are in reality philosophical *derashot*, adapted from oral sermons that bar Hiyya presumably delivered.)[20] The absence of contemporary Moslem homiletic literature may have been a factor in the lack of Jewish creativity in literary *derashot*. Moslem worship did not include a sermon based on Scriptural—that is, Koranic—exegesis; the sermons were exhortatory and rather formalized, and as a result no exegetically based sermon literature developed among the Moslems.[21]

Here it is worth noting that any treatment of the *derashah* as a distinct literary genre must take into account the fact that there is much homiletic material deposited in other literary genres, since it was not unusual for the *darshan* to turn his Scriptural interpretations into Biblical commentary and his ethical exhortations into essays on ethics and morality.

It is not clear when the transition from the midrashic style *derashah* to the medieval *derashah* took place, and indeed it is likely that it took place at different times in different places. In northern France and in Germany, the composition of midrashim in the old style continued, side by side with the creation of new *derashot*.

In twelfth-century Provence, where many of the smaller midrashim such as *Midrash Tadshei* were redacted, we have some of the earliest medieval Jewish sermons recorded. The *derashah* of Rabad for Rosh Hashanah is a good example of such *derashot*; it deals primarily with halakhic matters, but opens with homiletical considerations as halakhic sermons usually do.[22]

Casting a glance at the Ashkenazic communities, the following facts and features emerge. From the thirteenth century we have a few *derashot* such as those in *Kelalei Hamilah Lerabi Ya'akov Hakohen* and those of his son R.

[16] *Cuzari*, V, 20.

[17] *Responsa*, ed. Y. Blau (Jerusalem 1957-1961), pp. 190, 202.

[18] See references in Urbach, *Ba'alei Hatosafot*, pp. 385ff.

[19] See the analysis of B. Septimus, "Piety and Power in 13th Century Catalonia," in I. Twersky, ed., *Studies in Medieval Jewish History and Literature* (Cambridge MA 1979), pp. 215-218.

[20] See J. Dan, *Sifrut Hamusar Vehadrush*, pp. 69-75.

[21] See *Encyclopaedia of Islam*, s.v. Khutba; see S. A. Bonebakker, "Literary Rhetoric and Poetics in Arabic Literature," *Viator* 1 (1970) 76, who discusses the lack of development of a theory of oratory in Islam; J. Pedersen, "The Islamic Preacher," *Ignace Goldziher Memorial Volume*, vol. I, eds. S. Lowinger and J. Somogyi (Budapest 1948), pp. 226-250.

[22] See I. Twersky, *Rabad*, pp. 110-113; idem, *Kiryat Sefer* 32 (1957) 440-443.

Gershom.[23] Jacob Elbaum[24] has published and analyzed three Ashkenazic *derashot* from the thirteenth century which are close in style, methodology and content to the above-mentioned *derashot* and which bear similarities to passages in other thirteenth-century Ashkenazic works such as *Sefer Ḥasidim, Sefer Rokeaḥ* and *Arugat Habosem* of R. Abraham b. Azriel. From all the above literature Elbaum notes that *derashot* in Ashkenaz were often built up out of a mosaic of midrashim, similar to the *Yalkutim*, such as *Yalkut Shim'oni*, compiled around the same time. Sometimes the *darshan* would go beyond mere assemblage and paraphrase the passages or even develop new conclusions using the methods of *gematria* and *notarikon* prevalent among the circles of Hasidei Ashkenaz. The *derashot* do display thematic and structural unity, and it is there that we see a conscious effort to continue the development of the *derashah.*[25] In the fourteenth century and later, Ashkenazic scholars who were also *darshanim*, such as R. Hayyim Or Zaru'a, Maharil, and R. Israel Isserlein, left us many *derashot* which are primarily halakhic in content. Thus R. Hayyim Or Zaru'a begins a typical *derashah* with a midrashic theme, finds a transition to a halakhic topic and concludes on an aggadic note.

It should be noted that the place of halakhah in the *derashah* varies greatly as a function of time, place and the individual *darshan.* In some descriptions of the *derashah*, halakhah appears as an integral part. Thus R. Menaḥem Hame'iri in thirteenth-century Provence says that instruction in the permitted and prohibited was an integral part of the Sabbath *derashah.*[26] Sometimes the question of whether halakhah should be included in the sermon raises the tempers of those who advocate its inclusion, as we see in the sixteenth- and seventeenth-century figures Maharal of Prague and R. Joel Sirkes, who argue strongly for its inclusion.[27]

The thirteenth century provides us with the first extensive literary remains of the medieval *derashah*, both in Provence and in Spain. This is not surprising, for it comes during a period of increased concern with the formal aspects of sermons and sermon literature in surrounding Christian society. Preaching occupied a central role in Christianity from its start. The proclamation of the Gospel, which is the primary function of Christian preaching, has important theological significance in Christianity.[28] However,

[23]See *Zikhron Brit Larishonim* (Cracow 1892), pp. 67-68, 122.

[24]See J. Elbaum, "Shalosh Derashot Ashkenaziyot Kedumot," *Kiryat Sefer* 48 (1973) 340-347.

[25]See below on the *derashot* of R. Moses of Coucy.

[26]*Beit Habeḥirah* on *Shabbat*, p. 445.

[27]See *Netivot Olam, Netiv Hatokheḥah*, ch. 3; *Bayit Ḥadash* to *Tur Oraḥ Ḥayyim* 290.

[28]See E. Dargan, *A History of Preaching* (New York 1905; repr. 1954), p. 553; James J. Murphy, *Rhetoric in the Middle Ages* (Berkeley 1974), pp. 273ff.

the nature of the Christian sermon was different from the Jewish one, perhaps because the Christian laity was less familiar with Scripture. The goal therefore had to be to make them acquainted with the fundamental message of Scripture, as well as exhortative—urging the listeners to follow a Christian way of life.

The thirteenth century is important in the history of the Christian sermon because it was at this time that we find systematic reflection on the nature and character of the sermon. A whole literature known as the *ars praedicandi* sprang up which, influenced by classical theories of rhetoric, attempted to establish systematic norms for delivering the sermon. Often these works would contain typical sermons or materials such as *exempla* for preachers to use. In effect they often served the function of sermon encyclopaedias.[29]

While there is no direct evidence of influence of Christian sermonics on Jewish sermons in the thirteenth century,[30] the very fact that Christians were writing these sermon manuals, which occupied a place of importance in Christian life and literature, may have influenced Jews to produce a sermon literature of their own.[31] Thus in the thirteenth century we first find occasional *derashot* recorded, and then the beginnings of full-fledged sermon books—one of the first being *Malmad Hatalmidim* of R. Jacob Anatoli of Provence,[32] a son-in-law of Samuel ibn Tibbon.

Malmad Hatalmidim consists of philosophical *derashot* for most of the pericopes, *parshiyot*, of the Torah and some of the holidays. Its *derashot* are heavily philosophical-allegorical, for the author's intent was to popularize Maimonidean philosophy through the medium of the *derashah*. Each *derashah* begins with a verse apparently unrelated to the *parashah*, often from *Ketuvim* (Hagiographa), and then, by careful interpretation and associative

[29]On the *ars praedicandi* see James J. Murphy, *Three Medieval Rhetorical Arts* (Berkeley 1971), Introduction; idem, *Rhetoric in the Middle Ages*, ch. 6, esp. p. 310; idem, *Medieval Rhetoric* (Toronto 1971), pp. 71-86; Harry Caplan, "Classical Rhetoric and the Medieval Theory of Preaching," in R. F. Howes, ed., *Historical Studies of Rhetoric and Rhetoricians* (Ithaca 1961), pp. 71-89.

[30]See, however, the suggestion of Y. Gilat in *Tarbiz* 28 (1959) 55 concerning the possible influence of the mendicant orders on the preaching of R. Moses of Coucy. On the influence of Christian sermonics on Jews in the fifteenth century, see M. Pachter, *Homiletic and Ethical Literature* (below, n.46), p. 17; H. H. Ben-Sasson in *EH*, s.v. *derashah*, concerning R. Isaac Arama.

[31]Concerning the extensive sermon literature in Spain, see the remarks of A. D. Deyermond in his review of G. R. Owst, "Literature and Pulpit in Medieval England" in *Estudios Lulianes* (Palma de Mallorca) 7 (1963) 234-235.

[32]Although the book was not printed until 1866, it was widely known. For a full treatment, see I. Bettan, *Studies*, pp. 49-88; J. Dan, *Sifrut*, pp. 82-91, and I. Zinberg, *A History of Jewish Literature*, vol. II, pp. 173-180.

thought, relates this verse to the *parashah*. In the process Anatoli integrates discussions of relevant verses as well as Talmudic and midrashic statements, which he often interprets allegorically. Philosophic allegory is a dominant feature of Anatoli's *derashot*, something for which he was criticized and on account of which he even had to stop his preaching.[33] There is an outer-directed motive in Anatoli's preaching, that is, he is very conscious of Gentile arguments and he quotes non-Jewish interpretations of Scripture in the *derashot.*[34] The *Malmad* became an influential book in the dissemination of philosophical ideas and a controversial book as well—it is mentioned in the literature of the Maimonidean controversies.[35] Ibn Shu'eib himself cites the *Malmad* several times in the Derashot and is sometimes critical of its interpretations which are not in accord with the opinion of the Rabbis.[36]

In thirteenth-century Spain, the most important *derashot* we have are the four *derashot* of Naḥmanides. Three—on Ecclesiastes, for Rosh Hashanah, and the *derashah* entitled *Torat Hashem Temimah*—are major addresses delivered late in his life. These are not "typical" *derashot* that would have been delivered on an ordinary Shabbat; they are *derashot* in which it would seem that Naḥmanides consciously attempted to summarize many of his fundamental ideas before large and generally learned audiences. They range broadly over many themes and subjects, with Ramban in full control not only of the subject material but of the formal structure as well, using a central text out of which all the ideas seem to flow. The last of the *derashot*—the *Derashah Leḥatunah*—contains kabbalistic allusions, and it would seem that the *derashah* was delivered before a small group, perhaps of initiates into kabbalistic knowledge like himself. His *derashot* exerted a great deal of influence in their written form and are frequently cited.[37]

Two other thirteenth-century preachers of note should be mentioned here who, although they have not left any books of sermons, contributed significantly to the history of the sermon and its literature. They are R. Moses of Coucy and R. Jonah of Gerona. R. Moses of Coucy[38] in France belonged to the Tosafistic school and was the author of the popular and authoritative *Sefer Miẓvot Gadol*, a compilation of all the 613 commandments designed to provide practical guidance to its readers and amply provided with aggadic embellishments in order to motivate proper observance. R. Moses, unique

[33]See Zinberg (n.32), p. 175.

[34]See Dan, *Sifrut*, p. 82.

[35]See, e.g., I. Zinberg, *A History*, vol. III, p. 63.

[36]See, e.g., 28Dc, 36Ca, 53Aa, 69Cb.

[37]Ibn Shu'eib cites the *Torat Hashem Temimah* as מאמר תורת ה'. See the recent additions to the *derashah* published by E. Kupfer in *Tarbiz* 40 (1970) 64-83.

[38]See Y. Gilat, above, n.30; E. Urbach, *Ba'alei Hatosafot*, pp. 384-395.

among the Tosafists, was a wandering preacher who was particularly well known for his journey throughout Spain in 1236 where he preached to many of the communities and according to his own testimony succeeded in a campaign for religious reform. Many fragments of his sermons are imbedded in the *Sefer Miẓvot Gadol*, and from them we get the sense of a popular preacher who in a simple and direct manner exhorted his listeners to repent and live honestly with the fear of God in them. The *derashot* do not share the characteristics of contemporary Ashkenazic *derashot*, as J. Elbaum has pointed out, and it may be that R. Moses adapted his style to the style prevalent in Spain.[39] This would explain the closeness in style between him and R. Jonah of Gerona. It seems that R. Moses' sermons also dealt with halakhic matters, and the *Sefer Miẓvot Gadol* may be the literary record of some of his halakhic-aggadic sermons.

We have no sermons per se of R. Jonah but much of the material incorporated in his *Gates of Repentance* and his commentary on Proverbs may very well have originated in oral sermons. As Bernard Septimus has pointed out recently, "there is evidence that he was not without the rhetorical skill which he so valued: a neatly turned phrase, a stylistic flourish, a pithy proverb, a parable borrowed from the world of chivalry, a touch of humor and of course, there are R. Jonah's homiletical interpretations of the Bible."[40] One of the striking aspects of R. Jonah's preaching in Septimus' description was its combination of deep piety, a concern with the cultivation of observance and spirituality, with a strong pragmatic streak which valued meaningful economic activity and was not ignorant of the place of economic power in the rule of the community.[41]

Finally, at the end of the thirteenth century, R. Baḥya b. Asher of Saragossa recorded his *derashot* in two forms—as proems to each *parashah* of the Torah and others arranged according to themes in *Kad Hakemaḥ*.[42] In neither is there any likelihood that the sermons are recorded in the way that they originally were delivered, but both sets of *derashot* show a *darshan* of great erudition, range, clarity and craftsmanship. The proems to the *parashah* are like the *petiḥta*, the midrashic proem, which starts from an unrelated verse and weaves its way into the opening verse of the *parashah*; these proems most likely are fragments of *derashot* which dealt in detail with the *parashah*, *derashot* which may have formed the basis for R. Baḥya's running commentary to the Torah.

[39]See Elbaum (above, n.24), p. 344, n.27.
[40]See Septimus, above, n. 19. See too *EH*, s.v. *derashah* by H. H. Ben-Sasson.
[41]Septimus, ibid.
[42]See I. Bettan, *Studies*, pp. 89-129; J. Reifman, *Alumah* 1 (1936) 69-100.

In the *Kad Hakemaḥ*, we have the first Hebrew sermon manual—a book consciously composed to provide *darshanim* with easy organized access to sources for sermons. "I have arranged my work in alphabetical order so that every *miẓvah* and character trait will have its own entry...and when a man rises up and wants to preach he will look at the rhymes at the end of the book, and they will guide him to the high path."[43] Each *derashah* in *Kad Hakemaḥ* is devoted to a single theme—something which would not be characteristic of a typical oral sermon. R. Bahya does testify at the beginning of the introduction that these sermons were actually preached,[44] but it is likely that the *derashot* as they appear in the *Kad Hakemaḥ* are fragments of *derashot*, rearranged for this specific literary purpose. The *derashot* are in a clear popular style and contain a great deal of Rabbinic material, but only a very small amount of Kabbalah, unlike Baḥya's commentary to the Torah in which he included a great deal of Kabbalah.[45]

2. Form and Style in the *Derashot 'al Hatorah*

Rabbi Joshua ibn Shu'eib's Derashot are a turning point in the history of the literary *derashah*. We have no other full collection of *derashot* prior to this which matches the *Derashot 'al Hatorah* in richness of texture, scope, skill and artistry.[46] Ibn Shu'eib is prototypical of the protean *darshan* who is at home at once in philosophy and Kabbalah, in halakhah and *ta'amei hamiẓvot* (reasons for *miẓvot*), in Biblical exegesis and in aggadic interpretation, utilizing all these modes effectively and perceptively while remaining anchored in the exegetical framework of the classic sermon.

The overall structure of ibn Shu'eib's *derashot* follow a regular pattern, but ibn Shu'eib's skill as a preacher provided him with the flexibility to fashion *derashot* whose variety of strains and rhythms create a symphony of ideas, interpretations and directives that is engaging and appealing intellectually

[43]In his introduction to *Kad Hakemaḥ* (ed. C. Chavel, p. 18). See Chavel's introduction, p. 11 and n.2. See Pachter (below, n.46), p. 14.

[44]*Kad Hakemaḥ*, p. 17: קרבן שפתי אקריב לאל יוצר.

[45]See E. Gottlieb, *The Kabbalah in the Writings of R. Baḥya ben Asher* (Tel Aviv 1970).

[46]So little research has been done in the field of the medieval *derashah*, even basic bibliographical work, that any generalizations such as these may have to be modified. Many *derashot* exist in manuscript untouched and many collections of *derashot* such as those by ibn Shu'eib's contemporaries Ritva and R. Ḥayyim, author of *Ẓeror Haḥayyim*, have been lost. See now the important dissertations of Mordechai Pachter, "Homiletic and Ethical Literature of Safed in the 16th Century" (unpublished Ph.D. thesis, Hebrew University, 1976), particularly part I, chapters 1 and 2, and J. Elbaum, "Zeramim Umegamot Besifrut Hamaḥshavah Vehamusar Be'ashkenaz Beme'ah Hasheh 'Esreh" (unpublished Ph.D. thesis, Hebrew University, 1977), pp. 209-213.

and aesthetically. Only by reading a full *derashah* can the careful synchronization of all its elements be conveyed; I shall try, however, to describe some of the formal aspects of the *derashot* and some of ibn Shu'eib's rhetorical tools.

Each *derashah* opens with a proemial verse, often from *Ketuvim*, sometimes a verse from the Prophets or a mishnah from *Pirkei Avot*. Interpretation of the verse leads to the *parashah*, which ibn Shu'eib usually explains in great detail by taking up each of its themes successively. Although the exposition is thematic he does manage to weave into the *derashah* explanations of substantial parts of the *parashah*. This may be why the *derashot* are sometimes referred to as a *Perush.*[47]

Ibn Shu'eib uses the introductory verses in many different ways; almost always there is careful and detailed exposition of the verse. Often he will interpret the verse on three levels: the simple or literal level—*peshat*; the allegorical level—*sikhli*; and the midrashic level. Thus, for example, he cites as the introductory verse to the *derashah* on *Shemot* (Ex. 1:1-6:1): "As the cold of snow in the time of harvest, so is a faithful messenger to him that sendeth him, he refreshes the soul of his master" (Proverbs 25:12). He interprets it first according to the *peshat* level as praises of the faithful messenger who is like a cold refreshing wind (ibn Shu'eib emphasizes—not snow itself) on a hot summer day. He refreshes the soul of his master by his industry and sharpness. He then goes to the allegorical *(sikhli)* interpretation: the verses refer to Man, who is given a mission to fulfill in this world; one who fulfills it faithfully will be rewarded. Finally, according to the midrashic interpretation, the verse refers to Moses the faithful messenger—and here is the link to the *parashah*. In the course of presenting these explanations, ibn Shu'eib cites verses and Talmudic and midrashic passages that are relevant to the discussion.

Before proceeding to the third interpretation, the midrashic, ibn Shu'eib launches into an extensive digression by maneuvering into a verse from Psalms which leads to a detailed explanation of all the verses in that psalm. This digression provides him with an opportunity to offer some ethical advice and to allude to some kabbalistic ideas. Carefully cultivated digressions are an important part of ibn Shu'eib's Derashot. The verse that is the focus of this digression, which seems at first to have only a tenuous connection to the *parashah*, is later reinterpreted in a manner which relates it directly to the *parashah*. Often, however, the digression is an independent unit which may have been inserted into the *derashah* when it was written down. Digressions of

[47]See the title page to the Constantinople 1523 edition of the Derashot which says ספר אבן שועיב פירוש נחמד על התורה. Only in the Cracow edition is the book called *Derashot 'al Hatorah.*

course are quite common in midrashic literatre and indeed in medieval literature in general. E. R. Curtius' description aptly fits the *derashah* as well.

> The Middle Ages was far from demanding unity of subject and inner coherence of structure in a work of literature. Indeed digression was regarded as special elegance....Accordingly, the medieval conception of art does not attempt to conceal digressions by transitions—on the contrary, poets often point them out with a certain satisfaction.[48]

Rabbi Joshua ibn Shu'eib will often point out his digressions, perhaps also to help the reader/listener keep track of the flow of the *derashah*.

> We have entered into this matter *(gilgalnu kol zeh)* of *bitaḥon* [faith] for it explains the *miẓvah*[49]....We have dwelt on this and have left the central theme of the *derashah*; we have entered into this because it relates to the *parashah*. However, let us return to our theme.[50]

Often to add to his listeners'/readers' interest there is more than one point of connection between the *parashah* and the proemial verse or the verses following it.

The Derashot begin, then, with a proem; they almost always conclude with a Messianic wish which is sometimes thematically connected with the *parashah* but which just as often is somewhat artificially appended.

One of the salient features of the Derashot is its extensive use of midrashic material. Ibn Shu'eib uses midrashim in the course of his exegesis—sometimes in the form of a verse-by-verse commentary.[51] Often ibn Shu'eib will insist that the midrash be accepted literally, as in the case of the midrash that says that even embryos in the mother's womb said praises to God during the Exodus from Egypt.[52] Aggadot and midrashim are cited as support or as a basis for *minhagim* as is common in the *minhagot* literature.[53] At other times, ibn Shu'eib uses aggadot as a basis for certain ideas which he elicits by skillful interpretation. As an interpreter of aggadot, ibn Shu'eib displays great skill, utilizing the allegorical tradition of philosophy as well as kabbalistic concepts. We will elaborate on this below in Chapter VII. For now let us look at one striking example. In describing Abraham's activities as the publicizer of God's unity he says:

[48]E. R. Curtius, *European Literature in the Latin Middle Ages* (New York 1953), pp. 501-502.

[49]55Ac.

[50]80Aa; see also 25Cc, 28Ac, 64Dc, 75Ca, and many other places in the Derashot.

[51]See, e.g., his *derashah* to *Teẓaveh*, particularly the commentary to the Book of Esther, pp. 31-32.

[52]See below, chapters IV and VII.

[53]Ibn Shu'eib follows an old tradition. The use of aggadah in *Sefer Hamanhig* is extensive; see Y. Rafael's introduction to his edition (Jerusalem 1978), pp. 28f.

> This is the thrust of the statement by the Sages of blessed memory that a jewel was tied around [Abraham's] neck which shined for the entire world; the sick were healed by it, and when he died God took it and placed it in the solar sphere. The meaning of this passage is as follows: the jewel hanging around his neck symbolizes the principles he would publicize with his throat, with which he would heal the sicknesses of the soul brought about by incorrect opinions. When he died it was placed in the solar sphere, for it is that which demonstrates the unity and omnipotence of God as it is written "the heavens declare the glory of the Lord" (Ps. 19:2).[54]

Second only to his use of Talmudic and midrashic sources is his use of medieval sources, explicitly or without attribution. S. Abramson has already started the work of enumerating ibn Shu'eib's remarkably extensive and varied sources. Interesting from the point of view of style is that ibn Shu'eib's sources were not merely cited to prove this point or that, but were molded, extended and elaborated upon to express more fully ibn Shu'eib's idea. This is particularly true in his use of passages from the *Cuzari* and *Moreh Nevukhim*, with which he took great liberties by interpolating extensively.[55]

One of the most striking aspects of the Derashot, we have said, is the inclusion of a substantial amount of kabbalistic material. No other *darshan* before, to our knowledge, used Kabbalah so extensively in oral *derashot*, nor do most *darshanim* begin to use Kabbalah in their oral *derashot* until the sixteenth century.[56] The Derashot indeed are a bold attempt to popularize Kabbalah by integrating it into the very fabric of the sermon.[57] The attempt seems to have been without immediate historic reverberations. The kabbalistic allusions are sometimes very brief; sometimes a detailed knowledge of kabbalistic symbolism is required to understand the references. This supports the notion that ibn Shu'eib was preaching to a varied audience; his brief allusions to Kabbalah were undoubtedly intended to arouse the average listener's interest in Kabbalah, to show how organically it fits into Jewish

[54]5Db, based on Baba Batra 16b; cf. R. Moses Almosnino, *Me'ameẓ Koaḥ* (Venice 1588) 3b. See the similar interpretation by Michael Sachs cited by A. Altmann in "The New Style of Preaching in Nineteenth-Century German Jewry," in A. Altmann, ed., *Studies in Nineteenth-Century Jewish Intellectual History* (Cambridge MA 1964), p. 85. Concerning the source for ibn Shu'eib's interpretation, see below ch. VII, n.68.

[55]37ABC.

[56]Thus, e.g., R. Levi ibn Ḥabib expresses opposition to this kind of preaching in the sixteenth century; see S. Baron, *The Jewish Community* (Philadelphia 1942), vol. 3, p. 134, n.48.

[57]It is not possible to argue that the kabbalistic allusions were added only to the written version of the sermon because in many of the *derashot* Kabbalah is an integral part of the structure of the sermon. See below, chapter VIII.

tradition. The more complicated allusions may have been addressed as asides to the handful of kabbalistic initiates in his audience.

Ibn Shu'eib spiced his Derashot with devices that were undoubtedly introduced to appeal to the popular imagination—an important element particularly in the oral *derashah. Gematria* and *notarikon* and particularly parallel groupings of threes, fours, fives, sevens, tens and so on are some of his favorite devices. Thus he points to the three parts of the Torah which contain three types of material: stories, *mizvot, sodot*; three parts of the soul; the three opening words of *Sefer Yezirah: sefer, sefar, sippur*; three levels of wisdom: *ḥokhmah, binah* and *da'at*; the three levels of *Kohen, Levi* and *Yisrael*;[58] or four levels of existence, four elements, four spheres, four archangels, four faces on the Chariot, etc.[59]

These are old midrashic tools, but also tools which achieved popularity in medieval Latin literature in ibn Shu'eib's time, as he may very well have been aware. In any case E. R. Curtius' explanation that "number was sanctified as a form-bestowing factor in the Divine works of creation. It acquired metaphysical dignity,"[60] was certainly true of ibn Shu'eib's thought.

Short quotable epigrams are sprinkled throughout the Derashot, such as "Alexander would say after a battle, we have come from the small battle—now we must begin the great one" (that is, the battle with one's evil inclination);[61] or in a discussion of the importance of sensitivity to one's fellow man: one should say that "even if there was but one thread from a spider's web between myself and my friend it would not break, for when he pulls I release and when he releases I pull";[62] or "the wise man said that jealousy is like fire—when the fire has no wood to consume, it consumes itself";[63] and many others.

Concrete metaphors and parables, dramatic descriptions and short stories are some of the other standard homiletic techniques which Rabbi Joshua ibn Shu'eib uses throughout the Derashot. Some examples: the very detailed description of the personality of King David;[64] the dramatic rendering of the verses in Ezekiel at the beginning of the *derashah* in *Bo* where he describes the saving of Israel, which is compared to an abandoned child; the midrashic allegory which ibn Shu'eib tells in great detail of how the tongue proves to other parts of the body how only it holds in its hand life and death.[65]

[58] 26Dc; see 23Db for another listing of groups of three.
[59] 52C.
[60] E. R. Curtius, *European Literature*, p. 504; see also 501ff. and 508.
[61] 69Dc. See Abramson, Introduction, pp. 35-37.
[62] 87Bb and ibid.
[63] 62Db.
[64] 60Db.
[65] 65D-66A.

The Derashot thus show a mastery of the technique of an effective oral sermon. This raises the question—were these *derashot* actually delivered?[66]

This question can never be answered with complete confidence in the absence of any contemporary corroborating testimony; the possibility always exists that the Derashot may have been written for delivery without ever having been actually delivered orally. However, two factors support the notion that they were actually delivered. First, the presence of the sorts of rhetorical flourishes that were mentioned above suggest an oral composition. Second, there is the very fact that ibn Shu'eib published them as *derashot* and did not transform them into another literary form. While as mentioned above various scholars of the thirteenth century composed individual literary *derashot*, these are more like occasional essays. There was not yet an established precedent for the composition of books of *derashot* that preserved the *derashah* in a literary form close to its oral form. We may speculate that ibn Shu'eib composed a book containing *derashot* for the entire year's cycle of Torah reading and holidays in order to provide a model for other *darshanim*. If this is indeed so, we would expect such a book to come from the pen of a seasoned practitioner in the oral art rather than a theoretician sitting in his study, who would probably have given us some hint of the purely literary origin of the work if that indeed were the case.[67]

Concerning the language in which the Derashot were given if indeed they were delivered orally, there is again little evidence to provide guidance. While it is certain that his listeners would have had to know some Hebrew since many parts of the *derashah* revolve around Hebrew texts and their careful exegesis, we cannot preclude the possibility that, although the sources were cited in Hebrew, the discussion itself was in the vernacular.[68] There is only one possible hint in the Derashot themselves concerning language.

> Since it is a *mizvah* today to discuss matters relating to Passover and its laws, I will discuss some laws briefly. The *rishonim* [early authorities]

[66]On the problem of the transition from the oral sermon to the written, see J. Dan, *Sifrut*, chapter 2, esp. pp. 35-37; Peter Erb, "Vernacular Material for Preaching" *Medieval Studies* 33 (1971) 63ff.; Peter Burke, *Popular Culture in Early Modern Europe* (New York 1978), p. 67; M. Pachter, *Homiletic and Ethical Literature*, pp. 2ff.; A. Shinan, "The Aggadic Literature" (above, n.4).

[67]The consciousness of the need to preserve in literary form the essential structure and character of the oral sermon is represented in the next century by R. Joel ibn Shu'eib who makes this explicit in his methodological comments at the beginning of his *'Olat Shabbat*. See above, n.3. See M. Pachter, *Homiletic and Ethical Literature*, pp. 21-22, 25.

[68]Cf. J. Dan, *Sifrut*, pp. 45-46. Dr. Benjamin Gampel informs me that in Tudela the vernacular was a Navarrese-Aragonian dialect. See P. Burke, *Popular Culture*, on the problem of language in the Christian sermon.

already compiled *azharot*[69] to be said on this day in which the laws of Passover are mentioned, in order to fulfill that obligation, but most people do not pay attention to their meaning—indeed many do not even understand them. Therefore it is customary to preach in clear language [*lidrosh belashon mevo'ar*] to men and women, for indeed some *mizvot* are in the hands of women.[70]

These two words—*lashon mevo'ar*—and the need for women to understand may imply that the *derashah* was in the vernacular, although ibn Shu'eib may be talking only about the *derashah* for Shabbat Hagadol, with its special attention to the practical halakhic aspects of Passover.[71]

If indeed ibn Shu'eib did deliver his *derashot* orally, the *derashot* as they appear in the *Derashot 'al Hatorah* are not cut from one cloth. There are *derashot* that clearly preserve elements of the live *derashah* but appear in their present form to be a literary creation rather than a record of an oral sermon. Thus, e.g., the *derashah* to *Tezaveh* contains none of the asides, digressions, direct addresses or moral exhortations that characterize some of his other *derashot*. It remains instead almost entirely within a strict exegetical framework: first the exegesis of *Parashat Zakhor* and then of the Book of Esther. He closely follows the verses with exegetical comments on most important phrases but raises virtually no philosophic problems, inserts no kabbalistic allusions nor any discussions of ethics. In his interpretation of the Book of Esther he has an overall interpretational scheme which he superimposes on a midrashic commentary to the book, but there is no real integration of the theme and the commentary. One gets the impression that the commentary was added on to an existing homily of ibn Shu'eib's when the *derashot* were edited for the book. Differences also exist between those *derashot* that contain considerable kabbalistic material and others that are virtually devoid of Kabbalah.

The literary editing of the Derashot manifests itself in three ways:

1) The Derashot are extensively cross-referenced, and there are references to future *derashot* as well as past. Most of the cross-references can be located in our printed texts.[72]

[69]*Azharot* are poetic listings of the *mizvot*, intended for liturgical use.

[70]38Db.

[71]Alternately, לשון מבואר might be in opposition to the paytanic obscurity of the *Azharot*.

[72]3Db, 6Dc, 9Ba, 13Bb, 20Ca, 22Ab, 26Db, 27Cb, 28Ac, 29Aa, 34Ba, 34Ca, 34Cc, 34Da, 41Cc, 42Bb, 43Dc, 45Ab, 46Da, 47Db, 50Dc, 52Cc, 57Ab, 57Db, 59Ab, 67Ca, 69Bb, 69Cb, 70Aa, 72Ab, 73Ab, 74Aa, 78Bb, 80Bc, 83Aa, 83Cb, 84Cc (twice), 84Da, 84Db, 86Da, 87Ab, 87Ca, 87Cc, 88Ab, 90Ca, 95Ca. While the overwhelming majority of the references are to past *derashot*, there are four references to forthcoming *derashot*

2) Some *derashot* are clearly composite, with two separate independent sections. The *derashah* to *Bo* is a good example. It consists of two distinct sections, clearly separable yet not disjointed. That is, although the editing process is visible, there is a rationale to the editorial decision. The proem to the sermon revolves around several verses in Ezekiel. These verses are at first explained briefly, until ibn Shu'eib reaches a verse whose exegesis opens several avenues. It is around this last verse that he constructs the *derashah*, with the usual interweaving with the subject matter of the *parashah*. At one point he seems to abandon the proemic verses, only to return to them with a surprising twist. Then he suddenly veers to a completely new theme which may very well have originally been a completely independent *derashah*. And indeed later in the Derashot, ibn Shu'eib refers to a passage in this second part of the *Bo derashah* as the *"derashah* to *Parashat Hahodesh,"* clearly implying that this was an independent *derashah.*[73]

3) Whole sections of *derashot* are repeated verbatim. While this is rare in the printed Derashot, there are parts of *derashot* in manuscripts which are identical to the printed *derashot* but occur in different contexts. In the manuscript of the Derashot in the Library of the Jewish Theological Seminary of America, there is a *derashah* on *Parashat Shekalim* which does not appear in the printed Derashot yet contains material which appears verbatim in the printed version, integrated in different contexts.[74]

The Derashot circulated widely, and S. Abramson has listed a wide variety of writers who utilized the *derashot.*[75] Some of the names that can be listed are: the fifteenth-century philosophers and preachers R. Abraham Bibago and R. Isaac Arama; the fifteenth-century Italian poet Moses Rieti, who notes the popularity of the Derashot in Sicily and the other Mediterranean islands;[76] R. Joseph Caro, the towering halakhic authority of the sixteenth century; his uncle R. Isaac Caro in his *Toldot Yiẓhak*;[77] in Poland, R. Moses Mat, author of

(27Cb, 29Aa, 46Da, and 47Db). I have located the referred text in most of the cases, but there are a few which I have not succeeded in locating. Perhaps they will turn up in manuscripts.

[73]Ibn Shu'eib in the *derashah* for Rosh Hashanah, 90Ca, in discussing the power of the court to sanctify the new moon says כמו שכתבנו בפרשת החדש, which is an allusion to 24Cb, the *derashah* to *Bo.*

[74]Ms R1607 P. 224r lines 10-27; printed version p. 29A. See now my edition of the *derashah* in *Kovez 'al Yad*, forthcoming.

[75]See Abramson, Introduction, pp. 43-46.

[76]Rieti, *Mikdash Me'at* (Wien 1851), p. 101b, חכם — [הערת המחבר] אבן שועיב ראוי להודיה. גדול חבר **ספרים** ופ׳ חמשה חומשי תורה. פ׳ נוהגים בו באיסקיליא וביתר איי הים ההוא. Notice that he considers the Derashot פירוש. See C. Roth, *Gleanings* (New York 1967), p. 68.

[77]See below, ch. IX, n.47.

the influential book of customs, *Mateh Mosheh*; in the seventeenth century, R. Abraham Portaleone of Mantua, whose *Shiltei Giborim* reflects the author's wide Jewish, humanistic, and scientific erudition, and R. Joseph Juspa Hahn of Frankfurt in his *Yosef Omeẓ*; in the eighteenth, R. Isaac Lampronti, author of the encyclopaedia of halakhah, *Paḥad Yiẓḥak*; and others. They used the Derashot as a source for midrashim, halakhot, customs and their explanations and Biblical exegesis.

The popularity of the Derashot is attested to by another fact—the Derashot were used as a source for anti-Jewish polemics at the end of the fifteenth century. Y. Baer describes two books written for Inquisitors for their debates with Conversos which used the Derashot as a source.[78]

The Derashot were printed twice in the sixteenth century, once in Constantinople in 1523 and again in Cracow in 1573. The sixteenth century itself was a time of explosive productivity in homiletics, so that it is not surprising that a master *darshan* such as ibn Shu'eib would be popular both in Sefardic-dominated Constantinople and in Ashkenazic Cracow.[79]

The Derashot show a learned, erudite preacher skillfully employing the sermon as a vehicle for the education and instruction of his listeners without ignoring the aesthetic side so necessary to keep the attention of his audience.

[78]Baer, *Toldot*, p. 446 and p. 546, n.87.

[79]Some of the more important sixteenth-century *darshanim* were R. Isaac Adarbi, R. Moses Galanti, R. Moses Almosnino, R. Solomon Halevi, R. Moses Alshekh, R. Ephraim Luntschitz, Maharal of Prague, and his brother R. Hayyim. See L. Zunz and H. Albeck, *Haderashot Beyisrael* (Jerusalem 1954), chapters 22 and 23, and now the dissertations of M. Pachter and J. Elbaum (above, n.46).

Chapter III

Jewish Society in the Eyes of a Homilist

The dynamics of Jewish life in Spain in general and in Navarre in particular, the social classes and their relative authority, the intellectual and ethical ideals and realities of the Jews are all reflected in the Derashot. Although at times muted by the homiletical and exegetical composition of the sermon, the reality is often apparent enough for the critical reader to perceive.

In identifying and assessing this reality, one must be careful to differentiate between conventional assertions and special contemporary themes. Not every piece of exegesis necessarily reflects a contemporary social situation, for exegesis and homiletics have their own inner dynamic; yet there are occasions when the selection of one approach or one interpretation over other possible ones does provide us with some insight into contemporary events.

Rabbi Joshua ibn Shu'eib was not primarily a social reformer, as was R. Moses of Coucy or R. Jonah of Gerona,[1] and we do not find a great deal of crusading zeal in his Derashot.[2] But he does have definite ideas concerning community organization, social problems, and ethical standards. Some of these matters were universally accepted principles of the Jewish community; others were hotly debated in ibn Shu'eib's time in Spain. In the process of articulating his political theory, in classifying social realities, and in his ethical pronouncements, some of the contemporary tensions and conflicts surface. In all we find both confirmation of certain realities we already know to have existed in Spain and a more balanced perspective on others.

[1]See above, ch. II, pp. 25-26.

[2]Cf. however, *derashah* to *Pinḥas*, 73B-C ואנו כמה זמרי יש בדורינו רצוני לומר שהיו צריכים ליסרם ולבערם מן הארץ ולכלות קוצי׳ מן הכרם. See below pp 46-47, 53-54.

1. On Proper Government: Aristocracy and Authority

Ibn Shu'eib has occasion to expound his views on the proper governance of society in a number of places. The most complete treatment is in the *parashah* of *Koraḥ*. This Biblical setting (Num. 16:1-18:32) is ideal for an analysis of political authority for it tells of the objections of Koraḥ to the authority of Moses' leadership.[3]

Ibn Shu'eib accepts the view held widely among Jews, although challenged later by Abravanel, that monarchy is a desirable form of govenment and that the appointment of a king is a Scriptural command. The verses in Deuteronomy (17:14-15) are ambiguous, and Rabbinic tradition is divided on the question of whether the section discussing the appointment of a king constitutes a positive command or merely describes the proper procedure should the people desire a king.[4] Most medieval authorities, and Maimonides very emphatically, hold the view that appointing a king is a *miẓvah*, a Scriptural command,[5] and ibn Shu'eib adopts that view. A problem of fundamental importance in the Jewish notion of kingship is the opposition to the people's request for a king on the part of the prophet Samuel (I Sam. 8). Ibn Shu'eib explains this as opposition to the premature request of the people rather than a fundamental opposition to the principle of monarchy.[6] In this ibn Shu'eib follows the *Sifre*: "Why were they punished in the days of Samuel—because they asked prematurely."[7] Likewise, Maimonides explains

[3]Other exegetes have done the same, starting with Philo. According to him, the root of the uprising of Koraḥ was the question of whether the few who are qualified by merit should rule or whether the rule should be entrusted to the many, irrespective of their qualifications; see H. A. Wolfson, *Philo* (Cambridge MA 1962), vol. 2, p. 388.

[4]Sifre, Deut #156 (ed. L. Finkelstein, p. 208); Sanhedrin 20b.

[5]See, e.g., *Mishneh Torah, Melakhim*, ch. 1; Naḥmanides, Deut 17:15. Cf. R. Baḥya b. Asher's ambiguous formulation, ad loc., and Ibn Ezra and Abarbanel to the same verse.

[6]66Dc.

[7]Sifre, loc. cit. The text of the Sifre reads as follows: אמר ר׳ יהודה והלא מצוה מן התורה לשאול להם מלך שנאמר שום תשים עליך מלך. למה נענשו בימי שמואל, לפי שהקדימו על ידם. ככל הגוים אשר סביבותי, רבי נהוריי אומר לא בקשו להם מלך אלא להעבידם ע״ז שנא׳ והיינו גם אנחנו ככל הגוים ושפטנו מלכנו ויצא לפננו ונלחם את מלחמתינו. The punctuation is according to Finkelstein; in his notes, he cites two medieval commentaries which explain הקדימו על ידם as referring to the עמי הארץ who spoke before the זקנים and stated their request והיינו ככל הגוים. Similarly Radak in his commentary to I Sam 8:5 says ובדברי חז״ל מחלוקת, מהם אמרו למה נענשו על שהקדימו ככל הגוים. That is, he does not put a period after על ידם in the Sifre text but rather reads the Sifre ...שהקדימו על ידם ככל הגויים. Ibn Shu'eib, who does not quote the Sifre but merely says גדול ובעבור שבקשו מלך בימי שאול קודם זמנו שהיה שמואל שופט וממונה נחשב להם עון, sustains Finkelstein's interpretation (and Meir ish Shalom before him). See Ginzberg, *Legends*, vol. VI, p. 230.

that Samuel's objection to Israel's request was due to the manner in which they asked and their motive.[8]

According to ibn Shu'eib, the king has wide-ranging powers. Ibn Shu'eib, like Maimonides, adopts the Talmudic view that Samuel in his stern warning to the Israelites described the king's prerogatives and not his illegal abuses of power.

> He has the power to issue decrees against the laws, even without witnesses and warning, for the "law of the kingdom is the law,"[9] and whoever rebels is liable to the death penalty. He has the power to confiscate money and to impose taxes as he sees fit, as it is written "and he will take your fields" (I Sam. 8:14). As the Rabbis have written "everything mentioned in the warning of Samuel the king may do."[10]

The selection of a king is by Divine Will and the very fact that a person is king implies Divine sanction of his rule. The king stands at the top of a hierarchical structure, "for just as God chose man from among other living creatures, similarly he chose one nation from all others, one tribe from all the others, one family...and one man from that family.[11] Ibn Shu'eib illustrates this by pointing to David, whose family and tribe were chosen for rulership.[12]

Ibn Shu'eib then describes another hierarachical structure in Judaism, a spiritual one—"for we find that God chose Israel from all the other nations and the tribe of Levi from among the tribes, and that tribe itself is divided into three families—each one higher than the other...and Aaron was chosen for the high priesthood."[13] These divisions, ibn Shu'eib adds, parallel the divisions of the heavenly hierarchy, for *malkhuta de'ar'a*, the earthly kingdom, is like *malkhuta dereki'a*, the heavenly kingdom.[14] Ibn Shu'eib adds a third hierarchy, that of those who serve the king. "Some sit before the king, others stand in the king's court, others stand by the gate, and others are

[8]*Mishneh Torah Melakhim* 1:2. See n.7.

[9]Ibn Shu'eib applies the rule of דינא דמלכותא דינא to Jewish kings. Cf. R. Nissim of Gerona in his commentary to Nedarim 28a who holds that the principle applies only to Gentile kings. Rashba in a responsum (vol. I #637) applies *dina demalkhuta* to Jewish kings outside of Israel. Cf. Meiri and Rashba to Nedarim. See S. Shilo, *Dina Demalkhuta Dina* (Jerusalem 1975), pp. 99-108, esp. p. 102 n.117 and p. 103.

[10]84Bb. See Sanhedrin 20b; Mishneh Torah, *Melakhim* 4:1.

[11]66Db.

[12]See also 14Cc [Mistakenly numbered p. 15] כי המלוכה היתה סדורה וגזורה לשלמה.

[13]66Db.

[14]Note that ibn Shu'eib does not claim that there is a continuity between the hierarchy or Chain of Being on earth with the heavenly one. He says rather that the earthly kingdom is "like" מעין but not actually continuous. Cf. A. D. Lovejoy, *The Great Chain of Being* (New York 1960), p. 59. While ibn Shu'eib is discussing here the Jewish king, perhaps he would apply his theory to Gentile kings as well.

employed by the king and leave when they are paid."[15] This last hierarchy is also interpreted in spiritual, religious terms, referring to levels of Torah study and the performance of *mizvot*.

The purpose of these analogies is, first of all, to establish the Divine right of the Jewish king and perhaps of the spiritual leadership as well—a right which cannot be challenged.[16] The king, according to ibn Shu'eib, embodies not only the highest political authority but is also crucial to the organic functioning of society.[17]

The crucial importance of the king and the organic nature of society is emphasized in another context. Ibn Shu'eib says that a society requires four elements for its continued functioning: wise men who understand the ways of the world and particularly political theory—they are to society as the mind is to the body. Second, the king, who rules and instills fear and awe upon his subjects to prevent violence and bloodshed; the heart which rules the body is the organic analogue of the king in society. Next are the leaders and local chiefs who administer justice—they are like the senses. Finally, the workers and artisans fulfill the function of the rest of the limbs of the body.[18]

[15]66Db. מהם רואי פני המלך ומהם עומדים בחצר המלך ומהם עומדים בשער המלך מהם עושים מלאכת המלך בשכר והולכים להם.

[16]Cf. A. J. Carlyle, *Medieval Political Theory*, vol. 3 (New York 1960), p. 183. Derashot 66Da: שאין רשאי לאדם להתגדל לפני המלך באיזה ענין מן המלוכה או בשום מעלה מן המעלות מאחר שאותו המלך הוא לאותו המינוי.

[17]Ibn Shu'eib's attitude toward the authority and importance of Jewish kings would be expected in light of what we know about the relation of the Jewish aristocracy in Spain with the Spanish monarchy. As Prof. Y. H. Yerushalmi has pointed out, "In the Jewish Aristocracy's own relation to the Crown there was more than a grudging service. *Servi camerae* they may have been, but they were also the one group in Spain that worked heart and soul for the aggrandizement of the king and the increase of his power" (from "The Lisbon Massacre of 1506 and the Royal Image in the *Shebet Yehuda*," *HUCA* Supplements number 1 [1976] 38; see also the literature cited in n.91).

[18]53Ba. Cf. 52Bc: כי השם ב"ה חלק כל ברואיו לד' מדרגות כפי האמת וברא אותם מדרגות מדרגות. The king as the heart of the nation, or alternatively as its soul, has its echoes in contemporary medieval political thought. Aquinas uses the same two analogies—king is to the kingdom as the soul is to the body (*On the Governance of Rulers* [New York 1938]) and as the heart is to the body (*Commentary to Aristotle's Politics*, I,12, as cited in B. Netanyahu, *Abravanel* [Philadelphia 1968], p. 180; see Abravanel's commentary to Deut 17:15).

Maimonides uses a similar analogy ולבו לב האומה (*Melakhim* 3:5); however, it does not appear that this is ibn Shu'eib's source. He does not cite Maimonides but rather an anonymous "certain wise man" (although he does cite Maimonides' statement that man is political by nature or necessity: וכמו שכתב הר"מ ז"ל האדם מדיני מוכרח.) See *Guide* II, 40. In ibn Tibbon's translation האדם מדיני בטבע.

More important, however, is the context in which the statements appear. Maimonides' statement is meant to express the idea that the way the king acts, what he does and

Significant here is the separation of the spiritual and political functions of the rulers. In this ibn Shu'eib follows Maimonides.[19]

This hierarchical notion and the concept of the organic nature of society are not new, of course. In Jewish literature it was Judah Halevy who emphasized the hierarchical order which places plant life above mineral life, animal life above that, and humanity above animals; the final step in this ladder is Israel, which is separated qualitatively from the other nations by virtue of its possession of the Torah and performance of *mizvot.*[20] This notion of hierarchy was also developed by R. Abraham ibn Daud who directed his argument towards the necessity for variety in human society as a justification for the distribution of talents and abilities among men.[21]

Rabbi Joshua ibn Shu'eib, however, is concerned with something more than the pure theory of governance, for the thrust of his argument and the purpose of the three analogies mentioned above is to explain why

> Solomon warned us[22]...that no one should go beyond his own rank and challenge the status of appointed officials and those of high rank, for their position was given to them by God, as the Rabbis have said "Even the head of the water drawers was appointed by Heaven" (Bava Batra 91b).[23]

Before we go any further in analyzing ibn Shu'eib's polemic, we must look quickly at the nature and the structure of the Jewish community in Spain. The Jews in Spain inherited from the Jews in Babylonia an oligarchical form of government in which the affairs of the community were determined by a

how he feels, influences the people strongly. The implication of ibn Shu'eib's analogy is different; the king's functions in society are analogous to the heart's biological functioning in the body. Just as the heart is the organ that supplies vital life to the body, the king as a political ruler is the cohesive factor that sustains society. On the Islamic and Neoplatonic equation of king=heart see G. Blidstein (below n.19), p. 58, n.28.

[19]See G. J. Blidstein, "On Political Structures—Four Medieval Comments," *Journal of Jewish Sociology* 22 (1980) 47-58.

[20]*Cuzari* V, 20 (ed. Even Shmuel, p. 228); see H. H. Ben-Sasson, "Yiḥud 'Am Yisrael Beda'at Bnei Hameah Ha-12," *Perakim* 2 (Jerusalem 1974) 157-158. The notion of a hierarchy of beings, the great chain of being, is documented in Lovejoy's book (above n.14); see esp. pp. 58, 59 and 64. On Halevi's view on kingship see G. Blidstein (above n.19).

[21]*Emunah Ramah* (Frankfurt am Main 1853; repr. Jerusalem 1967), pp. 93-96. See Ben-Sasson, "Yiḥud," and Blidstein (above n.19).

[22]The reference is to Proverbs 25:6, which was the proemial verse to the *derashah.*

[23]66Db. Cf. Ramban, Deut 17:15, who uses this Talmudic statement to justify the notion that, if a person is king, Divine approval is implied; ibn Shu'eib uses it to justify all official positions, as does R. Baḥya b. Asher, ad loc.

relatively small percentage of its members, who formed a ruling hierarchy. Indeed, in Geonic times, outlying communities were often controlled by the heads of Babylonian Jewry through their ability to appoint the rabbinic leader of the community.[24]

In Christian Spain, Jewish communal administration varied considerably from kingdom to kingdom, and this variety is confirmed by Rashba's description of the different communal structures that existed in his time.

> No uniform practice exists in these matters. In some places the affairs of the community are conducted by its elders and their councillors; there are others in which even the majority is unable to do anything without the consent and agreement of the entire community; there are still other places where [the members of the community] appoint certain [or: well-known] men, and the [community agrees] to conduct themselves according to their decisions in all communal affairs. These men are the trustees of the community. I see that you have adopted the last procedure since you choose officials called *mukkadamin*. Wherever this practice is followed the others are ruled out.[25]

We do find instances in Spain where ordinances *(takkanot)* required the approval of the entire community. But the most common form of government of the Jewish communities in Spain placed ultimate control of the community in the hands of a few families, although sometimes administration was placed in the hands of a wider group. The formal arrangement differed from community to community, but most often the smaller group was a self-perpetuating body in which each member elected his own successor without a majority vote. This seems to have been done in order to assure the representation of certain factions of the community.[26] At times powerful and rich families, by virtue of their connections in the Spanish courts, succeeded in dominating communal life by controlling the ruling bodies of the community. The prominent Al-Constantini family is a good example.[27]

[24]See, e.g., H. H. Ben-Sasson, *Hakehillah Hayehudit Biyemei Habeinayim* (Jerusalem 1976), p. 12: פירש הגאון ר׳ שמואל בן חפני ״תבע לראש הדור אשר עליו החוב למנות שופטים על ישראל״. Generally, see H. H. Ben-Sasson, *Perakim Letoldot Hayehudim Biyemei Habeinayim* (Tel Aviv 1958), pp. 84-142, and S. Baron, *The Jewish Community*, ch. 6.

[25]Rashba's Responsa, part III #394. See Y. Baer, *A History of the Jews in Christian Spain* (Philadelphia 1961), vol. I, p. 219. My translation differs in some minor ways. See also H. Beinart, "Hispano-Jewish Society," *Journal of World History* 11 (1968) 226-237.

[26]See Rashba's Responsa, III #399; A. A. Neumann, *The Jews in Spain*, vol. 1, pp. 34-35 and notes.

[27]Y. Baer, *Dvir* 2 (1923), 316; B. Septimus, "Ma'avak 'al shilton ẓiburi bevarẓelona bitkufat hapulmus 'al sifrei harambam," *Tarbiz* 42 (1973) 389-400. See Yom Tov

The Tudelan community of Rabbi Joshua ibn Shu'eib's time had a number of different governing and administrative bodies. There is mention in *takkanot* from the end of the thirteenth century and the beginning of the fourteenth of *mukkadamin* who had some sort of administrative or executive function.[28] There was a council of "eleven important members of the community," one of whose functions was the authoritative interpretation of all community *takkanot.*[29] There was also a "council of the twenty" who legislated *takkanot.*[30] The real power of the community, however, seems to have rested in a group of about eight families, the members of which appear as the signatories of many of the Tudelan *takkanot*. Indeed in a *takkanah* probably from the last decade of the thirteenth century it is stated that no new *takkanot* can be legislated without the signatures of the *mukkadamin* and of representatives of the "eight families who usually gather at the community assembly." The families mentioned in the *takkanah* are Falaqera, Abbasi, Fasat, Shu'eib, Daud, Manir, Comis and Orabuena.[31]

Protest against communal authority arose from time to time and often controversy surrounded the apportionment of taxes. Sometimes the wealthier members of the community insisted that a new tax be spread evenly on a population basis, while the lower classes demanded that the taxes be imposed in proportion to wealth. There was relatively little protest, however, concerning the manner in which the community was administered.[32]

Rabbi Joshua ibn Shu'eib's homily, therefore, is significant, for he is responding to just such a protest movement against the very basis of aristocratic leadership of Tudela. "In this matter many err when they say 'we are all the children of one man—I am as good as so-and-so; why is he in this position and not I?' This is utter foolishness."[33]

A *takkanah* in Tudela from 1303 confirms the fact that protests were being lodged against the communal leadership, although the *takkanah* does not state precisely what the protests were.

Assis, "The Jews of Aragon under James II" (unpublished Ph.D. thesis, Hebrew University, 1981), pp. 328ff.

[28]See F. Baer, *Die Juden in Christlichen Spanien*, vol. 1, #586, pp. 949ff. The *mukkadamin* are mentioned in paragraph 3 of that group of *takkanot.* On the earliest use of the term, see S. Goitein, *A Mediterranean Society*, vol. 2 (Los Angeles 1971), pp. 68ff.

[29]Baer, *Die Juden*, loc. cit., par. 3.

[30]Ibid. #601 par. 1 (p. 983).

[31]Ibid. #586 par. 16 (p. 957). This *takkanah* is undated, but the previous *takkanah* (par. 15) which is dated 1288 has almost identical signatories.

[32]See Baer, *Toldot*, p. 127; *History*, vol. 1, p. 213. Concerning Aragon see Y. Assis, "The Jews of Aragon," pp. 334f.

[33]66Da.

> The community decided that no resident of this city should...participate in any gathering or any agreement whose goal is to annul a *takkanah* or *haskamah* that the community agreed upon through the agency of the "twenty" or the "eleven." Whoever violates the above or challenges actions of the community will pay a fine to the king.[34]

What is interesting in ibn Shu'eib's description are the premises upon which the protest is being lodged. The protestors reject the hereditary prerogatives of the leaders of the community. Birth endows no one with special rights over others, they argue.[35]

Ibn Shu'eib's reaction is diplomatic. From the point of view of theory, he says, you are wrong. As we saw above, he maintains that the political hierarchy exists in the image of the Divine hierarchy.

Furthermore, in his *derashah* on *Shoftim* ibn Shu'eib paraphrases the *Sifri* as follows: "One may not remove a *Parnas*, or a *Ḥazzan* or a slaughterer or a circumcisor or any communal appointee; he transmits his position as an inheritance to his descendants."[36]

Ibn Shu'eib could probably do no less than defend the leadership since his family was one of the eight families whose approval was required on all communal *takkanot*, and it is very likely too that for a time he himself was the family's representative to this council of the eight.[37] But ibn Shu'eib assures the protestors that there are rewards for submission to the political leadership. If indeed you are really better, then by submitting to the community's authority you will merit "honor in far greater proportion to the submission you show now."[38] Perhaps he is alluding to the fact that, although there was no room for mobility within the hierarchy of the political leadership of the Jewish community, there was the possibility of mobility through spiritual leadership. And this is perhaps the reason that ibn Shu'eib introduces the last of his analogies "those who sit before the king, those who live in the court, etc.," for, among members of this spiritual court, there is some degree of mobility.[39]

[34]Baer, *Die Juden*, #601 (p. 983). "The kahal decided" = הסכימו הקהל. It is not clear whether this meant that the community gathered for a decision or that the community leaders decided in the name of the kahal.

[35]Cf. Mishnah Sanhedrin 4:5.

[36]84Ca. ובספרי דרשו מכאן שכל פרנס חזן או טבח או מוהל ושאר מנוי הקהל שאין יכולין להעבירן ממנויין ומוריש מנוייו לזרעו Ibn Shu'eib adds to the Sifre text דכתיב הוא ובניו See Sifre, Deut 17:20 (p. 212) and *Tosefta Ki-Fshutah Mo'ed*, part IV, p. 694. My thanks to Prof. G. Blidstein for bringing these passages to my attention.

[37]See above ch. I, pp. 3-4.

[38]66Db.

[39]Thus in the passage cited ibn Shu'eib alludes to a spiritual intellectual hierarchy (ומן החכמים השלמים בתורה ובמצוות ובמעשים טובים רואים פני המלך) Cf. *Guide* III,51.

Rabbi Joshua ibn Shu'eib's identification with some of the social ideals of the aristocracy did not render him insensitive to the abuses of that group nor to the needs and requirements of the simply-educated Jew. Although one might have expected a monarchist to be oblivious to the needs of the common people, ibn Shu'eib shows himself to be a compassionate and understanding teacher and leader, a populist one might even say, in ethical theory, as we shall see below.

In his attitude towards members of the aristocracy, particularly the courtiers, he was painfully aware that many had abandoned the observance of traditional Jewish practice. In his *derashah* on *Beha'alotkha*, he cites the Mishnah (Avot 4:21) that says that "three things remove a person from this world—jealousy, lust, and honor." These three drives, he says, drives which could be sublimated for good,[40] are the sources of wickedness in many people. This he uses as a starting point for a critique of certain groups of Jews. From his description we shall see that he must have had in mind the courtiers of his time.

He begins with a description of the corroding effects that jealousy can have on a person. There are people, he says, who envy others for their wisdom, their wealth, or their ethical achievements, believing that these qualities should belong only to themselves. Jealousy is self-destructive, he says, for as "...one wise man said, God does not have to take revenge on jealous people; their own jealousy brings utter destruction upon them, for they spend their days in sorrow and suffering."[41]

It is, however, his description of lust and honor which strongly suggests that he is describing the courtiers of his time.

> Desire too when it exceeds its bounds is evil, for a person's evil inclination [*yeẓer*] rules over him and intensifies his desire to eat "coarse" [i.e., non-kosher] foods in great quantities and to indulge in other physical pleasures, particularly with women. This desire will lead to the destruction of his body because he will never be satiated, just as they said "man has a small organ: the more he tries to satiate it, the hungrier it gets; but when he deprives it, it is satiated." Whoever allows his desires to have controlling powers over him will never be satisfied. They will cause him to violate the entire Torah, even to commit idolatry. For to indulge his desire for food and sexual intercourse, he will violate

Although the context of ibn Shu'eib's arguments is the political hierarchy, I believe it is clear that he wants to allude to the possibility of mobility in spiritual intellectual contexts.

For contemporary notions of hierarchy and mobility in Spain, see Joseph F. O'Callaghan, *A History of Medieval Spain* (Ithaca 1975), pp. 466-468.

[40]See below, pp. 54-55.

[41]62Db.

the Sabbath, testify falsely, kill and eventually abandon his religion to be free of all the *miẓvot*.

The pursuit of honor can also go out of bounds when people want to be honored not for the sake of Heaven, but to seek power and frighten others in order to show their prestige and honor, all of which will eventually lead to the destruction of their bodies; for there are those who travel by ship and cross deserts, subjecting themselves to drought by day and frost at night, all to gather money so that they will be honored by and domineer over their generation and in order to seek high appointments from princes and kings.

All this will bring destruction to them, for they will become sick and die from the effort even if they reach their desired goal. If they do not reach it, they will die from worry and disappointment. Even if they succeed in coming close to the crown, they will be injured or die anyway, for they will be informed upon, just as the Sages have warned, "Do not fraternize with the authorities." They have said that Joseph died before his brothers only because he fraternized with the government and ruled over others. This is the reason kings die before their time at a young age...because the kingdom buries its masters before their time. This is what is meant that honor takes a person out of the world—this world—as well as the world to come, because it is impossible to escape many serious and great sins.[42]

Several items in this passage require comment. Ibn Shu'eib does not identify who the people are, but his words bring to mind Y. Baer's description of the decline of sexual morality in Spain among the courtiers.[43] During the last decades of the thirteenth century, the problem became particularly acute, and in Toledo a reform movement developed under the leadership of Todros b. Judah Halevi Abulafia. The problem was symptomatic of the state of affairs in Spain generally and mention of it recurs in the ethical literature throughout the fourteenth and fifteenth centuries, in works such as Menaḥem b. Zeraḥ's *Ẓedah Laderekh.*[44]

The matter of sexual promiscuity is mentioned only twice in the Derashot, but each time in very sharp and condemning language. The first is the passage quoted above. The second is in the *derashah* to *Pinḥas*, where ibn Shu'eib discusses Pinḥas' reward for his zealotry in killing Zimri as he lay with a Midianite woman (Num 25:6-15):

Our Rabbis have said, whoever has sexual intercourse with a Gentile, zealots may kill him. A person should zealously defend God's honor by

[42]62D-63A.

[43]Y. Baer, *Toldot*, pp. 150-154; "Todros ben Yehudah Halevi Uzemano," *Zion* 2 (1937), 19-55.

[44]See below, n.51.

> opposing this sin more than other sins....In the Yerushalmi "Rabbi Simon said, Zimri caused tens of thousands of Israel to die," and we, how many Zimris do we have in our generation? This is to say that we should punish them, eliminate them from the land and clear the thorns from the vineyard.[45]

Perhaps these same "Zimris" are the "sect" to whom he refers in another place. "...There is another sect who do the opposite, for they pursue pleasures and discard the worship of God behind their backs."[46]

Baer has pointed out the nexus of sexual promiscuity, apostasy and informing.[47] Above, Rabbi Joshua ibn Shu'eib connects sexual promiscuity with eventual abandonment of *mizvot* and then apostasy; below we shall see his polemic against informers, and both may be the same group.[48] Piecing together the fragments of ibn Shu'eib's polemic, what we see is a hedonistic, power-hungry courtier who turns informer and apostate. The motive for conversion, according to ibn Shu'eib, is pleasure, convenience and power.[49]

This situation can be further documented before ibn Shu'eib's time and after him. In Isaac ibn Sahula's *Meshal Hakadmoni*, there is a parable of an adulterous wife and her husband the pious penitent, a story with characters that very likely reflect real people in thirteenth-century Spain.[50]

In this context let us look at R. Menaḥem b. Zeraḥ's programmatic statement in *Ẓedah Laderekh.*

> ...for I have seen those who walk in the court of our master the king, who shield and protect His nation according to their stature and place. However, because of the unsettled time and because of their desire for luxuries and other unnecessary items they have declined in their observance of *mizvot*, particularly those who travel, the servants and those who sit before the king. They completely abandon the laws of

[45]73BC.

[46]94Ab.

[47]Baer, *Toldot*, pp. 141ff.; *History*, vol. 1, pp. 236ff.

[48]What is not clear in ibn Shu'eib is whether or not philosophic culture is also a source for undermining the religious observance of this class. He does bemoan (89A): שיש כת בעולם ארורה ורשעה שסוברת שהצרות הבאות על האדם אינם בהשגחה ועונש אלא במקרה. It is not clear who these people are.

[49]Cf. B. Netanyahu, "Establishing the Dates of the Books *'Ha-Kaneh'* and *'Ha-peliah'*," *Salo Baron Jubilee Volume* (New York/Jerusalem 1974), Hebrew section, pp. 264-265. See "Iggeret Yehoshua Halorki" in J. Eisenstein, ed., *Ozar Vikuḥim* (Israel 1969), p. 98.

[50]*Meshal Hakadmoni*, pp. 73-87; and 119-120. See also S. Stein, "Rationalists and Kabbalists in Medieval Allegory," *Journal of Jewish Studies* 6 (1955) 73-86.

> prayer, blessings, permitted and prohibited food, Shabbat and holidays, laws concerning women and laws of wines.[51]

All those sins mentioned by ibn Shu'eib are mentioned by his student, who explicitly associates them with courtiers. We shall see below, however, that despite his sharp criticism of these failings ibn Shu'eib does not respond by advocating an ascetic world outlook.

Pride, arrogance, pursuit of honor and power were also widespread failings among the courtiers, and criticism of them became a common theme in contemporary ethical literature. Undoubtedly, Isaac ibn Sahula is echoing the courtiers with the following words that he puts into the mouth of the raven in *Meshal Hakadmoni*:

> One must vaunt his pedigree; he should raise his eyes and be proud of his ancestors and his family, boast of his wisdom and knowledge and let the world know of his insight. He will thereby be high and exalted in their eyes...and should a stranger come by who knows not his stature...he must inform him.[52]

Kalonymus b. Kalonymus in nearby Provence ridicules the same posture of those who proudly vaunt their pedigree:

> Of praise and honor I am deserving
> For my ancestry is fine, and I am a man of learning.[53]

The claim to distinguished ancestry was often a result of the Jews' need to legitimize their settlement in an area by asserting their ancient roots,[54] but it often also resulted in the display of pride and arrogance and the desire for great honor on the part of the members of aristocratic families.

Ibn Shu'eib's remarks about the travels of these people is borne out by many sources which testify to the extensive travels of Spanish Jews. The extensive travels of the courtiers were an inherent part of their position.[55]

Particularly intriguing are ibn Shu'eib's comments about rulership and political power. Whereas we first saw him as an ardent monarchist and a defender of the political hierarchy, he was as well very wary of the dangers and pitfalls of political power. When he warned of the pitfalls, however, he had in mind the courtiers who served the Gentile governments, whereas his defense

[51]*Ẓedah Laderekh*, intro. p. 4a. See Beinart, "Demutah Shel Haḥaẓranut Hayehudit Bisfarad Hanoẓrit," in *Elites and Leading Groups* (Jerusalem 1966), p. 65.

[52]*Meshal*, p. 193; cf. p. 209.

[53]*Even Boḥan*, ed. A. Haberman (Tel Aviv 1956), p. 38. For the end of the fourteenth century, see Solomon Alami's *Iggeret Hamusar*, ed. A. Haberman (Jerusalem 1946), p. 44.

[54]Beinart, "Demutah," p. 63.

[55]62Dc. The travels of Jewish businessmen throughout the Mediterranean basin in pursuit of their business is well known. See S. Goitein, *A Mediterranean Society*, passim. For Spain of this time see Y. Baer in *Dvir* 2 (1923) 311.

of hierarchical rule was directed internally, within the Jewish community. But even if the critique of political power was intended internally as well, it still sits well with ibn Shu'eib's defense of that power as legitimate. Abuse by individuals or the possible corrosive effect that political power has on its holders does not invalidate the necessity for political institutions. While he realized the deficiencies of some courtiers, he did not reject the courtiers as as a class.[56]

2. A Typology of Tudelan Jewish Society

The Jews to whom Rabbi Joshua ibn Shu'eib preached were naturally a varied group. His categorization of them in his *derashah* for Shabbat Hagadol provides us with confirmation of what we know from other similar typologies but adds additional insights as well.

> The first group are those who study Torah and are meticulous in fulfilling the *miẓvot*, but they are a minority. The second group also studies Torah but are not meticulous in their observance of *miẓvot*. Then there are those who perform *miẓvot* and do good deeds but are not learned. Finally there are the idle people [*yoshvei keranot*] who have neither Torah nor good deeds.[57]

At the top of his list are Torah scholars—obviously the rabbinic leadership to whom he refers in other places as the "pillars of the world"[58] and are singled out like the tribe of Levi, who have an obligation to teach and instruct the public.[59] He compares them to those who sit before the king, the *ro'ei penei hamelekh* (cf. 2 Kings 25:19, Esth. 1:14)[60] a religious and intellectual elite who "study Torah in the best manner possible...They are special individuals (*yeḥidim*)."[61] The comment "but they are a minority" is perhaps not a judgment concerning the general level of learning but rather the realistic assessment that the religious intellectual elite are always a minority.

The second and third groups are perhaps most representative of his audience. Group two very likely consisted of upper- and middle-class Jews who had more leisure time for study but whose practice of *miẓvot* fell short of the ideal. R. Menaḥem b. Zeraḥ, ibn Shu'eib's student, gives a fuller description of this group in his own fourfold typology of Jews:

---

[56]In contrast Baer, *Toldot*, pp. 154ff. (*History*, vol. 1, pp. 261ff.), claims that the author of the Zohar expressed *hatred* of the wealthy, incontinent aristocracy: ‏"רוחש בעל הזוהר שנאה גלויה לחברה הפרוצה והאפיקורסית. כל תורתו של המקובל היא מחאה נמרצת נגד השקפתם האוירואיסטית."‏

[57]37D.

[58]53Ac.

[59]54Bb. ‏והיחידים שבדור החכמים צריך לקבוע להם מדרשות שהם כנגד שבט לוי‏

[60]66Db.

[61]52Dc.

[The willow branches] symbolize the rest who are learned in Torah and know Bible.[62] They are property owners whose belief is in the manner of the masses and who perform *mizvot* for glory and power.[63]

Although there is no reference in this passage to any lack of meticulousness in the performance of the *mizvot*, clearly the manner of observance is not desirable, and we have seen above R. Menaḥem's complaint against the laxity in ritual observance among the upper classes.[64] Ibn Shu'eib's relatively gentle criticism is consistent with his moderate tone throughout the Derashot. He does, of course, point out his audience's failings—as we shall see in greater detail below—often in the areas of synagogue ritual or Torah study[65] but always in very gentle ways.

Because of our sins the Temple was destroyed but our synagogues and houses of study which replace it are called Temples in miniature. We must therefore worship in them with awe, fear and trepidation as if we were worshipping before the *Shekhinah*. Our prayer must be with *kavvanah*.[66]

It is not enough to observe the *mizvah* 'approximately'; one must be exacting in its details as well.[67]

As we shall see below, he preaches usually not with polemical thrusts but with positive encouragement in the observance of moral and ethical qualities, and always in the path of moderation. Only rarely does he stray from advocating a Golden Mean ethic.[68]

The third group, "those who perform *mizvot* and do good deeds but are not learned," probably comprised a large section of his audience. Here R. Menaḥem's parallel characterization of this group adds not too much that is new, but is more poignant.

...they are the people of action, simple people ['amei ha'arez] empty of wisdom but filled with *mizvot* like a pomegranate.[69] They perform their

---

[62]Ibn Shu'eib characterizes his הם הקוראים בתורה שהיא שם יעקב (38Ab) as בעלי תורה שמדתו אמת והתורה נקראת אמת

[63]*Ẓedah Laderekh, ma'amar* 4 *kelal* 6, ch. 1. True, there is no allusion to any lack of meticulousness in the performance of the *mizvah*, but clearly the manner in which it is being observed is not desirable.

[64]This chapter, pp. 47-48.

[65]E.g., 14Db, 40Db; cf. ch. VI below.

[66]30Dc.

[67]39Bb.

[68]E.g., 88Bc which has some of the flavor of *Ḥasidei Ashkenaz:* כלומר שחייב אדם להשפיל ולהכניע האיברים שהוא חוטא בהם בעיניו הגבוהים וההסתכלות בנשים האסורות שיכניעם בבכי ובדמעות עד שוביהם. This type of advice is exceptional in the Derashot.

[69]See his *derashah* to *Tezaveh* which I edited in I. Twersky, ed., *Studies in Medieval Jewish History and Literature* (Cambridge MA 1979), p. 270, l.145, where ibn Shu'eib

> *miẓvot* for the sake of Heaven in a modest and lowly manner, not in a sophisticated or clever manner.[70]

These are the craftsmen, the artisans, the farmers in ibn Shu'eib's audience.

> ...the House of Israel; they are the craftsmen and artisans who are occupied with their business, who plough and sow, plant vineyards and who maintain the existence of society;[71] who pray morning and evening and perform *miẓvot*. It is they who sustain the world, for such was the purpose of creation for "the world was not created for naught."[72]

Ibn Shu'eib, who here accurately portrays a wide range of Tudelan occupations,[73] knows how to appreciate their crucial contribution to society and to encourage them in the study of Torah. He understands their difficulties and limitations and tries to help them improve.

> ...as it is said "some do more, some do less, [but what is important is that one's intentions be for the sake of Heaven"]....It is clear that as long as we are involved in Torah study according to our abilities whether little or much God will quicken the redemption.[74]

His gentle prodding and understanding emerges clearly from the following as well.

> The pressures of the exile and taxes prevent a person from fulfilling this *miẓvah* [the study of Torah] perfectly as the Rabbis have said: "the Torah was given only to those who eat Manna." Yet everyone is still obliged to fulfill the *miẓvot* to the best of his ability at least in his free hours....A person cannot properly study Torah while suffering—however, whoever tries, studies Torah or hears it [i.e., is instructed in it] during his free hours, particularly on holidays, and his heart is devoted to Heaven, Scripture considers him to have fulfilled the commandment of 'the words of the Torah shall not part from your mouth.' Therefore the Rabbis and the prophets would preach in special places on the Sabbath and holidays.[75]

uses a similar expression—להגין על הריקנים שבישראל שהם שולי העם ומלאים מצות כרמון (cf. Rashi, Shabbat 105b, שאין לך ריק בישראל שאין בו תורה ומצות).

[70]*Ẓedah Laderekh*, loc. cit. (n.63). See also H. Beinart's characterization of this group in "Hispano-Jewish Society," pp. 224-225.

[71]עוסקים ביישוב המציאות

[72]53Ac-Ba. Jewish tilling of the soil was often simply a plot of land next to the home. (See H. Beinart, "Hispano-Jewish Society," pp. 224-245.) The context of the statement in the text is also a fourfold classification of the Jewish people. However, here two of the groups do not seem to have any special social connotation.

[73]See Baer, *History*, vol. 1, p. 203 (*Toldot*, p. 121) and notes; Newman, *The Jews in Spain*, vol. 1, pp. 164-167; and M. Kayserling, *Die Juden in Navarre*, ch. 4.

[74]27Dc.

[75]38Ca.

These are the "empty ones in Israel, at the bottom of the nation, filled, however, with *miẓvot* like a pomegranate."[76]

Ibn Shu'eib's tolerance of the unlearned is notable, particularly in view of the negative attitude towards the *'am-ha'areẓ* (unlearned) one finds in some contemporary kabbalistic literature. The author of the *Ra'ya Mehemna*, for example, is usually critical of the *'amei ha'areẓ* and describes them as "crawling insects"[77] and "filth, whose daughters are crawling insects."[78] The difference between ibn Shu'eib and other kabbalists may lie in the definition of the *'am-ha'areẓ*. In kabbalistic literature, particularly in the Zohar, *'am-ha'areẓ* was associated with the neglect of *miẓvot*,[79] which was not necessarily the case in ibn Shu'eib's Derashot. His *'am-ha'areẓ* is the simple devoted but unlearned Jew[80] who is not therefore necessarily negligent in his religious duties.

The above groups are characteristic of Jewish societies in many times and places. There is a group, however, for which ibn Shu'eib reserves very strong words of condemnation, a group characteristic of Spain in his time. Perhaps they are the same as the *'amei ha'areẓ* or the *'erev rav* so severely condemned by the *Ra'ya Mehemna*, but ibn Shu'eib is neither so explicit nor so severe in his condemnation as the author of the *Ra'ya Mehemna*.

This group is the last in the typology presented above. In the continuation to that passage he says that,

> ...these verses [the proemial verse to the *derashah*, Proverbs 1:20] stand for these four categories. Referring to the first group, who are ignoramuses [burim] and empty of everything, far from the king's gate, the idlers [yoshvei keranot], the verse says "wisdom shouts [that is, in reproof] to those who are outside."[81]

This group is much lower than the *'amei ha'areẓ* who, though unlearned, at least fulfill *miẓvot*. They are "ignoramuses and mockers, who are part of Israel in name only."[82] Ibn Shu'eib's sharp polemic against this group is repeated in another passage with some additional characterizations.

---

[76]*Derashah* to *Teẓaveh*, cited above n.69.

[77]Zohar III 33A.

[78]Zohar III 277B. See Tishby, *Mishnat Hazohar*, vol. 2 (Jerusalem 1961), p. 214, and esp. 680-702. To be sure, Tishby notes an exceptional statement (p. 685 n.46), but the general tenor of the *Ra'ya Mehemna*, as opposed to the Zohar itself (p. 669 n.38), is negative. As Tishby points out, the *Ra'ya Mehemna* statements generally go beyond the negative statements in the Talmud (p. 686).

[79]Tishby, ibid., p. 685 from Zohar II 93a ־דהועיל ואיהו עם הארץ חשיד איהו על כלא ואפי לו על שפיכות דמים וגלוי עריות וע״ז

[80]Who is also classified on a very low level by the *Ra'ya Mehemna*; see Tishby, ibid., p. 684.

[81]38Aa.

[82]Ibid.

> ...One more group is so small that it is difficult to consider them as a sect. They are the sect of scorners [*kat haleẓim*] who do not contribute to society and certainly do not study Torah or observe *miẓvot*; they are indolent slanderers [*yoshvei keranot ba'alei lashon hara'*] who should be excluded from a *minyan*—even more—it is a *miẓvah* to destroy them altogether....They can be compared to the hair and fingernails which are waste products of the body. Thus when the Sages told us in [tractate] Pesaḥim that 'he who throws his fingernail clippings away is wicked, he who burns them is a *ḥasid* and he who buries them is a *ẓaddik*' they are alluding to this cursed sect who abandon life in the world to come and this world as well. Therefore he who tolerates their existence and throws them in with the others is wicked; he who burns them, a *ḥasid*, for he destroys them so that no memory of them is left; he who buries them, i.e., angrily rebukes them and imprisons them in an unseen place, is a *ẓaddik.*[83]

His use of the terms *kat haleẓim* and *yoshvei keranot* indicates that he is concerned with the same group as in the previous passage (or perhaps with part of that group, namely the *yoshvei keranot*, the indolent, who are also *ba'alei lashon hara'*, slanderers). From the verdict which he passes on them—"it is a *miẓvah* to destroy them...so that no memory of them is left"—and from the characterization "indolent slanderers," one suspects that ibn Shu'eib is dealing with informers, which would account for the severity of his verdict upon them. We know that informing was a very great problem for the Jews in Spain, and in Tudela itself an ordinance was passed in the year 1288 that states that an informer must be delivered to the Spanish authorities for a death penalty; if no death penalty is carried out, then the informer is excommunicated for fifty years. Death sentences were indeed carried out upon informers in Spain; the Spanish authorities were willing to give the Jewish community this most basic means of self-preservation.[84]

We know that there were informers among the courtiers who at times used their knowledge of happenings within the Jewish community to further their position with the monarch.[85] As Baer describes it—based in part on the poetry of the courtier and poet Todros b. Yehuda Halevi—there were courtiers "who were close to the royal courts, cold-blooded statesmen, strong-armed communal leaders who were concerned only with their own pleasure,

[83]53Bb. Cf. Beinart, "Demutah," p. 69: "ולא פעם הוצרכו ראשי הקהל לנדותם ולהוציאם מכלל ישראל"

[84]Baer, *Die Juden*, vol. I, p. 953 #8; S. Baron, *Social and Religious History of the Jews*, vol. 11, pp. 61 and 312 n.70. See D. Kaufman, "Jewish Informers in the Middle Ages," *Jewish Quarterly Review* o.s. VIII (1895-96) 217ff., and particularly the text of Rashba on p. 229.

[85]Beinart, "Demutah," p. 66.

renegades and heretics in their opinions, who did not fulfil the commandments of the religion."[86] Some eventually left Judaism. Ibn Shu'eib says of these, "[As for] the *meshumadim* [converts] and sinners of Israel who are already circumcised, the Holy One blessed be He extends their foreskins and ushers them into purgatory."[87] They were probably the same as those that he calls "the brazen ones in the generation from whom all destruction stems."[88] Noteworthy, however, is the fact that ibn Shu'eib does not classify the wicked as an economic class, a theme prominent in the *Ra'ya Mehemna*. This is to be expected, for, if ibn Shu'eib was indeed a member of the upper class, his battle was social and ideological but not economic.[89]

Ibn Shu'eib's typology thus reflects in some measure the variety of social and intellectual types in fourteenth-century Spain. The scholar, the upper-class Jew, the ordinary humble Jew and the arrogant courtier are all represented and addressed in ibn Shu'eib's Derashot.

3. Ethical Theory: Moderation, Sublimation, and Asceticism

The kind of polemic that ibn Shu'eib directed against the courtiers is rare in the Derashot. It is the gentle, moderate kind of statements that are more characteristic of his tenor and indeed fit in with ibn Shu'eib's ethical statements generally.

Following the mainstream of Jewish ethical thought,[90] ibn Shu'eib advocates moderation in ethical traits and moral qualities. Like Maimonides, ibn Shu'eib informs his listeners that: "the intention of our perfect Torah is that man should walk the middle path, eating what he must in moderation, drinking moderately, engaging in intercourse moderately, dwelling in society justly and honestly."[91]

[86]See Y. Baer, "Hareka' Hahistori shel Hara'ya Mehemna," *Zion* 5 (1940) 37.

[87]7Ac.

[88]88Ac. Cf. R. Judah b. R. Asher, *Zikhron Yehudah* #91 (quoted by Baer in *Zion* 2 [1937] 40).

[89]See below for his attitude towards wealth. Are they the same group mentioned on 73Bc for their sexual crimes and of whom ibn Shu'eib also says צריכים ליסרם ולבערם מן העולם?

[90]Maimonides is the most important representative of this school of thought (see next note) but, as many have pointed out, there is Rabbinic support for a Golden Mean ethic in the following passage (Yerushalmi Ḥagigah 2:1) התורה הזו דומה לשני שבילים אחד של אור ואחד של שלג. היטה בזו מת באור היטה בזו מת בשלג; מה יעשה יהלך באמצע See the comments of J. Dan and I. Tishby in *Mivḥar Sifrut Hamusar* (Jerusalem 1970), pp 263-264, where they point out that a Golden Mean ethic is implicit or explicit in the works of R. Saadia Gaon, *Beliefs and Opinions* 10:17 and 19; R. Baḥya ibn Pakuda, *Duties of the Heart* 3:4, 9:7; R. Judah Halevi, *Cuzari* II,50, III,5; R. Abraham ibn Daud, and others. See too Maimonides, *Guide* II,39; Commentary to the Mishnah 4:4.

[91]44Ab. See also 85Ac-Bb where he quotes Maimonides' *Shemonah Perakim*, ch. 4 which deals in detail with the Golden Mean. On the Golden Mean, cf. Steven S.

His moderation is coupled with a positive appreciation of worldly and material needs and desires. Man's material needs and desires were created by God and must therefore have a positive function in this world, for *lo tohu bera'ah*, "the world was not created for naught" (Isaiah 45:18), ibn Shu'eib says, and therefore a man "should allow his body its share of the pleasures of the world"[91]—in moderation, to be sure.

Lo tohu bera'ah tells us too that even the *yeẓer hara'*, man's evil inclination, must have a positive function in this world.[92]

> Therefore one who is truly a man will use the *yeẓer hara'* for the necessities of life, as they said "'be mindful of Him in all possible ways' (Prov 3:6) even in the performance of a transgression" (Berakhot 63a). They mean that, while eating and performing intercourse, which can bring about transgressions, Man should intend these actions to be for the sake of heaven.[94] According to others they meant a real transgression, as long as his intention was for the sake of heaven, as they said "a trangression done for His sake is greater than a *miẓvah* done not for His sake" (Nazir 23b)....They also said that a person will be held accountable for everything that his eyes saw and in which he did not indulge.[95]

In another passage a similar note is struck:

> Man must eat to sustain himself physically in order to worship God. Man's sexual drive is necessary for the performance of the *miẓvah* of "Be fruitful and multiply." When he uses this drive for the proper purpose, he is truly worshipping God.[96]

Thus for ibn Shu'eib sublimation provides the means through which material forces can be used positively. Indeed the pleasure derived from eating and drinking on the festivals becomes a spiritual experience.

> When we do the *miẓvot*, the soul derives great pleasure and at that moment even physical things, i.e., eating and drinking and other

Schwarzchild, "Moral Radicalism and 'Middlingness' in the Ethics of Maimonides," *Studies in Medieval Culture* XI (1977); but see I. Twersky, *Introduction to the Code of Maimonides* (New Haven 1980), pp. 459-468.

[92]94Ab; 95Bbc.

[93]86Bb.

[94]Cf. R. Jonah of Gerona in his commentary to Proverbs: עוד יש לפרש, בכל דרכיך דעהו, שיהיו כל מעשיך לשם שמים ואל תדרוש מן העוה״ז הנאה ותענוג וכבוד ועושר וכל חפץ רק להשיג עבודת השם ית׳

[95]See Yerushalmi Kiddushin 4:12 (end). Similarly, R. Joseph Gikitilia, *Ginat Egoz*, 96A,B (cited in Dinur, *Yisrael Bagolah*, Sidrah B vol. 4, p. 312).

[96]62Da. See above in this chapter for his polemic against sexual promiscuity. The abuses of a small group do not change his ideal.

> pleasures, become spiritual [*ḥozrim ruḥaniyim*] and part of the worship of God.[97]

All this is true, however, only if one's intention is proper, for

> if, God forbid,..a man intends to obtain physical pleasure from the celebration...the festival is called...'your festival"...about which it has been said "I despise your monthly celebrations and your festivals."[98]

Material things are thus not inherently evil. Only if misused can they lead to evil.

Physical labor has value as well. In a decidedly non-quietistic manner, ibn Shu'eib insists that labor is necessary for the sustenance of the world, again citing *lo tohu* as his basis. And since man was created to sustain the world physically as well as spiritually,[99] physical laborers are necessary for society. "Farmers who plough and sow and artisans maintain the existence of the world."[100]

Labor and work, therefore, have intrinsic merit. Rather than being considered punishment, they are a required element of existence.[101] Indeed, one may fulfill a positive commandment by working.[102]

> It should not occur to a person to rely solely on God and say that everything has been decided by Him. If that were the case, all human activity would cease. Man's hand and other organs would be useless. The Torah, ethical instruction and all study would be superfluous if everything was in the hands of Heaven.[103]

Trust in God *(bitaḥon)*, ibn Shu'eib continues, consists of the belief that it is ultimately God who controls man's success and failure. "Industry is futile if

[97]41Aa.

[98]Ibid. ובעשותינו המצות מתענגת הנפש תענוג גדול, ובאותה שעה אפ׳ הדברים הגופניים שהם המאכל והמשתה והתענוגים האחרים כולם חוזרים רוחניים והם עבודת השם ואם חס ושלום אינו כן אלא שהאדם מתכוון להנאת גופו ואינו עובד לשם יתעלה העבודה הראויה אינן מועדים ומקראי קודש ועל זה אמרו ז״ל אלא הם מועדי בזמן שאתם עושין המצות ומקדשין המועדות באסיפת העם בבתי כנסיות... ומשבחין לשם ועוסקין בתורה, אלא הם מועדי ואם לאו אינם מועדי אלא מועדיכם See too 37Bb.

[99]3Ac.

[100]53Ba. See also 54Bb: כי בית ישראל שהם העיקר והעוסקים במלאכה ועובדי האדמה הם המיישבים העולם דכתי׳ לא תוהו בראה.

[101]Cf. R. J. Z. Werblowsky, "Faith Hope and Trust: A Study in the Concept of Bitahon," *Papers of the Institute of Jewish Studies* 1 (1964) 124: "The point of all these theories of 'the duty of effort' *(hobath hahishtadlut)* is that they deny all intrinsic value to man's labours and refuse to relate his efforts to their apparent fruits." In ibn Shu'eib this is not apparent.

[102]14Dc. אמרי׳ במכילתא ששת ימים תעבוד זו מצות עשה לעשות מלאכה...וזה ראוי לעשות לכל איש משכיל שישתדל בכל יכלתו בעמלו וכל מעשה ידים

[103]14Cc.

God does not assist, but industry with *bitaḥon* is required of man."[104] Thus, as Werblowsky has put it, "[There is] danger, not in any kind of human activity, but in its divorce from dependence on God."[105]

The results of human labor and effort, namely material wealth, are also not inherently evil, and, as we have said, ibn Shu'eib does not at any point attack the wealthy. "Wealth is bestowed upon an individual for one of three reasons: for good—as a reward; as a trial and test; and as revenge and punishment."[106] Wealth is a spiritual blessing when it is used for charity, for in this way the owner demonstrates that he does not rely on his wealth for success, but rather on God.[107] Indeed the use of wealth is one of the four ways in which one worships God: with one's heart, that is, using the *yeẓer tov*, man's good inclination, and the *yeẓer hara'*; with his body, through the performance of *miẓvot* which are done by the hands and feet; through the tongue, by reading the Torah and reciting the *Shema'*; and through money, by spending it for the honor of God: by buying sacred books, by supporting scholars, by spending money for the Sabbath and holidays, and by giving charity.[108]

Ibn Shu'eib's call for moderation and his conception of the positive potential in material drives and goods is accompanied by a polemic against extreme asceticism. In this polemic, which is influenced by Maimonides,[109] ibn Shu'eib indicates that he has encountered ascetics both within and outside the Jewish community. Both Franciscans whom he may have known first hand and Moslem Sufis whom he probably knew only from literature are mentioned explicitly in the Derashot. In a passage which is attributed to the Cuzari[110] he says

> according to the beliefs of all the nations, those people are important who are despised and lowly and who impose suffering upon themselves; such is the case with respect to the Christian attitude towards the *minores* [*ze'irim*] and the Ishmaelite attitude towards the *al-abidan.*[111]

Consistently and repeatedly ibn Shu'eib criticizes ascetic practices such as

[104]14Dc. On the relationship between *bitaḥon* and asceticism, see Werblowsky (above n.101), pp. 127-128 and n.35.

[105]Werblowsky, p. 102.

[106]61Bb. See also 70Ab.

[107]Cf. the similar opinion of R. Eleazar Rokeaḥ quoted in H. H. Ben-Sasson's "The Distribution of Wealth and Intellectual Abilities According to Ashkenazi Hasidim" (Hebrew), *Zion* 35 (1970) 67-68. See too B. Septimus, "Piety and Power" (ch. II, n.19), pp. 218-221, on R. Jonah of Gerona.

[108]80B-C.

[109]*Shemonah Perakim*, ch. 4.

[110]It is really a paraphrase and expansion of *Cuzari* IV,20ff. and II,30ff.

[111]37Cb: והנה באמונת כל האומות חושבים למין האנשים הנבזים והשפלים והמסגפים עצמם כנוצרים לאותם **הצעירים** וכישמעאלים לאותן שקורין **אלעבידין**

extreme self-denial of food and physical suffering and the distribution of all of one's wealth.

> It is known that, among the sects of people, opinions are divided concerning the worship of God. There are those who inflict suffering upon themselves and do not want to derive any benefit from physical things and they abstain from everything. This is not a straight path, for it was not the intention of creation—*"lo tohu bera'ah*—the world was not created for naught."[112]
>
> A person should give his body its portion of worldly pleasures and he should not deny it, for this is not the soul's desire. Rather one should treat it in moderation, not affording all of its desires the way those who spend all their days and holidays pursuing luxuries...but he also should not cause his soul to suffer through denial and fasting and deprivation of pleasures.[113]

In another context ibn Shu'eib exhorts:

> "Do not be righteous overmuch and do not make yourself overwise" (Eccles 7:16). The explanation of this is that a person should neither cause himself to suffer by fasting nor give away all of his money to charity nor "kill" himself; such a person is called by our sages a foolish *ḥasid.*[114]

Similarly, "One should neither torture his body with fasting nor should he wear clothing of wool and hair and dwell in the deserts."[115]

It would seem that ibn Shu'eib is not merely repeating standard themes but is rather polemicizing against contemporary practices.

[112] 94Ab. Interesting are the five separate but ultimately interrelated contexts in which ibn Shu'eib uses the verse *lo tohu*: to affirm the importance of physical labor (54Bb); to negate ascetic practices (94Ab); to affirm the positive function of evil forces (26Bb); to support the notion that the world was created for man's use (59Ac); and to affirm the positive function of *'amei ha'areẓ* (MS. JTSAL).

[113] 95Bc: שיתן לגוף חלקו מהנאות העולם ולא יסגף אותן שאין זה רצון הנפש אלא להתנהג בזה על דרך האמצעי. לא שיתן לו כל תאות היצר כדרך העושים כל ימיהם כחגים ורודפים אחר המותרות שהן הבל הבלים כמו שאמר בתחלת ספרו הבל הבלים כנגד זמני השנה שהם זרע וקציר וקור וחום וקיץ וחורף ...ולא שיענה ויסגף נפשו בתענית ובמנוע ממנו קצת ההנאות See also 85Db, 62CD.

[114] 85Ba; 85Dab: אם רעב שונאך שהוא היצר ומתאוה תאוה חזק׳ או אם צמא האכילוהו לחם ומים and 61Da: על ההכרחיי שהוא צורך גדול בקיום העולם ואל תסגפהו לגמרי ואל תענה עצמך לגמרי (נזיר) וצריך בכפרה מפני שלא ילמדו ממנו ויעשו זה הדרך אם אינו צריך לכך שהוא חטא גדול See too 44Db concerning abstinence from meat.

[115] 44Ab. לא שיענה גופו בתענית וילבש בגדי הצמר והשער וישכון במדברות A little afterwards in the same *derashah* he refers to חסידים הראשונים ששמענו שמעם שלא היו אוכלין בשר בהמה גסה אלא בשר עוף כדי להוליד דם זך מאד וכל זה מכלל הקדושה שנא׳ והתקדשתם It is not clear whether they were contemporaries or not. Cf. Maimonides' *Shemoneh Perakim*, ch. 4.

In the Zohar we do find an ascetic tendency, although, as I. Tishby has pointed out, there are three different approaches in the Zohar to the nature and source of the human body, and only one of them leads logically to an ascetic world outlook.[116]

The three approaches to the nature of the body are: 1) It is by its very nature evil and cannot be changed. 2) It is neutral, composed as it is of the four elements, but it is open to the influence of the soul and hence may be sanctified by it. 3) The body, created according to the model of the ten holy *Sefirot*, is an important instrument for the attainment of sanctity and is part of the holy realm. This last approach is shared by ibn Shu'eib, as we shall see.

These three conceptions lead to three different manners of human conduct. The first implies an ascetic approach to life which denies the body's needs, since they are inherently evil. The second requires the sanctification of the body by raising its material nature to a spiritual one. The final approach, which conceives of the body as inherently sacred, says that all of man's physical actions have a sacramental character.

These analytic distinctions, Tishby points out, may not have been evident to the author of the Zohar himself, and the practical implications of the three theoretical positions may each be applicable under different circumstances. In any case, there are many passages in the Zohar which are in accord with the ascetic approach, which sees the body as inherently evil and which requires man to break his physical drives which stand in opposition to his spiritual needs. "The Holy One blessed be He breaks the body in order to impose the rule of the soul.[117]

The Zohar describes a society of *perushim*, separatists, who spend their days in the desert, supporting themselves on wild fruit and vegetables.

> R. Ḥezekiah said, I was among the Arabs and I saw men who were hiding in caves in the mountains who would come to their homes on the eve of every Sabbath. I said to them, "What are you doing?" They answered me, "We are separatists who study Torah every day...." I said to them "Would that my lot be with yours in the world to come. Blessed are you in this world and goodness will be yours in the world to come."[118]

While any definite link between the Zohar's *perushim* and ibn Shu'eib's *kat* cannot be proven, one may speculate that they are indeed the same group.

Ibn Shu'eib never hints or alludes to the notion found in the Zohar that the origin of the body lies in the *sitra aḥra* or the "other side" which symbolizes the forces of evil in the Zohar.[119] For ibn Shu'eib the body is a

[116]The following is based on I. Tishby, *Mishnat Hazohar*, vol. 2, pp. 84-87.

[117]Zohar I, 180; see Tishby, *Mishnat Hazohar*, 2, 85.

[118]*Zohar Hadash, Bereshit*, 15D *Midrash Hane'elam* (from Tishby, *M.H.*, 2, 584).

[119]Tishby, *M.H.*, 2, 85.

> distinguished vessel whose figure and limbs point to heavenly matters ....For this reason man must be very careful not to defile this distinguished vessel for there is no precious vessel more distinguished than it in the world.[120]

It is for this reason that the

> hands which are the most important of the limbs allude to important roots...and there is therefore great significance in the fact that Israel is blessed by the raising of the hands of the priests.[121]
>
> Man is an analogue of the Universe. He has ten fingers on his hands and on his feet symbolizing the "tens"....Therefore man is obligated to guard his holy image *(ẓelem)* and see that his limbs are kept in cleanliness and sanctity. He should not use them for *tum'ah*, defilement, like other animals.[122]

The importance of the body, he says, is that it "symbolizes the Divine structure,"[123] that is, the ten *Sefirot*. It is certainly for this reason that

> the soul from above desires to reside in the body, for it knows what an honorable abode it is. Indeed when the soul leaves the body it weeps as it is written "his soul mourns for him" (Job 14:22). This is the secret of the revival of the dead and the world to come.[124]

Now the body is composed of base matter, whereas the soul is completely spiritual; hence they are opposite in their very essence. Indeed

> According to the wise men of the nations...[the soul] emanates from the angels, but the sages of Israel elevate it more and say it emanates from a source even higher—from the *ẓeror haḥayim.*[125]

However, he adds, the soul desires the body and remains attached to it by virtue of the food and drink that the body consumes. The soul remains attached to the body only as long as the body consumes food.

Thus man's material nature sustains his spiritual nature. It is true that the body's material origin is the source of man's *yeẓer hara'*, his evil instinct, but this does not mitigate the body's importance as an image of the Divine order nor does it lessen its potential for *kedushah*—holiness.[126]

[120] 45Bc.

[121] 20Dc. Cf. *Sha'arei Ha'avodah*, attributed to R. Jonah of Gerona (Bnei Brak 1970), p. 10. See below, p. 93.

[122] 60Ca. See A. Altmann, "The Delphic Maxim in Medieval Islam and Judaism" in *Studies in Religious Philosophy and Mysticism* (Ithaca 1969), p. 28.

[123] והוא כנגד הבנין העליון 48Cc.

[124] 37Ac.

[125] 37Bb.

[126] See 91Ac: שהנשמה היא עליונה רוחנית והגוף הוא שפל ונבזה ארציי; 21Dc: שני הפכים בנושא אחד; 91Ac: וחייבה סוד הבריאה להיות מכח נפש הנשמה יצר טוב מנהיג לאדם בדרך טובה ומכח הגוף כח ממשיך אחר התאוה והוא השטן ויצר הרע והוא כמו שאור שבעיסה כי השאור לבדו הוא רע אבל כשמשימין ממנו בעיסה כשיעור וכראוי הוא טוב מאד

The emphasis on the inherent sanctity of the human body and its implications for the potential good in all of man's material drives accounts for ibn Shu'eib's opposition to extreme asceticism and his moderate ethical demands.

> When man uses his limbs and organs for the performance of *mizvot* they are sacred; if, however, he uses them for transgressions such as thievery or looking upon forbidden women, then they are impure.[127]

With a moderate ethic go compassion and understanding of the people in fulfilling their religious obligations.

> "Some do more, some do less, but what is important is that one's intentions be for the sake of Heaven." The Torah does not require that we fulfill all 613 *mizvot*, nor does it state that if we do not read the entire Torah we will not merit a portion in the world to come. This is not the case. Everything depends on one's intention.[128]

or again

> "Happy are you who sow beside all waters" (Is 32:20). As the sages have said, "water means Torah"....And so here "all water" means any water: even a little water does good, as it is said some do more, some do less, etc.[129]

Ibn Shu'eib does not attempt to hold up an impossibly high ethic for his listeners. He is a *darshan* who obviously knows the capacities and the limitations of his audience and tries to encourage them with sympathy and understanding, rather than with fire and brimstone.[130] It is in this light that we

[127] 48Dc.

[128] 86Cc. The passage continues: וכמו שאמרו על פסוק כי המצוה הזאת אשר אנכי מצוך היום וגו׳ כי קרוב אליך וגו׳ וכי מצוה אחת היא והלא הם תריג מצות. אבל אמר המצוה כי הכל אחר הכוונה שהיא מצוה אחת, ויעסוק אדם בהם כפי יכלתו

[129] 27Dc: אשריכם זורעי על כל מים, ודרשו ז״ל אין מים אלא תורה דכתיב הוי כל צמא לכו למים. ומה שאמר **כל** מים ר״ל שום מים אפילו מעט, וכמו שאמרו אחד המרבה ואחד הממעיט See Avodah Zarah 5b. Ibn Shu'eib adds that the emphasis here is on the word **כל**. On p. 38B he also discusses the obligation to study Torah, realizing that many people can only find the time to study on the Sabbaths and holidays. Those who take full advantage of their time are considered as having studied full time.

What is interesting is that he concludes the discussion by mentioning that the recital of the *Shema'* is a technical fulfillment of *Talmud Torah*, the obligation to study Torah, a notion which, as he points out, the Talmud says should not be expounded publicly (Menaḥot 99b). His contemporary, R. Isaac ibn Sahula, author of the *Meshal Hakadmoni*, berates his audience for only fulfilling this minimum requirement. See *Meshal Hakadmoni*, intro. p. 5: ויאמרו אלי בנפש מרה ודעת חסרה לתורה ולתעודה חתום תורה ודי לנו בקראת שמע בעונתה ותפילה כתקנתה. כי המקרים הזידונו וירעו אתנו המצרים ויענונו

[130] Cf. Rashba, Responsa V #238: דע כי לשון רכה תשבור גרם. צריך לעלות מן הקלה אל החמורה והחכם מעלים עין לעתים

may understand his reference to the Rabbinic criticism of the prophets Isaiah and Elijah for having accused Israel of sins.[131]

But sympathy and understanding do not mean that one must compromise, condone or overlook. Nor does it mean that one cannot set up guidelines. R. Joshua does chastise, rebuke, and criticize, even strongly at times, just as he does urge restraint in material consumption.

One favorite theme of his, already mentioned above, is Torah study. Another is prayer. "Those who neglect worship of God and prayer, who arise early but arrive late for the services of God, their actions are nothingness and emptiness."[132]

Other themes which elicit gentle rebuke are proper business ethics,[133] eagerness in the performance of *miẓvot*[134] mutual and communal responsibility,[135] the evils of slander[136] and anger,[137] and the virtues of modesty[138] and repentance.[139]

His calls for restraint in dealing with physical and material drives do not, of course, contradict his opposition to extreme asceticism and his belief in the possibility of sublimating one's baser instincts. Both sublimation and suppression are valid methods in achieving ethical restraint, according to ibn Shu'eib. Since the body and the soul are "two opposites in one subject,"[140] man must "suppress the *yeẓer* and rule over the desire which overcomes man."[141] Man should consume only what is absolutely necessary to sustain himself and should not intend his consumption to be for pleasure but "for the sake of Heaven."[142] That R. Joshua did not consider this as contradictory to the notion of sublimating the *yeẓer hara'* and directing its drives to positive ends is evident from the end of the *derashah* to *Ki Teẓei* where, immediately after quoting the Talmudic saying that a person will have to give an account

[131] 92Ab.
[132] 14Db. Cf. 30Dc and 81Db. See below ch. V.
[133] 20Dc.
[134] 40Db.
[135] 53B-C.
[136] 64C-66.
[137] 68A-B.
[138] 60-62.
[139] 84A, 85A, 88D.
[140] 21Dc.
[141] 87Ba.
[142] 20Dc. Advocating restraint and sanctity, ibn Shu'eib cites the well-known passage from Ketuvot 104a that R. Judah Hanassi claimed that he derived no pleasure from this world and explains that R. Judah did not mean to say that he did not enjoy any physical pleasure, but that his intention in any physical act was for the sake of Heaven.

for everything he saw and did not eat and that R. Jose tasted from every permissible species in order to resist his *yeẓer*, Rabbi Joshua adds "a person should do so just to sustain the world [his body] and only as long as his intention is to worship God and improve his soul."[143] This is followed by a long passage taken from *Ḥovot Halevavot* which describes the soul as a guest in this world and a permanent resident in the world to come.[144] Spiritual matters should be man's primary concern.

Restraint and abstention which, according to ibn Shu'eib, lead to sanctity and purity are required not only to suppress the body and develop the soul, which is the essence of man, but are of crucial importance since the structure of man's body is a reflection of the Godhead itself—*ẓelem elokim.*[145]

Thus ibn Shu'eib emerges as a striking figure, for he combines in himself the aristocrat, defender of the privileges of the institutionalized powers, positive in his attitude towards wealth and the wealthy together with the confirmed kabbalist who is yet decidedly anti-ascetic; patient and tolerant of the simple uneducated Jew but impatient with and full of invective for the arrogant courtier who casts his Judaism aside.

This image should serve as a balance to the picture painted by Y. Baer of Spanish-Jewish society and its kabbalistic critics, such as the authors of the Zohar and the *Ra'ya Mehemna*. According to Baer, the "single goal" of the whole current of mysticism was "to remove Judaism from mundane entanglements to the sheltered precincts of Halakha and Aggada and guide it towards a way of life, mytho-mystic in outlook and *ascetic* in practice."[146] This asceticism, according to Baer, is accompanied by an extended glorification of the virtues of poverty, extended sympathetic descriptions of the persecuted poor and a sharp attack on the morality, particularly the sexual misconduct, of the aristocracy. In addition, he says, the kabbalists' attack on rationalism in the name of faith are typical of all works of this period.

And yet in ibn Shu'eib we have a kabbalist of a different temperament and a different work outlook. He did not see any intrinsic connection between his kabbalistic theory and the ascetic outlook of some of his colleagues. One does not have to "despise nature which caused him to sin" as R. Jonah Gerondi taught in his *Sha'arei Teshuvah.*[147] Restraint and properly directed use, yes,

[143] 86Cb. See. Y. Kiddushin, 4:12 (end).

[144] *Sha'ar 'Avodat Elokim*, ch. 9.

[145] See above p. 60 and n. 122.

[146] Baer, *History*, vol. 1, p. 244 (italics mine). See *Toldot*, p. 145: מגמתו הפנימית הראלית, which is not quite so definite as the English, "the single goal."

[147] Section I par. 33 (ed. Lewin Epstein [Jerusalem 1961], p. 20). R. Jonah's asceticism needs careful study. B. Septimus in "Piety and Power in Thirteenth Century Catalonia," p. 218, has characterized R. Jonah's human ideal as "far from a

denial and despising, no.[148]

His attitude towards the poor shows sympathy and understanding for them, but we do not find ibn Shu'eib extolling the virtues of poverty, nor does he equate the rich with the wicked.[149] On the contrary, we have seen his positive statements about wealth and property. While he does polemicize sharply against informers, we find no blanket indictments of contemporaries such as we find in R. Jonah: "The sins of the generation are many; they violate the prohibition against needless vows, cursing, taking God's name in vain, slander, needless hatred, looking at forbidden women and not studying Torah, which is worse than all of them."[150] One could not characterize him as "standing in the vanguard of the fight against the Jewish courtly society and for a reform in the life of the Jewish community," as S. Stein has described "the kabbalist."[151] On the other hand, although ibn Shu'eib was a member of one of the aristocratic families of Tudela, a fact which may have influenced him in his tolerance of the wealthy, we see that it did not blind him to the abuses that his contemporaries pointed out. He was too deeply committed to halakhic observance to be unaware of these abuses.

Tudela circa 1300 was not very different from neighboring cities in Spain, and the types of abuses pointed out by ibn Shu'eib were as common elsewhere as they were in Tudela, as evidenced by communal *takkanot* and continued criticism in later ethical books such as Alami's *Iggeret Hamusar.*[152] The

passionless unworldly ascetic R. Jonah recognizes the positive function of pleasure." However this source and some of the others Septimus cites needs to be contrasted with the very explicit statements in *Sha'rei Teshuvah* such as the one above and in paras. 30, 31 and 32 as well.

[148]An exception to this generalization about ibn Shu'eib would be a paragraph in a *derashah* which will be published in a forthcoming *Kovez̧ 'al Yad* in which ibn Shu'eib incorporates a passage from the anonymous bok of ethics, *Sefer Hayashar*, which expresses contempt for this world in terms which would be congenial with an ascetic world outlook.

[149]See Baer, *History*, p. 266. To be sure, I may be guilty of setting up a straw man. I. Tishby rejects the notion that the author of the *Ra'ya Mehemna* upheld poverty as an ideal. While he shows great compassion and sympathy for the poor, there is no glorification of poverty as an ideal. See *M.H.*, 2, pp. 692-702. Cf. G. Scholem, *Major Trends*, pp. 234-235. B. Netanyahu ignores Tishby's critique and accepts Baer's (and Scholem's) assessment—see "Zeman Ḥiburam Shel Hakanah Vehapeli'ah" in *Salo Baron Jubilee Volume*, Hebrew section, p. 255.

[150]*Sha'arei Teshuvah*, part 1, par. 8 (p. 10).

[151]S. M. Stein, "Rationalists and Kabbalists in Medieval Allegory," p. 77.

[152]Concerning the relevance of the evidence from the *Kanah* and the *Peli'ah* see the article by Netanyahu (above n.149) who argues that they were written in Spain after the riots of 1391. But see now M.Oron, "Hapeliah Vehakanah, Yesodot Hakabalah

generally temperate tone of ibn Shu'eib's remarks thus reflect not his situation but his ethical theory of moderation; the underlying social realities that the Derashot reveal confirm the general picture that emerges from other contemporary works.

Shebahem" (unpublished doctoral thesis, Hebrew University, 1980), and Y. Ta-Shema, "Where were the Books *Ha-kanah* and *Ha-pliah* Composed?" in *Studies in the History of Jewish Society* (Katz Festschrift; Jerusalem 1980; Hebrew), pp. 56-63.

Chapter IV
Attitude Towards Philosophy

Ibn Shu'eib's attitude towards philosophy and his use of philosophic sources share the ambiguity that is characteristic of his teacher Rashba and Rashba's students. It was Rashba who was the author of the famous *ḥerem* in 1305 prohibiting the study of philosophy for anyone under the age of twenty-five, at the culmination of a long and bitter struggle against the study of philosophy.[1] Rashba, however, was also well read in philosophic literature, and he "used phrases from the vocabulary of rationalism and introduced concepts from the realm of philosophy" in his commentary to the Aggadot and in his responsa.[2]

Rashba was circumspect in his use of philosophic explanations; he was first and foremost a halakhist, and his world outlook, to the extent that it went beyond that of the Talmud and Midrashim, was dominated by the world of Kabbalah. Still, the premises, analyses and conclusions of Jewish philosophers did not necessarily stand in opposition to the kabbalist; indeed, as we have said, there were kabbalists who saw Kabbalah as a step beyond philosophy—each valid in its own sphere[3]—while others attempted to integrate the

[1]See A. H. Halkin, "Haḥerem 'al Limmud Hapilosofiya," *Perakim* I (1967-68) 35-55; idem, "Yedaiah Bedershi's Apology," in A. Altmann, ed., *Jewish Medieval and Renaissance Studies* (Cambridge MA 1967), pp. 165-184.

[2]I. Twersky, "Aspects of the Social and Cultural History of Provencal Jewry," *Journal of World History* 11 (1968) 203. See, e.g., *Ḥidushei Harashba 'al Aggadot Hashas*, ed. S. Wineberger (Jerusalem 1966), Bava Batra, pp. 87ff.; *Teshuvot Harashba*, I, ##9, 60, 94.

[3]E.g., Abraham Abulafia. See G. Scholem, *Major Trends*, pp. 23, 24; below, ch. V, n.63 and above, ch. I, pp. 17-18.

two and interpret one system in terms of the other.[4]

Ibn Shu'eib, as a student of Rashba, unquestionably shared his teacher's positive attitude towards Kabbalah. That R. Joshua's perception of God, the world, man, and Torah were framed in kabbalistic categories is clear to any reader of the Derashot.[5] But his kabbalistic orientation did not stop him from drawing extensively on the literature of medieval Jewish philosophy. R. Sa'adia Gaon, R. Baḥya ibn Pakuda, R. Solomon ibn Gabirol, R. Judah Halevi, Maimonides, R. Jacob Anatoli and others are cited in the Derashot and indeed, as we have said, ibn Shu'eib sometimes used the original Arabic texts and presented his own translation in the Derashot.[6] Sometimes his use of philosophic ideas and interpretations is done in a matter-of-fact way, betraying their quiet assimilation; other times a philosophic view is presented only to be argued against. To assess his attitude towards philosophy, let us examine his treatment of three central themes in medieval Jewish philosophy: providence and free will; miracles; and prophecy.

1. Providence and Free Will

The idea that God is free to guide the world providentially, to suspend the laws of nature, and the analogous notion that man has free will are concepts that were affirmed and reaffirmed in traditional Jewish thought from Biblical times and onward.[7] In medieval times, as Jewish philosophers tried to come to terms with the Greek philosophic tradition, they became aware of the many problems that philosophy posed to these concepts. Some problems were: the belief in immutable laws of nature and the consequent deterministic view of the world and man; the negation of individual providence and the consequent absence of individual reward and punishment for moral actions; the impossibility of the miraculous suspension of the laws of nature. No Jewish philosopher abandoned belief in the traditional principles completely, but Jewish philosophers did at times redefine those concepts, reinterpreting the Biblical and Rabbinic passages that had become problematic in light of philosophic conceptions.

In the Derashot, while there is no systematic treatment of any of these issues, there is certainly an awareness of the philosophic issues involved, expressed usually in the form of a strong defense of the traditional Jewish

[4]See E. Schweid, *Harambam Veḥug Hashpa'ato*, ed. D. Oriyan (Jerusalem 1968), pp. 186ff.; S. O. Heller-Wilensky, "Isaac ibn Latif, Philosopher or Kabbalist?" *Jewish Medieval and Renaissance Studies*, pp. 185-223. Cf. above, ch. I, n.78.

[5]See below, ch. VIII.

[6]See above, ch. I, n.17.

[7]See E. E. Urbach, *Ḥazal, Emunot Vede'ot* (Jerusalem 1969), chs. 6, 11, 15; H. A. Wolfson, *Philo*, chs. 6 and 8.

point of view with an occasional sharp polemic against the "philosophic" position.

Who were his philosophic opponents? Ibn Shu'eib does not tell us, but in light of the contemporary controversy over the study of philosophy and particularly the rise of Averroistic thought among Jews in the thirteenth and fourteenth centuries, which renewed the problems of determinism and freedom, his concern with these traditional philosophic problems may have had some pressing contemporary urgency. The issues which he raises and the positions which he defends and attacks are not new, and indeed are matters which had been thoroughly reviewed before him.[8] What is significant is that a preacher in fourteenth-century Spain would raise them and contend with them. A preacher may attempt to shape and mold the ideas of his listeners; but he must also respond to their needs. Despite, or more likely because, of his desire to inculcate an essentially kabbalistic world view, ibn Shu'eib came to grips with philosophic problems as well. Perhaps through trying to put to rest the doubts arising out of philosophic speculation, he also wanted to win the confidence of his audience in order to tutor them in a kabbalistic world outlook.

While he returns to the theme of God's providence many times in the Derashot, he deals with it at length in two *derashot*, to *Tazri'a-Meẓora* and to *Devarim.* The *derashah* to *Tazri'a* can serve as a focus around which we may place his comments in other places.

The proemial verses to the *derashah* are from Psalms (139:5)—"You have formed me fore and aft, You lay your hand upon me." Ibn Shu'eib begins with a polemic against those who deny God's providence:

> King David...based [this psalm] on the idea of providence. He included in it the song of the embryo, which teaches providence, that is, that all the occurrences in this world are watched over and do not occur accidentally. The creation and sustaining of the embryo in the mother's womb teaches providence and shuts the mouth of those who deny it....The Psalmist dwells at length on the subject of providence, bringing the creation of the embryo as proof to its truth, in opposition to those who strive against God, blessed be He, and speak evil, saying "the Lord has abandoned the land" (Ez. 8:12). Concerning them he says, "Do I not hate, O Lord, those who hate you...? I hate them with perfect hatred" (139:22). He dwelt at length opposing those who philosophize, to refute their opinions.[9]

[8]See, e.g., Radak's treatment in Frank Talmage, *HUCA* 39 (1968) 193-201. See C. Sirat, *Jewish Philosophical Thought in the Middle Ages* (Jerusalem 1975), pp. 347-360.

[9]46Ca.

This kind of polemic, which occurs more than once in the Derashot,[10] is a frequent theme in contemporary Jewish literature. For example, the same concern is expressed in R. Isaac ibn Sahula's *Meshal Hakadmoni,*[11] the Zohar[12] and in the works of R. Baḥya b. Asher.[13]

Ibn Shu'eib goes on, however, to define the nature of God's providence; following Maimonides, he says that providence is extended to all creatures, but in different degrees. To the animal world providence extends only as far as the species but not to individual members. Among mankind, although providence is extended to individual members, there are varying degrees of providence. The lowest level is extended to the nations of the world who are punished only for malicious lawlessness *(ḥamas)*. Among Israel, the more righteous the individual the greater his degree of providence; in addition, the Land of Israel is more closely watched over than the rest of the world, as Halevi before him emphasized.[14]

R. Joshua insists that it is really not necessary even to argue or defend the notion of providence, for "the Torah is replete with it." Nonetheless, he continues to argue for the Jewish conception of providence and against opposing views. Twice he enumerates various theories of providence which, while based on similar enumerations by Maimonides in the *Guide,*[15] differ from them somewhat. At the end of the *derashah* to *Tazri'a* he enumerates four opinions on providence which he says are characteristic of "the Lord's adversaries mentioned in the psalm."[16]

The first opinion is that God's providence extends only as far as the lunar sphere—the opinion that Maimonides attributes to Aristotle.[17] The second opinion is that God's providence extends over every single action in this world—the opinion Maimonides attributes to the Ashariya, who hold that God's actions in this world are arbitrary. The third opinion is that everything that occurs is predestined by decree of the stars. Ibn Shu'eib adds here that there is an acceptable version of this opinion, as we shall see. This opinion is substituted for the Mu'tazilite position in Maimonides' categorization. The opinion of Epicurus, the fourth opinion, says that there is no providence at all. Maimonides lists this opinion first; ibn Shu'eib shifts it to the end for

[10] 76Ac דעות ההשגחה שהם חמשה, השלשה מהם נפסדים הפסד גדול וחלילה מהם

[11] See particularly *Meshal*, ch. 5; see also S. Stein in *JJS* 6 (1955) 84.

[12] See the text cited by Baer, *Toldot*, p. 155 (*History*, vol. 1, p. 263); I. Tishby, *M.H.*, I, pp. 265ff.

[13] See his *Kad Hakemaḥ* in C. Chavel, ed., *Kitvei Rabeinu Baḥya* (Jerusalem 1970), s.v. *hashgaḥah*, pp. 135ff.

[14] *Cuzari* II, 10-12.

[15] II,17.

[16] 49Da.

[17] *Guide* III,17, opinion 2.

exegetical reasons. (For the same reason, he does not present the Torah's view on providence in this context.)

Before commenting on his substitution here of the astrological opinion for the Mu'tazilite view presented by Maimonides, let us look at ibn Shu'eib's parallel presentation of the various opinions in his *derashah* to *Devarim*. There, the first three opinions correspond to Maimonides' presentation, namely, the opinions of Epicurus, Aristotle, and the Ashariya. For the fourth opinion, ibn Shu'eib again substitutes astrological determinism for the Mu'tazilite view, but his discussion here merits close examination. Those who believe in astrological determinism, ibn Shu'eib says,[18] may be divided into two groups. First there are those who believe that "the decree is permanent and irrevocable," and as a result the rightous may at times suffer unjustly. There are, however, those who believe in astrological determinism only

> on the condition that the Lord above watches the individuals of the human race and changes the constellations so that one who is barren may have children, a rich man can become poor and a poor man rich, in accordance with the reward and punishment due them.[19]

He attributes this opinion to R. Abraham ibn Ezra, Rabad, and Naḥmanides, and he claims that it is widely accepted and is mentioned in the Bible and the Talmud.[20]

He cites many sources to sustain this position such as "'for it will be your wisdom and discernment in the sight of the people' [Deut 4:6]—this refers to the figuring of seasons and planets" (Shabbat 75a) which ibn Shu'eib understands as referring to astrological calculations,[21] or "children, longevity and sustenance depend not on merit but on the stars," (Mo'ed Katan 28a)[22] and others.

Confronting the obvious question—why do so many reject astrology?—he says that those who reject it do so for two reasons. First, it is a subtle and highly complex matter and many cannot master it. Second, since God's will may change the astrological decree, it appears as if astrologers have no precise knowledge.

Only the House of Israel, he goes on to say, when living in the Land of Israel is completely free of the influences of the planets. When they are outside of the Land of Israel, they are subject to the decree of the stars; but that decree, as we have said, is itself subject to change in the hands of God. Ibn Shu'eib

[18]76Ba.

[19]Ibid.

[20]Cf. I. Twersky, *Rabad*, pp. 281-282 and nn.48, 49.

[21]See I. Twersky, *Introduction to the Code*, pp. 381-387, for an analysis of the use of this verse in Talmudic and medieval exegesis.

[22]See below, n.47.

concludes with a discussion of various Talmudic statements (from Shabbat 156a) that touch on the problem of whether or not Israel is affected by the stars and reconciles them to the view he has put forward.[23]

After this long and rather enthusiastic endorsement of the modified astrological view, R. Joshua presents what Maimonides calls the fifth view. Maimonides himself presents two versions of this view: a version that he calls "the opinion of our Law"[24] followed by his own belief. It is the latter which ibn Shu'eib cites briefly.

> The providence of God, blessed be He, is over the human species as a group as well as over its individual members. To living things that are not rational, providence is extended only to the species but not to the individuals; for the individuals, everything is pure happenstance. All of man's actions are subject to reward and punishment, and Israel is not influenced by the stars for "the Lord's portion is His people" (Deut 32:9) and it is written (Deut 4:20) "but you the Lord took." The halakhah in the Talmud was decided that Israel is not influenced by the stars and those statements which say that Israel is subject to the stars represent only the opinion of individuals. This is the opinion of Maimonides as he wrote in his well-known book. It is a correct and pious view which he did not want to publicize.[25]

Returning now to the question of why ibn Shu'eib substituted the astrological view for the Mu'tazilite view, there are two factors which may have brought this about, factors which are characteristic of the uses to which ibn Shu'eib put philosophy in the Derashot. The Mu'tazilite view of providence is philosophically technical and ibn Shu'eib may have considered it too technical a view to consider or deal with in this context.[26] Alternately or in addition, it may have been considered irrelevant because of its lack of contemporary currency. The astrological view, particularly the modified version formulated by ibn Shu'eib, was popular not only among certain scholarly circles but among the laity as well. Thus, as is characteristic of many preachers, their sermons reflect not only the opinions that they want to inculcate into the people; they reflect also what the people want to hear.

To be sure, R. Joshua does not ignore the Maimonidean view, but his rather curt, even misleading, treatment of it, failing to mention the higher levels of providence to which the wise man accedes, when contrasted with his detailed treatment of the astrological view, clearly indicates where his sympathies lie.

[23] 76Cb.

[24] III,17, opinion 5.

[25] 76Cc: והיא סברה נכונה עם חסידות כי לא רצה לפרסם הענין. Note that ibn Shu'eib never refers to the *Guide* by name in the Derashot.

[26] See H. A. Wolfson, *The Philosophy of the Kalam* (Cambridge MA 1976), pp. 622-623.

Let us return now to the *derashah* to *Tazri'a*. Although he states forcefully at the beginning of the *derashah* that the Torah is so full of the notion of providence as to make arguments in its favor unnecessry, perhaps he meant this only rhetorically or only in connection with the opinion of Epicurus, for he does then set out to refute the other opinions on providence.

Against the argument that God acts out of the necessity of His being, ibn Shu'eib merely asserts that

> in the verse [Jer 9:23] "I am the Lord who practices lovingkindness, justice and righteousness in the earth," the prophet has listed the noble things that God does to creation. The first is lovingkindness: that is, "I have been absolutely kind to all of creation by creating them"; not one exists by necessity but rather by simple will, for He, blessed be He, alone is of necessary existence.[27]

Concerning Aristotle's argument that below the inner sphere everything is subject to generation and corruption and there is no providence over individual members of a species, only over the species in general, ibn Shu'eib argues in greater detail that

> even according to their corrupt opinion, why should they not believe in providence over man who possesses a spiritual soul? Even according to their theory of the soul, it is emanated from the angels and the Active Intellect, just as many scholars of the Torah who philosophize also believe.[28]

R. Joshua continues in a parenthesis that, according to the tradition of the Rabbis, the source of the soul is much higher than the angels

> as it is written "He blew into his nostrils the breath of life" (Gen 2:7) as our master Rabbi Moses ben Naḥman has written, for one who breathes into the nostrils of another gives of his soul to him.[29]

In any case, the soul in man, which is noble and spiritual, is immaterial and hence not subject to generation and corruption. It should therefore merit providence despite the fact that it resides in the material body. Characteristically, ibn Shu'eib supports this with a Biblical verse.

> "After my skin has been thus destroyed, then from my flesh *(mibsari)* I shall see God" (Job 19:26) meaning—as against those who...accept this wicked notion, that is, the absence of providence, I shall see God *mibsari*, which means from my soul, as it is written "my flesh [*bsari*] also dwells secure" (Ps 16:9). [thus, *bsari* can refer to the soul.] That is, from my soul I can support the belief in providence.[30]

[27] 52Ca.

[28] 46Dc-47Aa.

[29] 47Aa: כי הנופח באפי אחר מנשמתו יתֵן בו See M. Ḥalamish, "Limkoro shel pitgam besifrut hakabbalah," *Sefer Hashanah Lebar Ilan* 13 (1970) 219.

[30] 47Aa. His assumption is that only the soul is eternal and hence secure. Cf. Me'iri,

Concerning the other opinion,[31] the opinion of the Ashariya, ibn Shu'eib's refutation leads us to the problem of determinism and free will. The Ashariya

> wish to establish providence very firmly—the result being, however, that their notion is far inferior to the first [that is, Aristotle's view] for any member of a religion. The philosophers too have rejected it, for it denies potentiality; whoever denies potentiality denies free will and choice in man; whosoever denies free will eliminates religion, the commandments, and reward and punishment. It is impossible that God should command us to do something which we cannot do...or vice versa. God forbid such evil when the Torah shouts "see I set...before you life and good, death and evil...therefore choose life" (Deut 30:15, 19).[32]

While ibn Shu'eib's objection is certainly not new, the matter was crucial, for without free will the basis of morality may be undermined. In Jewish philosophy, God's freedom to act providentially in His rule of the world and of humanity by deviating when necessary from the laws of nature has its corollary in the freedom of man to exercise his will freely.[33] Man's free will is a theme repeatedly emphasized in Jewish philosophic and ethical literature, and ibn Shu'eib returns to the theme many times in the Derashot, dealing with aggadic passages and Biblical verses that might seem to contradict that view. In the *derashah* to *Va'eira*, ibn Shu'eib assembles a collage of Biblical and Rabbinic passages which would seem to imply that the events of the world have been predetermined, thereby limiting man's freedom of choice. An examination of his discussion there will demonstrate further his concern for the notion of free will. It will also incidentally illustrate the manner in which he integrates his sources into the sermon, interspersing them with original commentary.

Discussing the verse in Exodus (6:3) "I appeared to Abraham, to Isaac, and to Jacob as God Almighty, but I did not make Myself known to them by My name the Lord," ibn Shu'eib explains that this was not due to the superiority of Moses over the fathers. Rather, the time for the revelation of that name had not come. He continues:

> This is the meaning of the verse "A season is set for everything, etc." (Eccl 3:1) as [the Rabbis] expounded: The Holy One, blessed be He, specified a time to create the world and a time for Abraham to call on

ad loc. See A. Altmann, "The Delphic Maxim in Medieval Islam and Judaism" in A. Altmann, ed., *Biblical and Other Studies*, pp. 196-230.

[31]The opinion of Epicurus he rejects totally, for it denies entirely any providence. The astrological view, when modified, he accepts.

[32]49Cb.

[33]See, e.g., H. A. Wolfson, *Philo* I, pp. 424-455.

God's name, a time for Moses, etc.[34] This passage has been found difficult by some scholars, for it appears from it that all matters are determined. But that is not the case, for there is free will, just as the sage Rabbi Akiva said concerning these matters: "everything is foreseen, yet freedom of choice is given."[35] He uttered a profound matter in few words. For although all is written in His book, still all is not decreed. This [book] is [referred to in] the verse "the book of man's generations" (Gen 5:1) [about which] they said "God showed Adam each generation and its preachers, etc."[36] and the same is said concerning Moses too.[37]

This [book is also referred to in] the verse [in which Moses demands "Now if You will forgive their sin well and good, but if not] erase me from the book which You have written" (Ex 32:32). [This knowledge was accessible to] Samuel Yarḥina'a who was an expert in the secret of intercalation[38] and this is [the book referred to in] the verse "they were all recorded in Your book" (Psalms 139:16).

This is also [the meaning of] the Rabbis' statement that "there was an arranged order of things before [creation]."[39]...It is certainly true that everything is revealed and foreseen before Him. He looks and sees to the beginning of all the generations. But still, freedom of choice is given. Maimonides discussed the matter at length in the Book of Knowledge (*Teshuvah* ch. 5); his words are very proper—"the words from the mouth of the wise are gracious" (Eccl. 10:12). The truth [however?] is as we have said.[40]

[34]Cf. *Kohelet Rabbah*, 3, and parallel sources. I did not find ibn Shu'eib's formulation of this theme in midrashic literature.

[35]Avot 3:15. See Urbach, *Ḥazal*, pp. 229ff. and n.11.

[36]Avodah Zarah 5a; Sanhedrin 38b.

[37]*Seder Eliyahu Zuta*, ed. M. Ish Shalom (Wien 1904), p. 183.

[38]סוד העיבור. This phrase when used in a kabbalistic context (as ibn Shu'eib does on p. 51Aa) refers to the doctrine of the transmigration of souls. Here ibn Shu'eib is using it in its original Talmudic sense as knowledge of the workings of the calendar, that is, astronomical knowledge. The passage to which ibn Shu'eib must be referring is in Berakhot 58b: ואמר שמואל נהירין לי שבילי דשמיא כשבילי דנהרדעא which testifies to Samuel's knowledge of astronomy and astronomical phenomena. Ibn Shu'eib is equating it with knowledge of astrology; if the astrological knowledge is predictive, then it is as problematic as the "book" referred to in the passage above. Cf., however, R. H. 20b where Samuel does not seem to know the *baraita* of *Sod Ha'ibur*.

[39]שהיה סדר זמנים קודם לכן. Ibn Shu'eib digresses here for a moment to assure the reader/listener that the סדר זמנים referred to here does not imply eternity in the sense of uncreated ואין כוונתם חלילה שיטו דבריהם לצד הקדמות, חלילה חלילה, ולכן אמר סדר זמנים ולא אמר שיהו זמנים קודם לכן, אלא שהיה הכל **מסודר** לפניו Cf. *Guide* II,28.

[40]22Cab.

R. Joshua's solution is not new—it merely reiterates "the simple assertion of Philo and the Rabbis that both God has foreknowledge and man is free."[41] However, if one were to ignore the explicit assertions of free will in the passage, it would sound like a strong argument *for* determinism, based on Biblical and Rabbinic passages. Particularly striking is his association of Samuel's astronomical knowledge, the passage concerning an arranged order of things, and a deterministic outlook. One is tempted to speculate, therefore, that ibn Shu'eib is reproducing an actual debate on the matter, perhaps even one in which he participated.[42] Keeping in mind that a contemporary of ibn Shu'eib's was the Christian convert Abner of Burgos who put forward strong determinist views in his *Iggeret Hagezerah*, it is not inconceivable that such arguments reproduce some of Abner's own positions.[43]

Later in another *derashah*,[44] R. Joshua deals with the well-known saying, "Everything is in the hands of heaven except for the fear of Heaven" (Bera-khot 33b) and offers three interpretations. The first, his own, is that man is free in the performance of *miẓvot* which determine his righteousness, although his personal circumstances are determined by God—rich or poor, long lived or short lived, etc. He then cites the opinion of Rabad of Posquières, that even the circumstances surrounding the fulfillment of *miẓvot* are determined—for how can a person build a fence on his roof without a house or place fringes on a garment if he has no clothes—"except for fear of heaven which is a matter decided inwardly by man."[45] After indicating his preference for the first explanation, he cites Maimonides[46] who says that "everything" refers to the natural and physical circumstances of the world; however, man's actions, acquisition of wealth, personal and marital life, are all in his hands—he acts without constraints and is rewarded and punished based on his own actions.

In another passage he gives voice to the difficulties in the passage "Children, longevity and sustenance do not depend on merit but rather on the stars,"[47] and in still another place in passing he reaffirms that "God's

---

[41]Wolfson, *Philo* I, 461.

[42]Note his repetition of *ḥalilah ḥalilah.*

[43]See above ch. I, n.13, for the possibility that ibn Shu'eib debated with Abner. Concerning Abner, see also Y. Baer, "Sefer Minḥat Kena'ot shel Avner Miburgos," *Tarbiẓ* 2 (1940) 188-206; idem, "Torat Hakabbalah Bemishnato Hakristologit shel Avner Miburgos," *Sefer Hayovel likhvod Gershom Scholem* (Jerusalem 1958) 152-163. See also E. Schweid, "Critique of Aristotelianism in the Systems of Jewish Medieval Philosophy" (unpublished Ph.D. thesis, Harvard University, 1962), pp. 167-175.

[44]80Db.

[45]חוץ מיראת שמים שהוא מסור לאדם ואין צריך לממון.

[46]*Shemonah Perakim,* ch. 8.

[47]81Ab. See Moed Katan 28a. Urbach, *Hazal*, pp. 246-253, esp. 251. Ibn Shu'eib offers two solutions to the question which he cites in the name of רבים שאלו: 1) that it

prescience does not eliminate free actions."[48]

From the above discussions we see that ibn Shu'eib is genuinely concerned with providing his listeners with a correct outlook on a very difficult philosophical-theological problem, confronting the problem logically and interpreting the sources from Rabbinic literature.

2. Miracles

Another important conception associated with God's providence is the notion of miracle. Miracles are implicitly recognized in a providential scheme that includes individual providence, for it conceives of God as free to intervene in nature to reward and to punish. In medieval Jewish philosophy the possibility of miracles was virtually unquestioned, for, if God could create the universe, He could also upset the laws of the universe He created.[49] What one does find, however, is a tendency to limit the extent that God intervenes in the affairs of the world. A miraculous occurrence means the interruption of causality, of the regular workings of nature and, if nature is constantly interrupted, it would be difficult to speak of nature at all.

Three methods were developed to limit Scriptural miracles. The first was to explain certain apparently miraculous events as having arisen from natural causes, an approach developed already by Philo.[50] Another approach was to interpret miracles allegorically, the miracle itself having occurred not in reality but in a vision.[51] Finally, many saw miracles as a preestablished disharmony, a notion based on the Mishnaic statement that certain miraculous things were "created at twilight on the sixth day of creation."[52]

refers to the entire community—but individuls are judged by their merit; 2) he differentiates, as we have seen above, between the Land of Israel and outside of Israel. In the latter, the Jews are governed by the stars. See above, p. 71. The Meiri to Mo'ed Katan (p. 153) found the passage so difficult that he rejected it entirely: כי הוא מאמר יחיד, לא יסבלוהו דרכי הדת בשום פנים. See B. Z. Benedict, "Mezonei Bemazala Talya," *Torah Shebe'al Peh* 19 (1977) 223-246.

48 64Db: ידיעת השם לא תבטל האפשר ולא תכריחהו.

49 *Guide* II,25; Wolfson, *Philo* I, pp. 354-355. Maimonides argues that creation proves the possibility of miracles. Halevi and Naḥmanides, and ibn Shu'eib following them, argue that miracles prove creation. See *Cuzari* V,5. Naḥmanides, Exodus 3:16: המופת הנפלא מורה שיש לעולם א-לוה מחדשו; ibn Shu'eib 22Bc: כי בשנוי הטבע ובניסים מתאמת חדוש העולם See Wolfson, "Maimonides and Halevi on Design Chance and Necessity," reprinted in I. Twersky and G. H. Williams, eds., *Studies in the History of Philosophy and Religion*, vol. II (Cambridge MA 1977), p. 56.

50 Wolfson, *Philo* I, pp. 350-351.

51 See *Guide* II,42, the sharp response of Naḥmanides, Genesis 18:1, and the discussion among the *Guide*'s commentators, particularly Abarbanel's extension of Maimonides' principles; E. Schweid, *Ta'am Vehakashah* (Ramat Gan 1970), p. 191.

52 Avot 5:6; *Bereshit Rabbah* 5:5. See J. Guttman, *Philosophies of Judaism* (New York 1963), p. 170.

Both Maimonides and Judah Halevi adopted slightly different versions of this last idea, not in order to deny the miraculous nature of the events, but in order to "reconcile the possibility of miracles with God's expressed promise to observe laws which He has established in the Universe."[53]

Ibn Shu'eib, however, does not share the concern of these Jewish philosophers for the preservation of the regularity of nature, and rather consistently insists that the miracles described in Scripture occurred in the precise and literal manner in which the Torah seems to describe them. Thus Jacob's wrestling with the angel was real, not a dream and "all that occurred to Balaam was miraculous, as we said, and similarly that which occurred to his ass was also miraculous."[54]

In his discussion of the splitting of the Red Sea, ibn Shu'eib argues forcefully against limiting the miracles in Scripture through interpretation.

> If He could change the nature of flowing water and cause it to stand like a pillar, and He could change the nature of the celestial spheres, which if stopped would ordinarily cause the world to revert to chaos and void, yet they were stopped for a full day; then why should one doubt the possibility of any change in nature? For if we believe even in the slightest change, we must believe that He can change it many times. For He who established nature may change it, except according to those of little faith who believe that the world is eternal and uncreated, and that natural law is immutable. There are some people who believe that the Lord cannot even lengthen the wing of a fly. We, however, the House of Israel, born in His house, having been given possession of His Torah which teaches us that the world was created by the simple and undetermined will of God; who believe that He established the laws of nature and determined that fire should rise and water should fall, why should we have any doubt that He can change this nature? There is no difference between nature and deviation from nature except for the fact that nature preceded the deviation in time; should the deviation have preceded nature we would have said that that is the way it should be.
>
> There is no need to dwell at length on this matter for a person who has good and true faith must believe in the words of the Rabbis of blessed memory which they received by tradition from Moses our teacher.[55]

[53]Wolfson, *Philo* I, p. 351 n.24. See also idem, "Judah Halevi on Miracles," *Studies*, II, pp. 431-432.

[54]14Ac, 70Dc.

[55]26Abc. On the changes in the celestial spheres see Ralbag, *Milḥamot Hashem* (Leipzig 1866) 6:2:12, who claims that nothing about them can be changed. On the "wing of the fly" see *Guide* II, 22; Ramban, *Torat Hashem Temimah*, p. 246; S. Klein-Braslavy, "The Influence of R. Nissim Girondi in Crescas' and Albo's Principles," *Eshel Beersheva* 2 (1980) 182 n.9.

Nature is thus defined as what is customary rather than as what is necessary or determined. Ibn Shu'eib does admit in passing, however, that the normal manner in which God conducts His affairs is through nature. That is, there is an ordinary manner in which the world is accustomed to operate, and miracles are used only in extroardinary circumstances.[56]

Here again ibn Shu'eib raises a matter which sounds as if it were fitted into the homiletical context from a polemical one. He asks why it is that God should change one part of creation for one of his creatures—does it not imply a deficiency in His work? He answers by saying that, since the idea of Israel preceded creation and the world was created for man and his benefit, it is altogether proper to abrogate the laws of nature for the sake of man.[57] In other words, since the world was created for man's benefit, everything necessary for his continued benefit, whether natural or miraculous, is considered a fulfillment of the purpose of creation.

In summary, ibn Shu'eib endorses the notion of God's complete and unrestricted freedom to change the laws of nature, although he acknowledges that there is an ordinary manner in which God usually does conduct the world; in addition he abstains from endorsing any of the philosophic attempts to limit the extent of the Scriptural miracles, and hence we find almost no allegorical interpretation of miracles in the Derashot.[58]

3. Prophecy

Finally, let us consider R. Joshua's views on prophecy. These can be best understood within the context of Maimonides' discussion. Maimonides attempts to reconcile the philosophic notion of prophecy conceived of in naturalistic-intellectualistic terms and the religious conception of prophecy which sees prophecy as an act of Divine grace.[59] His resolution retains the religious insistence on grace but confines the recipients of that grace to those who have achieved the intellectual and moral perfection of the philosopher-prophet. Although Rambam has supporting texts for his position, there are contradictory texts as well, foremost of which is a midrashic statement about revelation: "A handmaiden at the [splitting of the Red] Sea witnessed more

[56]70Dc.

[57]94Bb.

[58]I found one allegorical interpretation (26Bb) of the bitter waters of Marah—bitter with incorrect opinions and sweetened with the waters of the Torah. Ibn Shu'eib, who bases the interpretation on a midrashic passage, did not intend denying the historicity of the event but rather intended adding symbolic value to it. That this must be the case is reaffirmed by the fact that this explanation appears just a few lines after his polemic against those who deny miracles.

[59]*Guide*, II, 32ff. See A. Altmann, "Maimonides and Thomas Aquinas: Natural or Divine Prophecy?" *AJS Review* 3 (1978) 8.

than Ezekiel the son of Buzi."[60] A revelation which is perceived identically by all is unacceptable to Maimonides because it is inconsistent with his notion that prophecy requires intellectual perfection. Therefore, with the help of a deft bit of exegesis of a midrashic statement, Maimonides maintains that, although revelation was a prophetic experience for the children of Israel, there was no communication of content. Their understanding of the content of revelation was accomplished only through Moses' instructions.[61]

Maimonides' position, particulary as it was interpreted by some of his followers, raised ibn Shu'eib's ire considerably. He lashes out at those who deny the literal meaning of the midrashic passage that states that even the infants and fetuses who were present at the Sea reached a level of prophecy and that even a simple maid at the Sea reached a higher level of revelation than did Ezekiel.

> They say: how is it possible for one who does not possess the prerequisites for prophecy to be fitted to prophesy; did not the Rabbis of blessed memory say that prophecy descends only on the wise—that is, on one who is perfect in his wisdom; on a man who has the courage to control his inclinations and desires, and who is rich, that is, content with his lot?[62] If so, how was it possible for women and maid-servants to attain prophecy at a level higher than even Ezekiel the prophet? How was it possible for an infant who has no understanding and speech or a fetus in his mother's womb to sing praises?
>
> As a result they said that these [aggadot] could not be taken literally, that they are metaphors and allegories. They invent strange interpretations and, although they intend to sanctify the Name, they make the sacred profane, for they believe only in what they see with their eyes and attain through their senses. They do not believe that which does not accord with reason or nature in the manner of the philosophers. But he who has faith in his heart and bears no hatred will believe that God creates new things in this world as the situation requires. With respect to this, David said, "I have chosen the way of faith" (Psalm 119:30), that is to say, I have chosen to believe that which has been passed down by tradition as a matter of faith, and I have not depended only on my senses and reasoning.
>
> Therefore why should we use allegories and metaphors to interpret the words of the Torah and the words of the Rabbis in a nonliteral

[60] *Mekhilta, Masehta Deshirah*, ch. 3 (p. 126).

[61] *Guide*, II, 33.

[62] Nedarim 38a. Notice how ibn Shu'eib integrates text and commentary. Cf. Mishneh Torah, *Yesodei Hatorah* 7:1.

> manner? If God bestowed a gift and abundant grace, and wants one to merit prophetic visions...then why should we reject this?[63]

R. Joshua's conception of prophecy coincides with Halevi's which, unlike that of Maimonides, does not require intellectual perfection.[64] As added proof, ibn Shu'eib cites the Talmudic statement "a wise man is superior to a prophet."[65] The statement implies that each category is exclusive, for if the prophet was also very wise, he would certainly be superior to the wise man who is not a prophet.[66]

Beyond this ibn Shu'eib argues, citing a responsum of Rashba, that the ability of God to grant prophecy is never limited by an individual's status, for He can grant prophecy to whomever He wishes. Only that which is logically impossible God cannot do; but that which nature limits, God can override. Thus the verse in Joel (3:1) "I will pour out my spirit on all flesh; your sons and daughters shall prophesy" may be taken literally and there is no need for Maimonides' rationalizing explanations. In the same manner in which ibn Shu'eib refuses to recognize any limits on God's power to perform miracles, he refuses to recognize any limit on God's ability to communicate with man.

R. Joshua thus insists upon the unrestricted freedom of God to carry out His will as a God of Providence who performs miracles and communicates with whom He pleases. He stands against the beliefs of members of philosophic circles who denied that God had that kind of freedom or who tried to modify the scope of Divine activities of that sort recounted in Scripture and Talmud. To those philosophers he states that reason has its limits.

4. Limits of Rational Thought

The limitation of reason is a theme found often among medieval Jewish philosophers. Maimonides acknowledged this limitation; R. Judah Halevi stressed it. Drawing on both Maimonides and Halevi, ibn Shu'eib espouses a theory that posits a suprarational faculty that transcends reason.

> How can one rely only upon the intellect when we see that the intellect vainly attempts to apprehend even material natural things, such as qualities of herbs, minerals, and spices....As the wise man has written, the intellect does not have the power to comprehend all sensory objects, certainly not those that are hidden like the magnet...how much more so spiritual Divine matters which are above the intellect.

Just as water cannot rise above its source, similarly the intellect cannot rise above its source: it cannot fully comprehend mataphysical matters whose

[63] 25Dab.
[64] See Wolfson, "Maimonides and Hallevy on Prophecy," p. 117.
[65] Baba Batra 12a.
[66] 25Db.

source is above it. That knowledge is accessible only through the prophetic intellect.[67]

Several times in the Derashot ibn Shu'eib elaborates on what he variously calls *hasekhel hane'eẓal* (the "emanated intellect"), *hasekhel heḥanun* (the "gracious intellect")[68] or *hasekhel hanevu'i* (the "prophetic intellect").

> There are three faculties, the natural intellect, the acquired intellect and the emanated intellect, which is also called the gracious intellect....The first one, the natural intellect which every man has, enables him to understand basic principles. The second, the acquired intellect, is like the wise man who studies wisdom and Torah, inferring one thing from the next, and acquires this intellect. The third intellect, however, which is emanated from the super-abundance of God's essence and spirit, occurs only among the prophets and only in Israel.[69]

In another long passage, which ibn Shu'eib presents as an excerpt from the *Cuzari* but which is mostly his own explanation with a few passages from the *Cuzari* woven in, he explains the function of this "prophetic intellect."[70] Sometimes one's sense of perception is misleading, as when one views the sun and it appears small. The acquired intellect corrects the mistaken impressions of the senses. Similarly,

> there is something above the acquired intellect, that is, the emanated intellect, and we who follow the Torah call it the prophetic intellect. Its function is to correct the mistakes of perception of the acquired intellect in the same manner that the acquired intellect corrects perceptions and sense experiences. Thus there are four levels: gross senses, subtle sensations, acquired intellect, and emanated intelligences, also called prophetic. Whoever is not a prophet or son of a prophet from Israel cannot attain it.[71]

This notion of a special suprarational faculty is already mentioned in the *Cuzari* (4:3) as "the inner eye" and elaborated upon by others such as Joseph ibn Aknin and in the letter written by an anonymous student of Maimonides to R. Ḥasdai of Alexandria. In that letter, the author informs us that "there is a level of intellegence above the level of the philosophers, and that is

[67] 47Aab. See *Perush Aggadot of R. Azriel*, p. 39.

[68] 36Db.

[69] 84Ac.

[70] 47B; see *Cuzari* IV,3; IV,19.

[71] 47Bc. כי יש ענין אחד למעלה מן השכל הקנוי והוא שכל נאצל, ואנו בני התורה קורין לו שכל נבואי, שיתקן מה שטועה השכל הקנוי שאינו משיגו, כמו שהשכל הקנוי מתקן המוחש והמורגש. והנה לפי זה הם ארבע מדרגות, החוש הגס, וההרגש הדק, והשכל הקנוי, והשכל הנאצל הנקרא נבואי. ומי שאינן נביאים בישראל לא ישיג זה ולא בני. (Cf. 49Db.) He continues that the idea that prophecy is limited to Jews is attested to by Gentiles as well. See Wolfson, *Studies* II, p. 99, who cites Justyn Martyr on the subject.

prophecy. Prophecy is a world apart and no rational proof or discussion is applicable to it....Prophecy is above rational demonstration which cannot achieve what prophecy achieves."[72]

R. Joshua quotes Maimonides in a similar vein (or at least he attributes such a passage to Maimonides—I have not found the source).

> ...therefore we must rely on those upon whom the Holy Spirit has descended and who have comprehended truth prophetically. For those who think that the philosophers have comprehended the true nature of all beings subject to generation and corruption and of spiritual beings too are mistaken, for there are many difficulties in those opinions.[73]

Thus, ibn Shu'eib emphasizes the limitations on rational inquiry rather than its importance; we have likewise seen that he is an opponent of some extreme philosophical positions. Although he displays a substantial familiarity with philosophical questions and a genuine concern for them, they clearly do not play a central role in the Derashot. One senses, moreover, that his concern springs mainly out of his concern for his audience, who were confronted by or interested in these problems. Ibn Shu'eib's own interest lay more in the direction of Kabbalah.

[72]*Iggerot Harambam* (Leipzig 1859), p. 23. The letter is attributed to Maimonides.
[73]48Cb.

Chapter V
Reasons for the Commandments

1. Sources of Obligation

Concern for the fulfillment of the *mizvot*, the commandments, of the Torah is central in Jewish thought, from the Bible and Rabbinic literature and onward through the Middle Ages and to the present. In the Derashot this concern appears in many different contexts and from different perspectives. Characteristically, ibn Shu'eib weaves together various strands, adding literary or exegetical flourishes while expanding on certain ideas.

From Rabbinic and medieval Jewish literature, ibn Shu'eib collates various explanations of the nature of Israel's obligation or motivations for performing *mizvot*.

> We, the House of Israel, are obligated to perform the commandments of God. There are four important aspects of the performance and fulfillment of the *mizvot*; each one alone would have obligated man, how much more so all four.[1]

The four aspects are: 1) The *mizvot* are expressions of God's will. That fact alone should cause us to desire to fulfill the *mizvot* even if we had not been directly commanded, just as Abraham, Isaac and Jacob kept the Torah without being commanded.[2]

2) But since we were commanded to fulfill the *mizvot*, our obligation is even greater. So, too, says ibn Shu'eib, is our reward greater based on the principle that "one who is commanded and performs the *mizvah* is greater than one

[1] 39AB. Cf. Urbach, *Ḥazal*, pp. 285-287.

[2] Here ibn Shu'eib adds an epigram כבודו של אדם רצונו (של מקום) which is the reverse of the usual epigram רצונו של אדם כבודו. See Yerushalmi Peah 1:1; *Sefer Ḥasidim*, ed. R. Margoliyot (Jerusalem 1957), par. 152.

who performs the *mizvah* without being commanded" (Kidushin 31a).[3] In support of the notion that commanded observance merits greater reward, ibn Shu'eib adduces the much quoted passage "What does God care if one slaughters from the neck or from the back? Rather, the *mizvot* were only given to purify man" (Bereshit Rabbah 44:1). By its use in this context, ibn Shu'eib suggests that the intent of the passage is that obedience to God's command is primary in halakhic observance. (We shall see below some of the problems that arise concerning this passage and ibn Shu'eib's interpretation.) In further support of the above principle, ibn Shu'eib explains that one who is commanded must contend with his evil inclination and is therefore worthy of greater reward.

3) The third argument for observance of *mizvot* is the self-imposed obligation that derives from the covenants of Sinai and the Plains of Moab, when Israel collectively took oaths to observe the *mizvot*.[4]

4) Finally, the promised reward for the commandments warrants their strict observance, for "one who faithfully observes the *mizvot* will not know suffering" although, he adds, this is the "least of all the reasons."[5]

In an earlier passage, ibn Shu'eib interpreted the verse in Ecclesiastes, "The word of the king is supreme and who may say to him, 'What doest thou'" (Eccl 8:4), in the following way:

> The decree of the king cannot be annulled, for there is no one who can give him orders. But one who keeps the commandments can annul decrees, as it is written, "'The Rock of Israel rules over man' (II Samuel 23:3); but who rules over Me? the righteous man, as it is written 'the righteous man *(zaddik)* rules over the fear of God' (ibid.)."[6]

Noteworthy here is ibn Shu'eib's extension to all observers of *mizvot* of the Talmudic notion of the *zaddik*'s ability to annul God's decrees.

The *mizvot* that we fulfill, ibn Shu'eib emphasizes, must be fulfilled in a precise manner, with awareness and understanding. One who does *mizvot* in an habitual and unthinking way was characterized by Jeremiah as "Cursed is he who trusts in man" (Jer 17:5) because this kind of person "relies on others' knowledge for the fulfillment of the *mizvah* and does not bother to know its

[3]Kiddushin 31a. See Urbach (above n.1), loc. cit.

[4]See Ramban on Deut 29:9.

[5]39Ba. See M.T. *Teshuvah* 10:5. The verse is from Eccl 8:5. I have translated שומר מצוה לא ידע רע as faithful observance in accordance with ibn Shu'eib's interpretation.

[6]39Ab. Based on Mo'ed Katan 16b. Concerning the last point ibn Shu'eib says: ואמר כאשר דבר מלך שלטון כלומר גזרת המלך אין אדם יכול לבטלה כי מי יאמר לו מה תעשה זולתי שומר המצוה שהוא מבטל הגזירה כמו שכתוב צור ישראל מושל באדם מי מושל בי, צדיק. וזהו צדיק מושל יראת א׳. See also 33C for expansion of this notion. RSV translates the verse (II Sam 23:3): "The Rock of Israel has said to me: When one rules justly over men, ruling in the fear of God...."

content and perform it correctly."[7] Those "people who are eager to perform *miẓvot*—and indeed to fulfill them—but are not so eager to fulfill the details of the *miẓvot* and are not exacting in their performance"[8] have to be reminded that "one who keeps a *miẓvah (shomer miẓvah)* will know not misfortune" (Eccl 8:5). Ibn Shu'eib emphasizes that as opposed to the word *'oseh*—doer —*shomer*, guardian, implies meticulous attention to detail which is the sine qua non for *miẓvot*. "It says in the Jerusalem Talmud that, when you perform the *miẓvot* properly, they are *miẓvot*, but if not, they are not considered *miẓvot*."[9]

The solution to this situation, ibn Shu'eib feels, is that a person should not only study the details of the *miẓvah* but should

> try with all his strength to...understand its content and reason; if he is not capable of this and finds no one who understands the reason, he should believe that there is a very important reason and he should perform the *miẓvah* bearing in mind its great significance, related as it is to the Divine chariot. He will receive a great reward and in addition he will have fulfilled his Master's command.[10]

By understanding the *miẓvah* "one fulfills *'befikha uvilvavkha la'asoto*: it shall be in your mouth and in your heart for you to do it' (Deut 30:14). *Befikha* stands for study and repetition; *bilvavkha* tells us that the *miẓvah* should be performed willingly, and not as a burden."[11]

2. Meaning in *Miẓvot*

R. Joshua's concern with finding ways to motivate committed observance of *miẓvot* led him to expound upon the meaning of the *miẓvot*, an enterprise with a long history.

Already in the Torah itself explanations or reasons are given for some *miẓvot*, and the Talmud and Midrash offer many more. Some are moral-symbolic or historical-symbolic: for instance, the four species—the palm branch, the *etrog*, the willow branch and the myrtle which are held on Sukkot—are interpreted as standing for four different types of people or alternatively for the four fathers of the Jewish people.[12] Some *miẓvot*, it is

[7]Ibn Shu'eib's interpretation is new. Cf. Joseph ibn Caspi's Will in *Hebrew Ethical Wills*, pp. 138-139: והמשל בזה כי אינו הכרח שנדע כולנו על כל פנים דין ארבעה שומרים...ואם הידיעה הזאת טובה רק די לנו אם יש לנו בימינו שופט או שופטים ידעו זה ושפטו את העם בכל עת

[8]39Aa.

[9]Shabbat 13:3.

[10]39Bb.

[11]Ibid.

[12]Leviticus Rabbah 30:9, 12. For a full discussion see I. Heinemann, *Ta'amei Hamiẓvot Besifrut Yisrael* vol. 1 (Jerusalem 1959), pp. 30-35; Urbach, *Ḥazal*, pp. 321-347. See also now David Halivni, *Midrash, Mishnah, and Gemara: The Jewish Predilection for Justified Law* (Cambridge MA 1986).

suggested, were commanded to atone for particular sins. The sages explain, for example, that the three *miẓvot* that are primarily in the woman's domain, namely, observance of the menstrual laws, the separation of the *ḥallah* and lighting the Sabbath candles, serve as atonement for the sin of Eve.[13] Others are explained as rewards for the actions of our ancestors; thus on account of Abraham's rejection of even a thread of booty in the war of the four kings (Gen 14), his children merited the *miẓvah* of *ẓiẓit*.[14] The sages of the Talmud also explained the moral logic of certain *miẓvot*. For instance, they suggested that the thief, who steals in secret, is punished more severely than the robber, who steals openly, because his fear of man was greater than his fear of God; the robber at least made them equal.[15]

Both philosophers and kabbalists in the Middle Ages continued and expanded upon the attempt to provide a basis for understanding the *miẓvot*. Maimonides, for example, devotes a large part of the *Guide of the Perplexed* to the question. The philosophers were motivated both by the need to understand God's laws, an understanding which would lead to the love of Him,[16] and by the need to justify the *miẓvot* to the non-Jews, to show the nations of the world what a "wise and discerning nation" (Deut. 4:6) is the nation of Israel.[17]

Kabbalists too dealt extensively with reasons for *miẓvot* and occasionally even argued for the logical understanding of *miẓvot*. R. Jacob b. Sheshet, who explains that the laws of kashrut are commanded in order to preserve the purity of the soul, says:

> I know that there are among the righteous and the wise of Israel those who will criticize me for having written explanations for two or three *miẓvot* of the Torah, which may provide an opening for offering rational reasons to many of the *miẓvot*. I shall bring a proof that any wise man may offer an explanation for any *miẓvah* whose reason is not explained in the Torah; there is great usefulness in this and his reward is great, because he lends esteem to the *miẓvah* in the eyes of the nations, for they say that "surely this nation is a wise and discerning people." They argue against us, what is the reason for that *miẓvah* or the other, saying that they are only allegories. However, when we offer them reasons based on wisdom which they cannot contradict, they will say, "Come let us go up

[13]B.R. 17:8.
[14]B.R. 43:9.
[15]*Mekhilta, Mishpatim*, 15.
[16]See, e.g., *Mishneh Torah, Teshuvah* 10:6.
[17]*Guide for the Perplexed*, III,31. See I. Twersky, "Concerning Maimonides' Rationalization of the Commandments: an Explanation of Hilkhot Me'ilah VIII:8" in *Studies in the History of the Jewish Society in the Middle Ages and in the Modern Period Presented to Prof. Jacob Katz* (Jerusalem 1980), pp. 24-33.

to the house of God, to the house of the Lord of Jacob. Let us be instructed in His ways and walk in His path" (Is 2:3). The only way Abraham our father, who knew all branches of wisdom, could have known the *miẓvot*—for with the exception of eight he was not commanded to do them—is through the use of reason....I have no doubt that Abraham's knowledge of them came through wisdom and not prophecy. Wisdom preceded prophecy not only for Abraham but similarly for all prophets. Since Abraham recognized his Creator through wisdom, he was certainly able to understand the *miẓvot* worthy of Him and His Torah. Therefore no scholar or *ḥasid* should find fault with offering reasons for *miẓvot* whose reasons are not explicit in the Torah; the only stipulation is that one should not say that the reason given is the primary reason that the *miẓvah* was commanded. Rather, one should say, had the *miẓvah* not otherwise been given it should have been given for such and such reason.[18]

The similarity to Maimonides is striking: the rational accessibility of all the *miẓvot* and the public demonstration of their wisdom are two prominent themes in the *Guide*.[19]

This was not, however, R. Jacob b. Sheshet's main approach to explaining *miẓvot*, nor was it the way other kabbalists approached the matter. Beginning with *Sefer Habahir* and continuing through the Gerona kabbalists, R. Moses de Leon, the *Ra'ya Mehemna*, R. Baḥya b. Asher, R. Menahem Recanati and many others, the explanation of *miẓvot*, which occupies a central place in their kabbalistic systems, was directed toward Jews and was accomplished through the use of kabbalistic categories.[20] These explanations were perhaps not accessible to all; what was important was that they existed. As Todros Abulafia said in *Oẓar Hakavod*,

> Even though they are called statutes [*ḥukkim*] implying that they are the decrees of the king, still and all...the king does not issue decrees and establish them as law unless he has a reason known to himself and a few of his wise men...even though it may be obscured from the masses. How much more so the King of Kings, the Holy One, blessed be He, would not have issued a decree for naught.[21]

According to the kabbalists the Divinity reveals itself in ten stages or aspects. Among these ten stages or *Sefirot* there exists a dynamic tension

---

[18]R. Jacob b. Sheshet, *Sefer Meshiv Devarim Nekhoḥim*, ed. G. Vajda (Jerusalem, 1968), p. 83 (see, however, below, p. 106); see too Recanati's introduction to *Ta'amei Hamiẓvot* and Todros Abulafia's *Oẓar Hakavod* (Warsaw 1879), p. 44.

[19]See above n.17 and sources in Prof. Twersky's article.

[20]Twersky, "Maimonides' Rationalization," p. 25, n.4.

[21]*Oẓar Hakavod*, p. 44.

between those forces which symbolize *Ḥesed*, lovingkindness, and *Din*, strict justice. *Miẓvot*, according to the kabbalists, on the one hand symbolize the dynamic life of the *Sefirot* and on the other hand go beyond symbolism by constituting a spiritual reality which actually intersects and affects the upper worlds.[22] Such an approach could not but enhance the individual's awareness of the significance of *miẓvot*.

The different kinds of explanations used by the Rabbis, philosophers and kabbalists, while based on different premises, were not seen as mutually exclusive, and it is therefore not surprising to find a popular and eclectic preacher such as ibn Shu'eib using all three different kinds of explanations for the *miẓvot*. Eclecticism in such cases could be a strength.

3. Kabbalah and the Commandments

R. Joshua was foremost a kabbalist, and, while the number of *miẓvot* explained kabbalistically in the Derashot may not be large, he clearly believed that the kabbalistic reason was the true reason for the *miẓvah*.

> I have brought all of this in order to make these matters more intelligible and to aid in understanding them somewhat. For we have already said that the true reason for sacrifices is the most concealed.[23]

The concealed reason is of course the kabbalistic reason which interprets the details of the *miẓvah* in symbolic terms.[24]

[22]See G. Scholem, *Hakabbalah Bigeronah*, pp. 327-333; I. Tishby, *Mishnat Hazohar*, vol. 2, pp. 431-442.

[23]37Cbc: הבאתי כל זה לקרב הדברים אל השכל ולשכך האוזן קצת. ועל האמת כבר בארנו שטעם הקרבן האמיתי הוא נעלם מאד.

[24]That the phrase "concealed reason" (טעם...נעלם מאד) refers to kabbalistic interpretations is borne out by other passages in the Derashot. E.g., on p. 45Ab:
וכבר כתבנו בפרשת ויקרא והארכנו בזה (טעמי קרבן) ועל זה אמר שלמה. אורח חיים למעלה ולמשכיל כלומר המצות הנכבדות שהם אורח חיים שמדריך האדם ומזכהו לעוה״ב **טעמה נעלם ונסתר** והם למעלה מן השכל הקנוי, אלא למי **שחננו השכל החנון** שגלה סודו לעבדיו הנביאים וקבלו מהם חכמי ישראל איש מפי איש.

According to ibn Shu'eib שכל החנון is the agent which comprehends kabbalistic secrets. Thus on p. 36Db we find the following (I have corrected the text according to the readings in Munich ms. 9):
היה תמה מן החכמים בעלי תורתינו היאך רוצים לפרש המצות על ידי השכל כי סודות תורתינו והמצות הנכבדות הם חוץ מן השכל. כי מה ענין לתפילין ולד׳ בתים שבהם...בדרך השכל...אבל מצותינו המעולות **הם חוץ מן** השכל ואינן ידועין אלא למי **שחננו השם שכל החנון** כמו לנביאים ומסרום לחכמים איש מפי איש.

Further proof can be adduced from the following two pages. On p. 41Bb:
ועל כן אמר שלמה שלשה המה נפלאו ממני ואמרינן במדרש זה פסח מצה ומרור. ולכן נצטוינו במצרים קודם הגאולה להורות שאין טעמם לזכור היציאה לבד אלא טעם אחר יש בהם נעלם.

On p. 39Db he is explicit that: ואכילת מצה מצותה גדולה על דרך הקבלה כי החמץ רמז למדת הדין הקשה...אבל פסח כלו רחמים. See below.

Let us look at some examples of ibn Shu'eib's use of Kabbalah to explain the *mizvot*. The prohibition on eating *ḥameẓ* (leavened bread), he says, is very strict because *ḥameẓ* is a symbol of God's stern justice—*middat hadin ha-kasheh*—which punished the Egyptians by killing their first-born and drowning their army in the sea. Passover is entirely *Raḥamim*—compassion—and the introduction of an iota of *ḥameẓ* would be like benefiting from idolatrous objects. One who does so is considered as if he were *mekaẓeẓ bintiyot*, literally, "one who cuts the shoots" but metaphorically a heretic in respect of the mystical nature of God.[25] Thus, objects through which *miẓvot* are performed or prohibitions are violated symbolize the *Sefirot*, the Divine worlds; the performance or violation of *miẓvot* becomes a matter affecting not only the religious obligation of the Jew but entailing a symbolic disruption of the Divine inner order.

The different sounds of the shofar heard on Rosh Hashanah symbolize the interplay of *Sefirot* on that day. *Zikhron teru'ah* is the way Rosh Hashanah is referred to in the Torah (Lev 23:24), and the name itself, according to R. Joshua, alludes to the character of the day. The *teru'ah*, the short staccato blast of the shofar, alludes to the tenth *Sefirah, Malkhut* or *Shekhinah*, in its capacity of administrator of justice; the *teki'ah*, the plain undifferentiated blast which is alluded to in the word *zikhron*—remembrance—symbolizes *Raḥamim* or compassion. Rosh Hashanah then is a day when justice is tempered by mercy and therefore the *teru'ah* blasts are surrounded by the *teki'ah* blasts; by contrast, the blasts of the Israelite camp marching forward in the wilderness consisted only of *teru'ot*, indicating that the attribute of stern justice alone was at work. R. Joshua supports his ideas with many verses interpreted kabbalistically, as well as aggadot similarly interpreted; the cogency of the proofs would not be obvious to the uninitiated, and one suspects that only those with a good working knowledge of Kabbalah could follow ibn Shu'eib's argument.[26]

Another example of kabbalistic symbolism in the *miẓvot* is his interpretation of the four species—the palm branch, myrtle branch, willow branch and *etrog*. As we have said, a Rabbinic midrash makes these symbols of Abraham, Isaac, Jacob, and Joseph. These in turn, says ibn Shu'eib, embody the four aspects of the *Merkavah*, the Divine Chariot. "For this

[25] 39Dbc. A very similar explanation, perhaps ibn Shu'eib's source, is in R. Moses de Leon's *Nefesh Haḥakhamah* (Basle 1608; Jerusalem 1969), section 15. *Kiẓuẓ Bintiyot* as mystical heresy stems from Hagigah 14b; see Tishby, *M.H.* I p. 222.

[26] 90AB. The basis of his explanation is Naḥmanides' commentary to Lev 23:24. Contemporary kabbalistic literature is helpful here as in other places in unravelling ibn Shu'eib's kabbalistic allusions. See, e.g., Recanati, R. Baḥya, *Be'ur Sodot Haramban* and *Keter Shem Tov* to the verse in Leviticus; Moses de Leon, *Nefesh*, loc. cit. See also Tishby, *M.H.*, 2, pp. 223-226.

reason," he says, "you should understand why the *'aravah* is on the left, the *hadas* is on the right, the *lulav* is in the middle, and the *etrog* is by itself."[27] (Left represents strict justice; right represents mercy.)[28] Another midrash which ibn Shu'eib quotes says that each of the four species stands for God; ibn Shu'eib does not explain what the midrash means, but he does say that this midrash reveals more of the secret of the *lulav* than others and "raises the matter higher than the first midrash."[29]

Another recurring theme in midrashic and medieval Hebrew literature is the symbolism of the various parts of the Tabernacle. According to ibn Shu'eib, the parts of the Tabernacle correspond to the different parts of the world and of man. The parallelism is developed in great detail; each part of the Tabernacle parallels some aspect of creation and some part of the human body. The midrashic basis for this exposition is elaborated and developed in intricate detail, not only by ibn Shu'eib but also by other kabbalists as well. Ibn Shu'eib says,

> There is no doubt that all these configurations are significant and contain important secrets—who can comprehend their details!—but most important is to remember that the configurations of the Tabernacle parallel the configurations in the spiritual worlds.[30]

Hokhmah (wisdom), *da'at* (knowledge) and *tevunah* (understanding) lie at the basis of, or play a role in the creation of, all three: man, world, and Tabernacle (see Ex 35:31); in addition, they are associated with the highest and most profound of the *Sefirot*, as we shall see below.

Sometimes the kabbalistic connection lies in the numerical structure of the *mizvah*, seven and ten being two such numbers to which significance has been attached in Kabbalah. Seven is important because it is the lower seven *Sefirot* which represent the active revelation of God in this world and which

[27] 94CD.

[28] See, e.g., G. Scholem, *Kabbalah*, pp. 106-107.

[29] 94CD. Although the midrashim interpreted by ibn Shu'eib are quoted in contemporary literature, ibn Shu'eib's explanations are not widely found. See, however, Zohar I (additions, p. 267b): וענף עץ עבות, ענף לשמאל עבות לימין ונמצא עץ באמצע. See now Jacob Katz, "Halakhah and Kabbalah—First Contacts" in *Yitzhak F. Baer Memorial Volume* (Jerusalem 1980), p. 154.

[30] 30Bb. Cf. 60Bbc. See A. Aptowitzer, "Beit Hamikdash Shel Ma'alah al pi Ha'agadah," *Tarbiz* 2 (1931) 137-153, 257 and 285; I. Tishby, *M.H.*, 2, p. 183-194. The symbolic interpretation of the Temple is very widespread. Prof. Twersky brought to my attention R. Moses Isserles' comment in his introduction to *Torat Ha'olah* (Tel Aviv n.d.), p. 2a: כל חכם מחכמינו המציא טעם נכון...בהויית הקרבנות והמשכן

For an analysis of the *derashah* to *Terumah* in which ibn Shu'eib dwells at length on the symbolism of the Tabernacle, see Henk J. Huyser, "The Medium is the Message" (unpublished Ph.D. thesis, Katholieke Theoligische Hogeschool Te Utrecht, 1980).

constitute its spiritual reality. Indeed each such *Sefirah* is considered a "day of creation."

"She has carved her seven pillars" [Prov 9:1]. This refers to the seven supernal days of creation which cannot be confined by time. All sets of seven allude to these seven days.[31]

Sets of seven abound in Jewish tradition; there are seven *miẓvot* connected with the holiday of Sukkot, seven weeks between Passover and Shavu'ot, seven years to the *shemittah* (sabbatical cycle), seven *shemittot* (sabbaticals) to each *yovel* (jubilee), and seven years of service for the Hebrew bondsman. In all of the above, ibn Shu'eib tells us, the number seven is a significant aspect of the *miẓvah*.[32]

Ten, the total number of *Sefirot*, is also alluded to by many *miẓvot*; the ten days of repentance between Rosh Hashanah and Yom Kippur; the Ten Commandments; the Priestly Blessing, which is uttered with ten raised fingers;[33] many objects in the Temple which were made in groups of ten or in dimensions of ten,[34] such as the wings of the cherubim which were ten cubits wide; and many more. Here again the common number connects the *miẓvah* with the *Sefirot*.

Another major theme in ibn Shu'eib's kabbalistic explanations of the *miẓvot* is the association of some *miẓvot* with the forces of evil. As we shall explain in more detail in chapter IX on the problem of evil, ibn Shu'eib reiterates the belief that Satan or Sama'el is a real force in this world and is the immediate source of evil in the world. Satan derives his power from the primeval *naḥash*, snake, which is synonymous with or derivative from the Left side of the *Sefirot*.[35]

Many *miẓvot* and their details are conditioned by these forces or are gestures to them. Contact with a human corpse results in *tum'ah*, ritual defilement, because death was introduced into the world as a result of Eve's pollution by the snake when she violated God's command.[36] The *tum'ah* of the menstruant also has its source in the sin of Eve; indeed the reason that certain types of blood cause *tum'ah* and others do not[37] was because "the Rabbis knew which blood came from the side of purity, the right side, and

---

[31]29Db. See Ramban, Gen 1:3. He speaks only of six days which parallel six *Sefirot*, as does the Zohar I 3b. Cf., however, *Be'ur Sodot* to the verse in Gen.

[32]94Bc (seven *miẓvot* of *Sukkot*); 28Da (Hebrew bondsman) and others.

[33]20Dc. Above, p. 60 and n.121. The source is the Commentary of R. Ezra to *Shir Hashirim*, p. 530; see editor's notes. See J. Katz, "Halakhah and Kabbalah" (above n.29), p. 166.

[34]30Bc.

[35]See Tishby, *M.H.*, 2, p. 264.

[36]47CD.

[37]See, e.g., Niddah 19a.

which came from the side of provocation and *tum'ah*, the side of the *naḥash*, the Left."[38]

The forces of evil play a role in the goat for Azazel, a notion which ibn Shu'eib derived from Ramban (Lev 17:8). Since the purpose of *miẓvot* is to maintain the proper balance between opposite powers within the Godhead as manifested in the *Sefirot*, some *miẓvot* are associated with *Ḥesed* (force of lovingkindness) and others with *Din* (stern justice). The powers of the Left side, emanating from *Din*, or from the last *Sefirah, Malkhut*, are personified by Satan, Sama'el, and the Prince (that is, the guardian angel) of Esau or Edom and are restrained and put to rest through our obedience to particular *miẓvot*; the goat in particular symbolizes these forces of evil. By sending it to Azazel, atonement is afforded for Israel.

Ramban, and ibn Shu'eib following him, emphasize that the goat is not offered as a sacrifice to these forces but is dedicated to God, Who through the medium of the lottery determines that it be sent to the wilderness of Azazel. This is to eliminate the appearance of sacrificing to the forces of evil.[39]

One more example of ibn Shu'eib's use of Kabbalah is his brief kabbalistic explanation of the laws of incest, an explanation his audience would find difficult to follow without understanding the kabbalistic principles involved. Following R. Ezra of Gerona,[40] he says that the prohibition of incestuous relations was in order "to prevent the union of the root and the branch." According to the detailed explanations of this idea found in *Be'ur Sodot Haramban* and other commentaries on Naḥmanides on Leviticus 18:6, the lower seven *Sefirot*, also called "springs" *(ma'ayanot)* and "roots," were the sources of all reality during the seven days of creation. Everything that came into being was a branch of one of the roots. But after the first seven days, all creativity stems not from the "roots" or the "springs" but from the existing

[38] 47C:

כי לפי דעת רבותנו ז״ל הטומאה באה על עון חוה...וחכמים היו בקיאים במראות הללו והיו מכירים איזה טמא ואי זה טהור, שהיו יודעים אם הם באים מצד הטהרה מצד הימין או מצד הקטרוג והטומאה מצד נחש מצד שמאל.

His source might be *Tikkunei Zohar, Tikkun* 40 (p. 90a in Vilna edition).

ואינון כגוונא דדם טהור ודם נדה דצריך לאפרשא בינייהו בגין דההוא זוהמא דהטיל נחש בחוה גרים לערבא מיין דדכיו עם מיין דמסאבו, ובגין דא תקינו תקנא דא לחובה לאפרשא בינייהו.

[39] Ibn Shu'eib adds as a postscript that the identity of Samael (derived from שמאל) with the Prince of Edom (symbol of Christianity) is significant for it is symbolic of the essence of Edom which is derived from the Left. That is why, he adds, they write from left to right כי שם שרשם...כי שם יצר הרע (51Dab).

[40] 51Aa; see R. Ezra's commentary to *Shir Hashirim* (ed. Chavel, *Kitvei Haramban*), p. 546; in the printed text of the Derashot the reading is ר׳ אברהם בן עזרא ז״ל, but, as S. Abramson has pointed out (Intro. p. 20), many of the passages attributed to ibn Ezra are really by R. Ezra.

"branches," that is, the natural forces already brought into being through the activity of the roots.[41] An incestuous relationship is analogous *(dugmah lazeh)* to the creation of new branches by a branch uniting with its own root, something prohibited after the first week of creation; only Cain and Abel were permitted to marry their sisters[42] since the seven members of the first family (perhaps Adam, Eve, Cain, Abel, and their three sisters) were analogous to the seven "springs" which could procreate one with another.[43]

R. Joshua combines this idea with another explanation, one which Ramban offers in his commentary to the Torah. Ramban, after admitting that he has no received tradition with which to explain *'arayot*, forbidden sexual relations, suggests that the prohibitions are linked to the *sod ha'ibur*, the transmigration of souls. According to Recanati's explanation of Ramban, improper sexual relationships result in the improper placement of the nascent soul.[44] (Recanati himself offers a third explanation of *'arayot* which sees each of the prohibited *'arayot* as affecting a specific *Sefirah*.)

In addition to pointing out the symbolic counterparts of the *mizvot* in the world of *Sefirot* and the interplay of forces within that world, ibn Shu'eib also tells us that each *mizvah* has a metaphysical counterpart in the upper world to which the performer of the *mizvah* connects when fulfilling the *mizvah*. In the name of R. Ezra[45] he says:

> The *mizvot* and the transgressions occupy a place in the upper world, and performer of the *mizvah* connects himself to that supernal *mizvah*;

[41]*Keter Shem Tov*, Recanati in his commentary, and in his *Ta'amei Hamizvot*.

[42]According to the Midrash, one was born with one twin sister, the other with two sisters. See Ginzberg, *Legends*, V, p. 188 n.17.

[43]51Ac:

והכלל כי כל הבא על אחת מכל אלו העריות הוא מכחיש במעש׳ בראשית כמו שכתב ר׳ (אברהם ן׳) עזרא ז״ל שלא להשיב דבר הנפרד לשרשו והענף לעקרו שהאחים שנבראו בששת ימי בראשית הן דוגמת שבע המעיינות ולכן הותרו בתאומותיהן. וזהו חסד כמו שדרשו ז״ל חסד עשיתי וכו׳. ומלת תבל שמבלבל הענין והזרע הבא מהם אין לו השארות, כי לא יצלח ואין תועלת באותה ביאה אלא זימה, כלומר מחשבה רעה, כי כוונת המשגל לקיום המין והשאר מאוס ורחוק ומזה סוד העבור והיתר יבמה.

My own explanation, based on the one in the *Be'ur Sodot Haramban*, is cited by its author as taken from מגילת סתרים כתוב בכתב ידו (של הרמב״ן). See also G. Scholem, "Perakim Mitoldot Sifrut Hakabbalah," ch. 8 (K.S. 6 [1929] 417). R. Shem Tov ibn Gaon in *Keter Shem Tov* reproduces the text in *Be'ur Sodot*. See also Recanati in his commentary and *Ta'amei Hamizvot*. Cf. Tishby, *M.H.*, 2, pp. 622-623, and n.136 where he points to the origin of the terms שורש and ענף in Maimonides' *Guide*, III, 49.

[44]Recanati presents the two as distinct explanations. Ibn Shu'eib combines them, believing that they are both applicable. See previous note. Cf. 60Ac where he relates עריות to כלאים and says כלומר שידבק כל אחד בבת זוגו ובמין שלו וזהו טעם איסור כלאים והרבעה.
לכל דבר יש כוח במרום ולא יערבב את הכוחות. וזהו טעם איסור עריות

[45]The text reads והחכם ר׳אברהם בן עזרא ז״ל. See n.40.

> that is the meaning of the passage, "the reward of a *mizvah* is a *mizvah*." The doer of the *mizvah* ties himself to the *mizvah* itself, which is the name of the Holy One, blessed be He. The result is that his soul is constantly bound up with the *mizvah*. The word *mizvah* comes from the word *zvt* (bind).[46]

The *mizvah* thus becomes a unique tool for achieving closeness to God.

Looking at the range of *mizvot* that ibn Shu'eib explains kabbalistically, he does not seem to limit his kabbalistic explanations to any one group or type of *mizvot*, an approach consistent with his contemporaries such as Recanati, the anonymous author of the *Ra'ya Mehemna*, and R. Baḥya b. Asher.

In his theoretical statements concerning the classification of *mizvot*, on the other hand, he follows the earlier Gerona kabbalists. As G. Scholem has pointed out, according to R. Ezra and Ramban only certain *mizvot* have kabbalistic reasons, such as oaths and vows, *kilayim* (mingled seeds), the sabbatical year, *tefilin*, sacrifices, and a few others. After Ramban, however, we find kabbalistic explanations for all types of *mizvot* in most kabbalistic works.[47] Ibn Shu'eib follows the latter approach in practice, although his classificatory statements might seem to imply the opposite.

In several places in the Derashot, R. Joshua presents classifications of *mizvot* and, although there are differences between some of the classifications, differences that can be accounted for by exegetical considerations, they are all similar in their conceptual formulations. In the *derashah* to *Vayikra* ibn Shu'eib cites Micah 6:8: "He has told you O man what is good and what the Lord requires of you; only to do justice *(mishpat)* and to love goodness *(ḥesed)* and to walk modestly with God *(hazne'a lekhet)*." These categories, according to ibn Shu'eib, encompass all the *mizvot*.

[46] 86Db:
כי המצוות והעבירות יש בעולם העליון מקום שנקשר בו עושה המצוה וזהו ששכר מצוה מצוה. שנקשר במצוה עצמה שהיא שמו של הקב״ה שהוא תמיד נפשו שם צרורה. מלשון צות.
The closest passage in R. Ezra that I was able to find is in his commentary to *Shir Hashirim* (in *Kitvei Haramban*), p. 528: כי עשיית המצוה היא אור החיים והעושה אותה למטה מקיים ומעמיד כחה, וכן הוא אומר כי נר מצוה ותורה אור Similar is R. Moses de Leon's statement in *Nefesh Haḥakhamah* (page following L3) כי המצוה שאדם מחזיק בה היא נמשכת אליו להעלותו וליחדו אליה. מכאן אמ׳ רז״ל ששכר מצוה מצוה ושכר עבירה עבירה. See too R. Baḥya on Avot (p. 596) ששכר מצוה מצוה כלומר גמול המצוה, המצוה בעצמה כי אור המצוה שואב נשמתו וכן גמול העבירה, עבירה עצמה See G. Scholem, "Te'udah Ḥadash Letoldot Reshit Hakabbalah" in *Sefer Bialik*, ed. Y. Fikhman (Tel Aviv 1934), p. 159. R. Ezra says
אתה ידעת כי טעמי התורה רובם מפורשים ומהם נסתרים ונעלמים כגון הנדרים והשבועות והכלאים והערלה והשמטה והיובל והמלה והעריות והלולב ואתרוג ותפילין וציצית שהם מצות אלוהיות, ועמהם הקרבנות.
Cf. his similar statement in his commentary to *Shir Hashirim*, p. 496. See chapter VIII on Ibn Shu'eib's Kabbalah.

[47] See also G. Scholem's discussion on the matter in *Hakabbalah Bigeronah*, p. 338.

> Subsumed under the word *mishpat* are most of the rational *miẓvot (miẓvot sikhliot)*. *Ḥesed* includes *miẓvot* such as visiting the sick and burying the dead, as well as the obligation to perform *miẓvot* beyond their technical requirements. *Haẓne'a lekhet* refers to the *miẓvot* of obedience unique to the Torah *(hamiẓvot hatoriyot hashimiyot)* which are called *ḥukkim* [statutes] whose reason is hidden, that is to say covered; the prophet therefore used the word *haẓne'a* [modest] to indicate *miẓvot* whose reasons were not made explicit. The most important *miẓvot* in this category are declaring God's unity and love and fear of Him....Also included are the *miẓvot* of *tefilin, ẓiẓit, lulav, sukkah*, and others that are similar.[48]

Thus while *miẓvot* in the first two categories have reasons which may be obvious or revealed, the *miẓvot* in the last category have hidden meanings.[49]

What ibn Shu'eib means by hidden may be adduced from another classification of *miẓvot*. At the beginning of the *derashah* to *Aḥarei Mot* he presents a fivefold classification of religious duties based on the verse in Proverbs (9:10), "The beginning of wisdom *(ḥokhmah)* is the fear of the Lord *(yir'at hashem)* and the essence of understanding *(binah)* is knowledge *(da'at)* of the holy *(kedoshim)*." Five stages are listed in this verse, R. Joshua notes: *da'at, binah, ḥokhmah, kedushah* and *yir'at hashem*. The first three represent three groups of *miẓvot* and stand for three aspects of man's intelligence.

> *Da'at* stands for man's natural intelligence...and associated with this Intelligence are *miẓvot sikhliot* such as murder, adultery,[50] thievery, false testimony and robbery. *Binah* [understanding] is applied to man after toiling in the study of Torah and wisdom, by inferring one thing from another....Standing for this Intelligence are *miẓvot* which man's natural intelligence would not have inferred such as *ẓiẓit, tefilin, lulav,*

[48]36Ab. Ibn Shu'eib's interpretion is based on Radak's commentary to Micah and Halevi (*Cuzari* II,48). When the *Cuzari* cites the verse from Micah, the *ḥaver* explains that the verse talks about חקים השכליים which are a prelude to the מצות האלוהיות השמעיות

The implication of the paragraph is that only עשות משפט ואהבת חסד represent the שכליות. Radak is more explicit and obviously ibn Shu'eib's direct source. Ibn Shu'eib's novel twist lies in the last category. Radak says ,הוא יחוד האל ית׳ ואהבתו בכל לבבו ובכל נפשו ואמר הצנע, כי הדבר הזה מסור ללב., i.e., *miẓvot*, the fulfillment of which is hidden or covered. Ibn Shu'eib transforms this to *miẓvot* **שטעמם** נסתר כלומר מכוסה. Some of his examples, however, are identical with Radak's יחוד ואהבת השם.

[49]Noteworthy is the inclusion of the unity of God under *shim'iyot* and not under *sikhliyot* as do others. See, e.g., *Ḥovot Halevavot*, Introd. (ed. Kafaḥ [Jerusalem 1973] p. 27). Although Maimonides does not use the terminology, he considers God's unity as provable rationally.

[50]Cf., however, 60Ac where adultery is linked to *kilayim*.

> *ḥameẓ* and *maẓah*, whose reason man can fathom only by toiling in the Torah and inferring one thing from another. This group is called *'edot* [testimonies]. *Ḥokhmah* which is the Emanated Intelligence [*hasekhel hane'eẓal*] is unique to Israel; God graciously granted it to those who fear Him and revealed His secret to His servants the prophets. Symbolizing this Intelligence are the *miẓvot* called *ḥukkim* such as the goat that is sent to *Azazel*, the red heifer, *kilayim*, mixing meat and milk; they are all attacked by the evil inclination and criticized by the nations of the world, for their reason is profound and can only be comprehened by the *sekhel hanevi'im* [the prophetic intellect], for they are beyond all rational perception.[51]

The third group here, *ḥukkim*, is not merely covered or hidden but also "beyond rational perception." As we discussed above, the "prophetic intellect" here, *sekhel hanevi'im*, is probably identical with the "gracious intellect," *sekhel heḥanun*, of which ibn Shu'eib says (in the name of Rashba)

> our superior *miẓvot* are above reason and can only be known to one who is graced by God with the gracious intellect like the prophets who in turn handed the reasons down to the Sages person to person.[52]

Ibn Shu'eib's repeated emphasis on *miẓvot* which are "beyond reason" points obviously to his belief that these *miẓvot* have kabbalistic explanations, but which *miẓvot* fit into which category varies in ibn Shu'eib's classifications. Of all the groups of *miẓvot*, the *ḥukkim* are the most important; their very obscurity indicates their importance.

> I have heard from my teacher Rashba that the hidden matters in the Torah, like the sacrifices and similar *miẓvot*, point to their greatness, for being covered and hidden indicates great importance, like the Godhead whose essence and matters are hidden from humanity, indeed even from the angels.[53]

[51] 49Dbc:
והחכמה הוא השכל הנאצל שוהוא מסוגל בישראל וחננו השם ליריאיו וגלה סודו אל עבדיו הנביאים וכנגד זה השכל באו המצות הנקראים חקים שיצר הרע מקטרג ואומו׳ העולם משיבים עליהם כשעיר המשתלח וכפרה אדומה וכלאים ובשר בחלב, כי טעמם עמוק לא יושג אלא בשכל הנביאים כי הם חוץ מכל שכל.
Cf. R. Baḥya, end of ch. 3 of Avot in *Kitvei R. Baḥya*, p. 592.

[52] 36Db. Noteworthy is the fact that ibn Shu'eib considers these explanations to have been revealed prophetically. Kabbalists, of course, believe their tradition to have been handed down as an esoteric tradition from Moses on Sinai. In a passage strikingly similar to Maimonides' description of the esoteric tradition of philosophy in the *Guide* I,71, R. Moses de Leon in his *Shekel Hakodesh* (p. 22) traces the tradition of wisdom back to Adam. Other kabbalists develop the same idea; see, e.g., R. Ezra, Introduction to *Shir Hashirim*, p. 479; Todros Abulafia, *Oẓar Hakavod*, p. 44; R. Meir ibn Gabbai, *Avodat Hakodesh*, part 4 *(Sitrei Torah)*, ch. 1.

[53] 36Db: שמעתי למורי הרשב״א perhaps "I heard in his name." Cf. R. Baḥya, Lev 23:24:

Similarly, in explaining why so little is said about the *mizvah* of *shofar* in the Torah, ibn Shu'eib says:

> This matter our Rabbis wrote about in the *Tosefta* in tractate *Eruvin*. They say there that, concerning the *mizvot* which are the essence of the Godhead, such as *shofar, tefilin, lulav* and *zizit*, there are few verses in Scripture but many *halakhot*; however, concerning the holidays whose reasons are obvious and which teach about ex nihilo creation and miracles, there are many verses, for the teachings are well known among the nations.[54]

Thus it is precisely the *mizvot* whose meaning is obscure, as the Godhead itself is obscured, that have kabbalistic meaning and are therefore the most important *mizvot*.[55]

That the very obscurity of *hukkim* points to their importance is not original with ibn Shu'eib or even Rashba. R. Judah Halevi already developed the theme that the *hukkim* which are unique to the Jewish people show the wisdom and the greatness of God.[56] R. Joshua's contribution here is

כי כל מה שהענין יותר נעלם ויותר פנימי הוא יותר סתום. Cf. Naḥmanides, Lev 26:15, who says that the hiddenness of the חוק can lead to its rejection by fools. See above, ch. I, n.26.

[54]89Dc. This passage requires some comment. The context of the passage is an explanation why shofar is hardly discussed in the Torah.

וגם זה הענין כבר כתבו אותו רבותינו ז"ל בתוספתא דעירובין שאומרין שם כי במצוות שהם עיקר האלוהות כגון שופר תפילין לולב ציצית, מקרא מועט והלכות רבות. אבל במועדות שטעמן נגלה ומורין על החדוש ועל הנסים, מקרא מרובה. שהענין ההוא מפורסם בכל האומות.

S. Lieberman comments in *Tosefta ki-fshuta* (part 3 of Order Mo'ed [New York 1962], p. 468) that our Tosefta contains no such passage. Our Tosefta *(Mo'ed, Ḥagigah*, p. 379) reads **הלכות שבת** חגיגות ומעילות כהררין תלוין בסערה מקרא מועט והלכות מרובות אין להם על מי שיסמוכו On the basis of a passage in *Mekor Ḥayyim* of Samuel J. Zarza, Lieberman suggests that ibn Shu'eib's reading of the Tosefta was רגלים חגיגות ומעילות וכו' and this is how the text of the Derashot should be read: בתוספתא דעירובין שאומרין שם [רגלים וחגיגות מקרא מועט והלכות מרובות] כי במצות שהם עיקר האלהות כגון... According to this, ibn Shu'eib is explaining the Tosefta: "How can one say the holidays have little Scripture?" His answer—the Tosefta is referring to the *mizvot* of the holiday, but the holidays themselves have much Scripture. Lieberman's explanation, however, does not account for *tefilin* and *zizit* in the grouping (Lieberman omitted *tefilin* from his quotation of the ibn Shu'eib text). Perhaps ibn Shu'eib included them because they are often grouped together as in the passage from R. Ezra, cited above and the end of n.46, which may have been the basis for ibn Shu'eib here. Cf. R. Baḥya, *Kad Hakemah*, p. 347: המצות המקובלות שהן הן עיקר הקדושה

[55]Whereas ibn Shu'eib considers its obscurity the source of its importance, R. Baḥya (*Avot*, Ch. 3, p. 592) says in one place that their importance will be recognized by appreciating the wisdom inherent in the *mizvot* whose reason is open. However, see above n.53 and E. Gottlieb, *The Kabbalah in the Writings*, p. 244. Cf. I. Heinemann, *Darkhei Ha'agadah* (Jerusalem 1954), p. 12.

[56]*Cuzari,* II,48 and III,7.

exegetical, for he supplies a Rabbinic passage to serve as the source for the idea. He goes further than others by calling these *miẓvot 'ikar ha'elohut*, the essence of the Godhead, thereby lending them unique status.

The categories and their members are not ironclad, and he varies the groupings in different contexts. *Tefilin, ẓiẓit*, and *lulav*, which are some of the *miẓvot* which are here called "*'ikar ha'elohut*" are classified in another place as testimonies, *'edot,*[57] that is, *miẓvot* whose reasons are difficult to understand but are accessible to rational explanation *(hasekhel moreh 'aleihem).*

The inconsistency is due to exegetical considerations, but it also reflects ibn Shu'eib's position that particular *miẓvot* may have both kabbalistic interpretations and other kinds of explanations. The above classifications taken by themselves might have seemed to imply that only certain *miẓvot* could have kabbalistic meaning. In practice, however, as we have said, many more *sodot* or kabbalistic explanations are alluded to.

R. Joshua believed that the kabbalistic explanation, if one was forthcoming, conveyed the "true meaning" of the *miẓvah.* For example, *maẓah, maror* (bitter herbs) and *ḥameẓ* (unleavened bread) all served to remind us of the Exodus from Egypt, but there is another "concealed reason, very great and outstanding."[58] In another place after citing R. Judah Halevi's explanation of sacrifices (with his own additions) he says: "I have brought all of this in order to make these matters more intelligible and to aid in understanding somewhat. Verily we have already said that the true reason is most concealed."[59]

"To aid in understanding...the true reason is most concealed" are the two poles between which ibn Shu'eib's explanations of *miẓvot* move. On the one hand we see a determined attempt to inform his listeners of the kabbalistic meaning of *miẓvot*, an attempt rooted in the belief that the kabbalistic meaning is the real meaning of the *miẓvah* and based on the premise that the kabbalistic understanding of the *miẓvot* will motivate dedicated and committed observance of the *miẓvot*. For this reason kabbalistic explanations are offered also for *miẓvot* whose social and ethical utility is obvious.[60] On the other hand ibn Shu'eib appears also to share the feeling of rationalists (and some kabbalists, as we have seen) that it is important to make the *miẓvot* rationally intelligible.

[57]49Dc. See J. Katz, "Halakhah and Kabbalah"

[58]41Bbc.

[59]37Cbc.

[60]The kabbalistic explanations of *miẓvot* that are no longer observed of course show that motivation was not his only concern. An integrated kabbalistic view of the Torah motivated him as well.

4. The Rationalists and the Commandments

He knew, of course, that the attempt to make *mizvot* rationally palatable had its limits. The following passage which he quotes in the name of Rashba shows strong disapproval of rational explanations.

> He [Rashba] also said that he was puzzled as to why scholars of our Torah should want to explain the *mizvot* rationally, for the secrets of the Torah, the exalted *mizvot*, are outside of reason; how can one rationally explain *tefilin* with its four sections, *zizit* and all of its strings, the red heifer, or *kilayim*. Our superior *mizvot* are outside of reason and can be known only to someone who has been graced by God with the "gracious intellect" [*sekhel hehanun*] like the prophets who handed down this knowledge to wise men orally.[61]

Rashba's opposition to rational explanations seems to be rather strong; although he is quoted approvingly here, ibn Shu'eib does not accept his position entirely.[62] The Derashot are full of rational explanations of *mizvot* drawn from such places as Maimonides' *Guide* and *Malmad Hatalmidim* of R. Jacob Anatoli. Although, as we shall see below, he often makes it clear that these explanations do not reflect the true or the real meaning of the *mizvah*, his very use of them, the very fact that he introduces them into the Derashot, shows his concern with the importance of making *mizvot* intelligible.

There is a dialectic involved in using rational explanations for *mizvot*. It is true that ibn Shu'eib acknowledges that rational understanding motivates observance, and it is for this reason that he uses them. This does not contradict his belief that the kabbalistic explanation is really the true explanation, much in the manner of Abraham Abulafia who saw both the rationalist and kabbalistic approaches as valid but considered Kabbalah

[61] 36Db. The Cracow edition reads היאך רוצים לפרש המצות על דרך השכל **ביסודות** תורתינו והמצות הנכבדות הם חוץ מן השכל. I translated according to the Constantinople edition and Munich MS (Munich MS #9) which read: היאך רוצים לפרש המצות על דרך השכל **כי סודות** תורתינו המצות הנכבדות הם חוץ מן השכל. See 39Bc where ibn Shu'eib identifies מעשה מרכבה as the explanations of the *mizvot* (and below this chapter).

[62] The context of the quotation is significant and reflects ibn Shu'eib's use of sources. Ibn Shu'eib is dealing with various explanations for sacrifices. After finding the rational explanations of Maimonides, ibn Ezra and *Malmad ha-Talmidim* inadequate, ibn Shu'eib tells us that there must be a secret, hidden meaning to sacrifices since they are so important. The relationship of the hidden meaning to the act itself is analogous to the relationship of the soul to the body, for the soul is hidden and unseen and its importance is evident from its actions. Then, to emphasize the importance of the hidden, i.e., kabbalistic explanation, he quotes the above passage from Rashba followed with a paraphrase from the Guide (I,31) which discusses the limitations of the human intellect. Thus he uses Maimonides' own statement almost against himself. It is therefore not surprising that he quotes Rashba to prove a point ad locum without consistently following his premises.

superior, more subtle and deeper.[63] Yet certain dangers are perceived as ever present in these types of explanations as we shall see shortly. First let us turn to some of his explanations and see what he actually says.

Many *miẓvot* in the Torah, he says, are *sikhliot*, rational: for example, the *miẓvot* in the Decalogue from "Honor your father and your mother" until the end are *sikhliot*, as are all the *miẓvot* which are acts of *ḥesed*, lovingkindness.[64] In one place, after ibn Shu'eib lists the *miẓvot sikhliot* in the Decalogue, he suggests, as we have already seen, that the *miẓvot* classified as *'edot* such as *ẓiẓit, tefilin*, etc., can be understood with a great deal of intellectual effort.[65] The *sikhliot* thus are *miẓvot* which man would have legislated on his own without Divine aid; the *'edot* are *miẓvot* which can be explained rationally once they are given.

> The third group are *miẓvot sikhliot*, rational commandments such as charity, honoring one's father and mother, acts of lovingkindness, [the prohibition of] robbery, thievery, and desire, which were commanded for the welfare of the body....Standing for this third group are the words *yir'at hashem* [fear of God]. *Miẓvot sikhliot* endow man with modesty and fear; they purify his body and improve his moral qualities; and they cause justice and truth to prevail between man and his fellow man.[66]

Thus, this group of *miẓvot* seeks to aid man in setting up a society guided by laws which will fashion his political life and which will inculcate opinions necessary for proper ethical and moral behavior. In line with this approach, ibn Shu'eib uses psychological, sociological, historical, esthetic, ethical, and practical-utilitarian categories as well as theological concepts to explain the *miẓvot*. Here are some examples.

R. Joshua presents an interesting explanation for one of the laws dealing with false witnesses. *'Edim zomemim* are witnesses whose testimony was proven false by two other witnesses who testify that the first group was located at some other place when the incident about which they testified took place.[67] The false witnesses are punished by imposing upon them the penalty that would have resulted from their testimony—but only if the sentence has

---

[63]See G. Scholem, *Hakabbalah Shel Sefer Hatemunah*, ed. Y. Ben Shlomo (Jerusalem 1969), pp. 127-128. Citing Abulafia (של שכל הפועל) ועם היות שתי ההגדרות מפידהו
והקבלה הגדה יותר דקה וחכמה יותר עמוקה מן החכמה המושגת בשכל החמרי.

[64]36Aa. See the commentary of ibn Ezra to Exodus 20:2 where he asserts that all the *miẓvot* in the Decalogue, except for the Sabbath, are rational (כי הם נטועים בשקול הדעת). See too *Cuzari* III,11 and *Guide*, II,33, where it is clear that other parts of the Decalogue, particularly the first two commandments, are counted among the rational. See I. Twersky, *Introduction to the Code of Maimonides*, p. 458 and n.247.

[65]49Dbc.

[66]59Ca. See Guide III,27.

[67]Deut. 19:17-19; Makkot 2a.

not been carried out; if the sentence has been carried out then false witnesses are not punished.[68] The two problems which these laws raise, namely, why the second pair of witnesses are believed over the first and why the false witnesses are not punished if the sentence has been carried out, are widely discussed by medieval Talmudists.

Ramban in his Torah commentary says that, if the verdict was carried out, it must have been God's will, for He would not allow the Sanhedrin to unjustly mete out capital punishment.[69] Ibn Shu'eib cites Ramban's explanation but then presents another explanation which he heard "from the mouth of a French rabbi."

> Until their testimony has been carried out, their death will atone for their sin, for the purpose of the death penalties imposed by the court is atonement. However, if the defendant was executed, the false witnesses are not killed because there is no atoning for their sin; they will be an eternal horror.[70]

Ibn Shu'eib goes on to compare their case to the sin of sacrificing to *Molekh*, for which one is culpable only if some of one's children are delivered to *Molekh*, but not if all are delivered. "All of this I have heard," he concludes.[71] In any case, it is the enormity of the crime and thus the impossibility of atonement that frees them from society's punishment. The Divine punishment will be inflicted.

The social impact of *miẓvot* is assessed in ibn Shu'eib's explanation of the *miẓvah* to wear *ẓiẓiyot* (fringes) on four-cornered garments for "He distinguished us from all the nations and therefore we must remain distinguished in everything, even our dress. For this reason we were commanded to observe the *miẓvah* of *ẓiẓit*."[72]

[68]See Rashi, Deut. 19:19, and Rashi, Hullin 11b, who seems to have coined the widely used phrase כאשר זמם ולא כאשר עשה based on the phrase in Makkot 2a כאשר זמם וליכא and the gist of Makkot 5b; Maimonides, Mishneh Torah, *'Edut* 20:2. Maimonides distinguishes between capital testimony to which this special law applies and other testimony to which it does not apply. See commentaries, ad loc., who discuss the possible source of this distinction which is not mentioned explicitly in the Talmud.

[69]See Rishonim and Aḥaronim on Makkot; see R. Baḥya b. Asher (including the puzzling explanation in the name of Ri); *Sefer Haḥinukh, miẓvah* 524; *Derashot Haran, derashah* 18; Abarbanel, and the explanation of R. Isaac ben Yedaiah cited by M. Saperstein, *Decoding the Rabbis*, pp. 157-158.

[70]28Ca.

[71]Hame'iri in *Beit Habeḥirah* to Makkot 3a (ed. S. Strelitz [Jerusalem 1965], p. 9) gives the same explanation in the name of "Ge'onim." Karo uses the idea without citing any source although he knew the Derashot. See, e.g., *Beit Yosef, Oraḥ Ḥayyim* 493. See also *Kesef Mishneh* on Mishneh Torah, *'Edut* 20:2. Ibn Shu'eib may have taken the idea from the Me'iri; more likely, they drew from a common tradition.

[72]60Aa.

The laws of kashrut were explained by Ramban as designed to insure the purity of the soul, for the prohibited animals cause coarseness to come upon the soul.[73] Ibn Shu'eib presents Naḥmanides' explanation,[74] but in one passage he expands upon it by emphasizing the physiological effects of eating non-kosher animals.

> It is well known that the reason the Torah prohibited these foods ...was in order to inform us that they confuse the mind and the heart ...and defile the pure soul which God has breathed into our nostrils....Know that among these prohibited species are the predators which the Torah prohibited because they produce impudence. They make the blood hot and cause burning and illness, make the heart coarse and confuse it.[75]

While the danger lies in the spiritual effects, the physical impact is important as well.[76]

Esthetic factors are the basis for his preference of prayer over sacrifices as we shall see below.[77] Insight into the workings of human nature provided the basis for an explanation of the importance of remembering the Exodus from Egypt. "When we remember his lovingkindness and the wonders He performed we will worship Him with zeal and perform the *mizvot* that God established for us...."[78]

Some of Maimonides' historical explanations of *mizvot* also appear in the Derashot. Thus when discussing the reasons for sacrifices, ibn Shu'eib presents Maimonides' historical explanation, that is, that the purpose of sacrifices was to wean the Israelites away from idolatry in a gradual manner by redirecting and limiting their sacrificial practices. This is immediately followed by Naḥmanides' sharp critique of Maimonides' explanation[79] and a

[73]See Ramban, Ex. 22:30, Lev. 11:13, Deut. 14:3, although he does allude to some negative physical consequences resulting from consuming certain animals (Lev. 11:13).

[74]51Cc. On Ramban's explanations of the *mizvot*, see Ḥ. Henoch, *Haramban Keḥoker Umekubbal* (Jerusalem 1978).

[75]44Cab.

[76]Cf. *Meshiv Devarim Nekhoḥim*, p. 82, l.113. אילו יאכל המאכלים הטמאים ההם שהם מולידים כל חולי לדעת חכמי הרפואות, אין ספק שיארע לו חולי--וכבר הבטיחנו אשר יעשה אותם האדם וחי בהם.

[77]Ch. VI, pp. 123-124.

[78]40Dc.

[79]Naḥmanides' original critique of Maimonides (Lev. 1:9) is directed against a passage in the Guide (III,46) where Maimonides says that the reason certain animals were used for sacrifices is that these animals were objects of worship and the purpose of sacrifices is to stamp out these incorrect opinions. Ritva in *Sefer Hazikaron*, ed. K. Kahana (Jerusalem 1956), pp. 55f., already notes that Naḥmanides fails to mention

mild defense of Maimonides (but not of his reason), that Rambam wrote his explanation to silence critics of *mizvot* by making them more rational.[80]

On another occasion ibn Shu'eib cites Maimonides' explanation of the prohibition of eating blood: it was a pagan practice and therefore it was prohibited. Naḥmanides, ibn Shu'eib points out, takes exception to this explanation, not because he rejects Maimonides' premises as he does in the case of sacrifices, but rather because the Torah itself implies that there is something intrinsically wrong with the act of eating blood.[81]

We find a dialectic in ibn Shu'eib's attitude towards explaining the *mizvot* in rational terms. While he occasionally makes use of such explanations, he is often critical of them. This is evident again in his use of Maimonides' explanation of *etrog* and *lulav*. According to Maimonides, the four varieties that are taken on Sukkot are fresh and pleasant smelling; the fresh vegetation celebrates the arrival of the Jewish people to the Land of Israel, a land rich in vegetation. R. Joshua says: "Even though Maimonides gave a trivial explanation [*ta'am nakel*]...there is no doubt that he said this in order to ease the understanding of those who criticize the need for the four *minim.*"[82] Maimonides himself would never have claimed to be giving the real reason, says ibn Shu'eib, like many other defenders of Rambam. Maimonides was merely giving an explanation for the *hamon 'am*, for the masses, just as the Sages themselves did, while still believing that the real meaning lies somewhere else.[83]

III,32 in the Guide where Maimonides says that sacrifices were instituted as a mode of worship because all the surrounding nations used sacrifices, and the Torah's purpose was to redirect the worship of the Israelites, using familiar modes of worship. Ibn Shu'eib, when citing Maimonides, sumarizes both passages in the Guide and then follows with Naḥmanides' critique. One may ask: why did Naḥmanides only criticize the Guide III,46 and not III,32? Secondly, why did ibn Shu'eib combine them into one explanation? See next note.

[80]This defense is like Ritva's in the *Sefer Hazikaron* (previous note) which indicates that ibn Shu'eib was familiar with Ritva's comments. Perhaps ibn Shu'eib is defending Ramban against Ritva by implying that Ramban's critique is directed against Maimonides' entire explanation and not just part of it, and that is why ibn Shu'eib quotes the entire Maimonidean explanation, something which Naḥmanides omitted.

[81]Naḥmanides, who rejects Maimonides' explanation of sacrifices here, accepts in principle his explanation of *dam*. Perhaps the difference is that sacrifices involve a positive act which according to Maimonides has no intrinsic meaning but is merely an act of protest against idolatry. The prohibition on eating blood, however, is a type of abstention. Naḥmanides may have found it less objectionable to see acts of abstention as originating in historical circumstances than positive acts.

[82]94Ca.

[83]He applies Ritva's defense (see note 80). See I. Twersky, *Introduction to the Code of Maimonides*, p. 403 and n.122.

Ibn Shu'eib does not explain his objection to the "trivial explanation" of
Maimonides, but it is clear from other contexts that he is concerned with
criticism and ridicule of *miẓvot* which ultimately lead to neglect of *miẓvot*. He
complains that there was one group who denied the validity of anything which
was not immediately ascertainable *(huẓ lasekhel)* such as the revival of the
dead and the coming of the Messiah. They "ridicule the *miẓvot shim'iyot*
which are outside of reason. How much more so do they ridicule the words of
tradition, the Talmud, and they do not fulfill the *miẓvot*."[84]

This of course is not a new theme. The notion that rational skepticism
results in antinomian behavior is a recurrent theme in thirteenth- and
fourteenth-century anti-philosophic polemics. R. Jacob b. Sheshet, whom we
saw above justifying rational explanations as possible explanations,
polemicizes against the neglect of *miẓvot* that results from explaining them in
utilitarian terms.[85] R. Isaac Polikar complains that "philosophers ridicule
some of our beliefs, insult our wisdom and our scholars, and do not want our
statutes; they do not observe God's religion, do not attend services, have no
fringes on their garments, no *tefilin* between their eyes, and no *mezuzot* on
their doors...."[86]

But despite his fears of the possible undermining effects of certain
explanations, we also find ibn Shu'eib emphasizing that the understanding of
miẓvot is crucial to their proper performance. The passage quoted above in
which ibn Shu'eib urges understanding when fulfilling *miẓvot* has an
interesting conclusion:

> "Cursed is the man who puts his trust in man..." [Jer 17:5], that is,
> who relies on the understanding of others when he performs a *miẓvah*
> and does not attempt to understand its content and to perform it
> properly....A person should try with all his might to understand its
> content and reasons as much as possible; if he is not capable of this or
> finds no one else who knows the reason, he should believe that it has a
> very important reason and he should perform the *miẓvah* bearing in
> mind its great significance, related as it is to the Chariot. For this alone
> his reward will be great, and in addition he will have fulfilled the
> commandment of his Master. Certain misguided individuals of our
> nation believe that the only purpose in performing a *miẓvah* is the

[84]56Ba. Cf. Rashba, *Minḥat Kena'ot*, Ch. 7, p. 40.

[85]R. Jacob b. Sheshet, *Sha'ar Hashamayim* in *Oẓar Neḥmad*, ed. I. Blumenfeld
(Vienna 1860), vol. III, p. 163.

[86]R. Isaac Polikar, *Vikuaḥ Hatorani im Hapilosoph* in *Ta'am Zekenim* (Frankfurt,
1855), p. 14a.

carrying out of God's will, testifying thereby to His Lordship, and that there is nothing else involved.[87]

Ibn Shu'eib continues that these people base themselves on two Talmudic passages; the first—"What does God care if one slaughters from the neck or from the back? Rather, the *miẓvot* were given only *leẓaref et habriyot*—to purify man"[88] (B.R. 44:1). The *miẓvot* cannot be particularly important, they argue, if they are arbitrary commands. Furthermore, a second Talmudic passage (Sukkah 28a) calls "the work of the Divine Chariot" "great matters" whereas "small matters" are "the questions of Abbaye and Rava." Since these people understand "the questions of Abbaye and Rava" as the parts of the Talmud dealing with the details of the *miẓvot* and "the work of the Divine Chariot" as philosophy and natural law, "the result of this explanation is that they are not exacting in the performance of *miẓvot*, ignoring some *miẓvot* entirely, such as prayer and tefilin[89]—something which will bring destruction and death."[90]

Ibn Shu'eib is thus concerned that the attribution of meaninglessness and the relegation of the *miẓvot* to a position of secondary importance will lead to the abandonment of religious observance. Ibn Shu'eib wants to combat this by insisting on the meaningfulness of *miẓvot*. Indeed, *ma'aseh merkavah*, the work of the Divine Chariot, he claims, refers not to philosophy and natural law but to the hidden meaning of the *miẓvot*. The Talmud does not present us here, ibn Shu'eib insists, with a hierarchy of values, philosophy then *miẓvot*, but rather is telling us the importance of understanding the *miẓvot* themselves, the details of which were analyzed in the "questions of Abbaye and Rava."

Continuing his refutation, ibn Shu'eib says that *leẓaref* does not imply arbitrary decrees which have no meaning. *Leẓaref* means literally to temper or melt or refine metal. The passage may be explained therefore in three possible ways. (1) The *miẓvot* were given to strengthen and ensure the continued

---

[87]39Bb. This passage has been analyzed by my teacher Prof. I. Twersky in his article "Berur Divrei Harambam" (below chapter VII, n.31), p. 33. The "misguided individuals" תועי רוח and טועי רוח are mentioned first in a letter of Rashba which was printed by A. Frumkin in his *Siddur Rav Amram Gaon* (Jerusalem 1912), pp. 78-80; it seems that the entire passage was taken from Rashba with minor changes and variations. Part of the letter was used by Meir Aldabi in *Shevilei Emunah, netiv* 8 (Warsaw 1887), p. 161—see below n.91. See there also the article by Katz who raises the question to what extent are we dealing wih a real group and to what extent is this a literary stereotype?

[88]Rashba adds והטועין חושבין בענין לצרף לדעת אם ילכו בתורתו וצואתו

[89]In Rashba's letter בתפלה ובתפילין ובהיתר ואיסור. Rashba follows this with the expression of concern that ואינן נותנין דעתם רק בלמוד ספרי חכמי האומות פילוסופיא וטבע which is not mentioned in ibn Shu'eib.

[90]39Bb.

existence of Israel or (2) they were given to bring Israel close to the truths embodied in the Torah, or (3) to purify Israel by removing sources of injury, that is, incorrect opinions and despicable moral qualities, just as purifying metal removes the impurities imbedded in it.[91]

From the above we see ibn Shu'eib following an approach that is already implicit in Maimonides' treatment of *ta'amei hamiẓvot.*[92] Maimonides too was concerned that the trivialization of *miẓvot* by characterizing them as arbitrary decrees, bereft of meaning, would serve as a justification for the abandonment of the observance of *miẓvot*.[93]

[91]Ibn Shu'eib's version of the passage is problematic. A comparison between the three versions of the passage found in Rashba, ibn Shu'eib and Aldabi yields the following. Rashba offers two explanations for the word *leẓaref*: 1) to strengthen; 2) to join, i.e., to join people to the truths. To these, Aldabi adds a third, purifying by eliminating dross, i.e., incorrect opinions. Ibn Shu'eib seems to have elided the second and third opinions when he says או לצרפן אל האמת מכל סיג כמו אמרוות טהורות כסף צרוף which may be a combination of Aldabi's second explanation והנה מלשון מצטרפין לומר שנתן לו הבורא ית׳ את המצות לצרף אותנו אל האמיתות הנרמזות בתורה with his third: והשלישי מלשון כסף צרוף הכסף שמכוון להוציא ממנו כל סיג נתן לנו הבורא המצות כדי למנוע ולהוציא ממנו כל נזק או אמונה רעה או מדה מגונה... For comparison here are the three versions:

אבן שועיב ל׳ט,ג	אלדבי	רשב״א
ולצרף הבריות הוא לחזק כמו שאמרו הגיע לצירוף, או לצרפן אל האמת מכל סיג כמו אמרות טהורות כסף צרוף כל אמרת אלוה צרופה	ולצרף כולל ג׳ ענינים. הענין הא׳ לחזקן ולהתמידן מלשון הגיע לצרף. והשני מלשון מצטרפין לומר שנתן לו הבורא יתברך את המצות לצרף אותנו אל האמתות הנרמזות בתורה שבהם נזכה לחיי העוה״ב. והשלישי מלשון כסף צרוף הכסף שמכוון להוציא ממנו כל סיג כן נתן לנו הבורא המצות כדי למנוע ולהוציא ממנו כל נזק או אמונה רעה	ולצרף כולל שני ענינים: לחזקן ולהתמידן מלשון הגיעו לצרף. והשני מלשון מצטרפין לצרף אותן אצל האמיתות הנרמזות בתורה

It would appear that ibn Shu'eib's version is derived from the other two, or else Aldabi drew from a source common to him and ibn Shu'eib. Concerning the definition of הוויות אביי ורבא as a דבר קטן, see the discussion below, chapter VII.

[92]See Twersky (above n.87).

[93]In ibn Shu'eib there is only a brief allusion to the fact that the תועי רוח are philosophers, and that is when he tells us that these people identify מעשה מרכבה as פילוסופית וטבע *(sic)*. The thrust of ibn Shu'eib's polemic is against the alleged arbitariness of *miẓvot* and their resultant neglect. Rashba's additional concern and Aldabi's primary concern (judging from the context, which is discussion of the importance, greatness, and authority of *Ḥazal*) is with priorities of study as well: Rashba

To be sure, ibn Shu'eib is not arguing here necessarily for rationalistic explanations of the *miẓvot*. But R. Joshua believes that it is of crucial importance for inspiring halakhic observance to explain *miẓvot* in a systematic fashion so that they have meaning beyond mere obedience to the will of the Commander *(meẓaveh)*. The end result, he insists, however, must be *ma'aseh*, action, without which there is "destruction and death." Indeed performance of *miẓvot* is crucial, for just as the patient who takes the doctor's prescription which the pharmacist prepares is cured even if he does not know how the medicine helps, so must we perform *miẓvot* as instructed by the scholars of the Talmud—the pharmacists—who follow the "doctor's" orders in describing the *miẓvot*.[94] There *are* reasons, however, and they can be understood by those scholars who are capable of understanding them.

5. Halakhah and Halakhic Explanation

Often, ibn Shu'eib will combine the sort of aggadic, kabbalistic, and philosophic explanations that we have seen above with halakhic explanations, including a brief summary of Talmudic discussion on the matter.[95] He slips easily from one to the other without any attempt to indicate transition from one frame of reference to the other.

For example, when trying to account for the extreme caution that the halakhah requires one to exercise to ensure that no bit of *ḥameẓ* remain in one's possession, when in other instances forbidden foods, whose consumption merits identical punishment, need not be so carefully eliminated, ibn Shu'eib first uses halakhic categories.

> Forbidden fat [*ḥelev*] and blood are items that are never permitted and hence people distance themselves from them; *ḥameẓ*, which is commonly found all year long, may be accidentally eaten and hence requires burning.[96]

But this reason seems insufficient to ibn Shu'eib, because the Nazirite, for whom wine was once permitted and now is forbidden, is not required to eliminate totally the foods now forbidden to him. Ibn Shu'eib therefore presents a kabbalistic explanation. We have discussed this passage above, but let us review it here. In all of creation God combined *Din* (stern justice) with *Raḥamim* (compassion) "and therefore on *Aẓeret* (Shavu'ot), *ḥameẓ* and *maẓah* are mixed" but Passover is entirely *Raḥamim* and therefore only *maẓah* is permitted with the Passover sacrifice and *ḥameẓ* is prohibited. We are commanded to eliminate it like idolatry and whoever eats it is considered

says, ואין נותנין דעתם רק בלמד ספרי חכמי האומות פלוסופיא וטבע וחושבים שהוא מעשה מרכבה
שלא הניח ריב״ז.

[94] On the sources of his *mashal*, see J. Katz, "Halakhah Vekabbalah" (below, chapter VII, n.24).

[95] E.g., 40Ba, concerning the prohibition of eating bread and *maẓah* on Passover eve.

[96] 39Db.

mekaẓeẓ bintiyot "one who cuts the shoots." Therefore its prohibition applies even to minute amounts and it never loses its identity, just like objects of idolatry. This is the reason that the Torah joined the prohibition on idolatry to the commandment to observe Passover, as it is written "You shall make no molten gods for yourselves. You shall observe the Feast of Unleavened Bread..." (Ex 34:17,18).[97] Notice the Scriptural proofs ibn Shu'eib brings to support his ideas, something his audience would certainly appreciate.

Thus for ibn Shu'eib the boundaries between halakhic reasoning and other types of explanation were not rigid. While this is also true for the Talmud itself, R. Joshua goes beyond the Talmud in posing halakhic and kabbalistic propositions almost in the same breath.

The laws of *niddah*, the menstruant, are an area of halakhah which is particularly treated in the Derashot in a systematic manner. Popular outlines and summaries of the *niddah* laws were a common feature of the medieval halakhic landscape then, as they have been since.[98] The pressing practicality of the material and its complexity, combined with the need for constant admonition inherent in sexual restrictions and mores, were all factors that encouraged the writing of such manuals.

One difficulty in explaining *niddah* laws lies in the fact that as presently practiced they consist of many layers of Rabbinic ordinance which surround the basic Scriptural-Talmudic law. In order to understand the present practice of the law it is important to see its development and change from Talmudic practice to its present state. Basing himself on Maimonides' presentation in the Mishneh Torah,[99] ibn Shu'eib deftly presents this development. Local variations in customs are noted,[100] and particularly interesting are the warnings against overstringency in certain *niddah* laws.[101]

[97] 39Dc:
...כמו הבריאה ה׳ אלהים שתף מדת הדין במדת הרחמים ובראו ולכן בעצרת המזיג חמץ ומצה אבל בפסח כלו רחמים ולכן באה המצ׳ בדין הקרבן ונאסר החמץ. רצונו להרחיקו כענין עבודה זרה והאוכלו מקצץ בנטיעות ולכן איסורו במשהוא ולא בטיל כעין עבודה זרה ממש. ולכן סמכו התורה לעבודה זרה דכתיב אלהי מסכה לא תעשו לך את חג המצות תשמור וכמו שצוה בעבודה זרה ולא תביא תועבה אל ביתך וגומר.
R. Baḥya b. Asher explains why *Din* is eliminated entirely on Passover (Exodus 13:3).
ומפני שישראל השיגו היד הגדולה שהיא מדת הדין, על כן אסר והרחיק להם את החמץ לרמוז להם שירחיקו מלהאמין במדת הדין לבד שלא יקצצו בנטיעות ושלא יאמינו שמדת הדין בלבד עשתה זאת.
Ibn Shu'eib's addition is that קיצוץ בנטיות is heresy just as idolatry is and therefore the nature of the prohibition of *ḥameẓ* whose purpose is to prevent this heresy is similar to the prohibition on idolatry.

[98] E.g., Rabad's *Ba'alei Hanefesh*; Ramban, Rashba, and Tashbeẓ all contributed to the literature. See I. Twersky, *Rabad*, pp. 86-97.

[99] Mishneh Torah, *Issurei Bi'ah*, particularly ch. 11.

[100] E.g., 47Da, variations between Spain and France concerning *dam tohar.*

[101] 47Db.

These warnings are significant for they show that ibn Shu'eib is clearly aware of the dialectical tension inherent in the *niddah* laws. On the one hand stringency is urged and encouraged because the punishment for violation is severe, and in addition menstrual blood is seen as so harmful that even the glance of the *niddah* can be dangerous.[102] On the other hand excessive stringency in the law may lead persons to violate that which is being so carefully hedged.

In his usual manner ibn Shu'eib weaves aggadic and kabbalistic motifs into his halakhic discussions. Here, he supplies the underlying kabbalistic reason for the status of the *niddah*. While discussing the halakhah that certain kinds of blood do not render a woman *temei'ah* (ritually impure) while others do, he says:

> According to our Rabbis, *tum'ah* is a result of the sin of Eve, one of the nine curses with which she was cursed. However, only red blood renders a woman *temei'ah* as they wrote in Tractate Niddah [19a]. "There are five types of red blood, some of which are permitted and some prohibited...." The Sages were expert in these showings of blood and could recognize which is *tamei* and which is *tahor* [ritually pure], for they knew whether they came from the side of *taharah* [purity, i.e., the right side] or from the side of prosecution and of *tum'ah*, from the side of the *naḥash* [snake], the left side.[103]

For kabbalists the Left side, the attribute of stern justice, *Din* or *Gevurah*, is also the source or the cause of evil in the world. One of Eve's punishments was that by submitting to the snake, that is, the evil inclination, the blood that flowed from her was affected by the snake—the powers of evil—and is therefore *tamei.*

Consistent with this explanation of *niddah* is ibn Shu'eib's belief, which we mentioned, in the harmful effects of menstrual blood. However, he does try to mitigate the practical implications of this approach. After mentioning that some avoid conversation with a *niddah* or walking in the same ground that she tread, he says "one should not be stricter than the later sages, as Maimonides wrote."[104] Thus the laws of *niddah* are presented both with their halakhic details and their kabbalistic underpinning.

[102] 50Dc.

[103] 47Ca.

לפי דעת רבותינו ז״ל הטומאה באה על עון חוה והוא מן התשע׳ קללות שנתקללה, ועל זה אינו מטמא אלא דם האדום וכמו שכתבו זכרם לברכה במסכת נדה כי חמשה מיני דמים אדומים הם. יש מהם מותרים ויש מהן אסורין...וחכמים היו בקיאים במראות הללו והיו מכירים אי זה טמא ואי זה טהור שהיו יודעים אם הם באים מצד הטהרה מצד ימין או מצד הקטרוג והטומאה מצד נחש מצד שמאל.

[104] 47Db. It should be noted that, from an halakhic point of view, the *tum'ah* of *Niddah* is inoperative when there is no Temple. The only aspect of *Niddah* regulated by

The *tum'ah*, incidentally, which kabbalists such as ibn Shu'eib associated with *niddah*, did not affect the positive assessment of the conjugal act by many of them. Ibn Shu'eib adopts the position of, and liberally quotes from, the *Iggeret Hakodesh*, a kabbalistic tract on proper sexual behavior written in the thirteenth century,[105] which asserts that the conjugal act when performed with proper *kavannah* is a sacred act, symbolizing as it does the harmonious unity within the Godhead itself.

6. Customs and Their Meaning

Minhagim, customs, have always played an important role in Jewish life, and alongside of halakhic manuals—or sometimes integrated with them—books of customs became widespread, particularly in the thirteenth century.[106] The customs mentioned in the Derashot cover many areas—indeed, if collated, they would form a small book of customs themselves. Some are Talmudic, others contemporary in origin. Many of the *minhagim* that ibn Shu'eib mentions have some connection with synagogue ritual; thus ibn Shu'eib tells us how to put on the *talit*, throwing the *ẓiẓiyot* behind us,[107] stoutly defends the custom of adding the fifth blessing in the *Ma'ariv* service preceding the *'Amidah,*[108] tells us when to insert *Zokhreinu Leḥayim,*[109] to stand at *Vayekhulu,*[110] how to read the thirteen attributes of mercy,[111] how to read the *Tokheḥah,*[112] how to read the last verses in the

halakhah is the prohibition on sexual intercourse, which is logically and halakhically separable from *tum'ah*, which regulates access to the Temple.

105 See *Kitvei Haramban*, ed. C. Chavel, vol. 2 (Jerusalem 1963), pp. 315-337. See now S. Abramson, "Iggeret Hakodesh Hameyuḥesset Laramban," *Sinai* 90 (1982) 232ff., who suggests that the author is R. Ezra, based on ibn Shu'eib's identification.

106 See the comments of I. Twersky, *Rabad*, pp. 241-242.

107 See below ch. VII, n.4.

108 24Da. See Berakhot 4b, Tosafot s.v. *de'amar*; Abudraham, p. 140.

109 79Bc:

ולכן היה מורי זכרונו לברכה מוחה בתפלת ראש השנה ועשרת ימי תשובה כשמפסיקין למען שמו באהבה ואומר זכרנו. אלא שיסיים מלך עוזר ומושיע ומגן ויאמר זכרנו כי כל המלות יש להם ענין ויותר באלו השלשה מלות כי הוא מלך עוזר ומושיע ומגן כי יש מלכים ואינן יכולים לעזור והוא עוזר ואם יעזרו אינן יכולין להגן בעדם ממלך אחר גדול והוא מגן לחוסים בו.

110 27Ca. In discussing how Sabbath testifies to God as Creator of the universe, he adds that therefore ויכולו is recited standing just as all testimony offered in court is given standing. See *Hamanhig*, ed. Y. Raphael, p. 138 and sources.

111 92Ba. After stating that on Yom Kippur thirteen covenants were made with Israel, symbolic of the thirteen attributes of God's mercy, he adds:

שנחלקו הקדמונים באלו הי״ג מדות. יש מהן מונין ה׳ ה׳ שתי מדות וכן נראה מנהגינו ולכן החזן אומר ויקרא והצבור אומרים ה׳ ה׳. ויש אומר כי השם הראשון הוא שם העצם ולכן יש בו פסוק ומונין פוקד עון אבות שהוא מן המנין. ויש מונין נוצר חסד לאלפים שתי מדות כי לאוהביו הוא לאלפים ולשומרי מצותיו מיראה לאלף דור. וי״א כי אין היחיד זוכרם וי״א שהיחיד המרבה תפלה בעת צרה זוכרם.

Cf. Abudraham, pp. 251-252.

Torah,[113] when to stand and when to sit during *Seliḥot,*[114] and others.

Outside of the synagogue too, one can compile from ibn Shu'eib an impressive list of customs, for example, the setting up of Elijah's chair at the circumcision,[115] removal of the knife before the Grace after meals,[116] the semi-

[112]The laws of reading the תוכחה are appropriately discussed in the *derashah* to *Ki Tavo* 87D. He discusses a) the Talmudic injunction against breaking up the תוכחה into portions; b) the manner in which they should be read; c) the Ge'onic advice not to leave the synagogue when it is to be read; d) who should read the תוכחה. Some excerpts:
ורז״ל אמרו אין מפסיקין בקללות משום דכתיב אל תקוץ בתוכחתו...ויש מפרשים אל תקוץ מלשון קוצים שלא יקרא אותם אדם במרוצה כהולך על הקוצים וברקנים אלא שיקרא אותם בנחת ובהכנעה ולא יקוץ בהם אלא שיקבלם בסבר פנים יפות...אמרו הגאונים שלא יצא כשיקראו לו התוכחות שלא יראה כמי שקץ בהם ואינו רוצה לשמעם לקיים והייתם נקיים מה׳ וישראל. ואין לזלזל בקריאתם לקרות אותם החזן...ונהגו בקצת מקומות לקרותן למי שאינו רגיל לקרות אלא בזה המקום שכל זה נראה כמי שמזלזל אלא שיקרא בזה המקום כמנהגו במקום אחר. ושמעתי כי מנהג הראשונים היה לעלות לקרותם זקן וחכם לקיים מוסר ה׳ בני אל תמאס.

[113]96Cd. See S. Abramson, Introduction, pp. 31-32. At the conclusion to the *derashah* for *Shmini Aẓeret* ibn Shu'eib presents four interpretations of the Talmudic statement that the last eight verses of the Torah יחיד קורא אותן (Baba Batra 15a). They are: 1) the verses may be recited without a *minyan* because of הואיל ונשתנו (which is interpreted in two ways) (see Mishneh Torah, *Tefilah* 13:6); 2) they are read without interruption (see Rabad, ad loc., and Rashi and Tosafot to B.B.); 3) they are read as a separate unit and not with the other verses (see Me'iri and R. Joseph Migash); 4) just the person called to the Torah reads them, without the *ḥazan* repeating after him, as was the custom once with respect to other parts of the Torah reading (see Tosafot, loc. cit., and Rabad). Cf. *Hamanhig*, ed. Y. Raphael, p. 420.

[114]85Ab. It appears in the *derashah* to *Shoftim* which is always read at the beginning of Elul. Sefardic practice was to begin the recitation of *Seliḥot* at the beginning of Elul (see *Hamanhig*, p. 329) and hence he introduces the relevant customs at the end of the *derashah.*
ונהגו תחלה לישב כשאומרין הפסוקים דרצויין ורחמים ואח״כ עומדים כשמתחיל הסליחות עד שעת נפילת אפים וסמכו על הכתובים שאמ׳ משה במ׳ יום הראשונים ואשב בהר, ובאמצעיים ואתנפל, ובאחרונ׳ ואנכי עמדתי בהר וגו׳. מהם בישיבה ומהם בנפילת אפים ומהם בעמידה.
See Abramson, Introduction, p. 33.

[115]12Cb. Elijah's chair enters into the discussion in an incidental manner; when discussing the children of Leah and Rachel he notes:
וכל זה לראיה שהיו נביאות ועל זה היו אומרות בבני שפחותיהן ואבנה גם אני ממנה כי הבנים שלהן הוא...ויש בקצת הדרשות שנולד ממשפחתה (של לאה) אליהו הנביא ומזרע גד הוא ונקרא גד על שנולד מהול מלשון גודו אילנא ולכן נקרא אליהו הגלעדי ולכן משימין כסא לאליהו בבית המלה עד שהוא מהול. ועוד שיהי׳ במ״ט כמו גד שהוא מזל כמו שאז״ל גד גדי וסינוק לא בא גד בא מזל טוב
See *Hamanhig*, p. 155; on Elijah's chair see Ginzberg, *Legends* VI, p. 338, n.103.

[116]30Da. At the end of *Terumah*, when discussing the prohibition against using metal on the stones of the altar, ibn Shu'eib adds that the custom to remove the knife from the table during *Birkat Hamazon* derives from this *miẓvah* and the midrashic analogy of the table as the altar. See R. Baḥya b. Asher, *Shulḥan shel Arba'* in *Kitvei R. Baḥya*, p. 478; see too *Orḥot Ḥayyim*, part 1, p. 72A.

mourning period during the *'Omer* period and its accompanying practices,[117] the placing of the two loaves of the Sabbath meal between two white cloths,[118] and the custom of not sleeping on Rosh Hashanah.[119]

R. Joshua is not only a defender of proper *minhagim* but occasionally a sharp critic of improper ones. Those who recite the reader's repetition of the *'Amidah* along with the reader are in error, ibn Shu'eib points out.[120] Also, shaking the *lulav* in a northerly or southerly direction is based on an "outside" (= heretical) opinion.[121]

Two matters relating to the laws of *niddah* receive particularly sharp criticism—the custom of waiting fourteen days after finding even a drop of menstrual blood and the custom, characterized by him as heretical (presumably Karaite),[122] of waiting 40 and 80 days respectively after the birth of a boy or a girl before resuming sexual relations.

Just as ibn Shu'eib presents us with a sustained attempt at presenting *ta'amei hamiẓvot*, so does he try to explain and justify *minhagim*, and many of the same types of explanations that we find in his *ta'amei hamiẓvot* we find too in his explanations of *minhagim*. The reasons are sometimes original, but more often they are taken from the books of customs of the preceding century as well as from midrashic and kabbalistic literature. Some of his explanations appear in contemporary literature, such as *Orḥot Ḥayyim.*

Sometimes the explanations are based on the inherent logic of the law; e.g., concerning the joining of the *Ge'ulah* (redemption) prayer to the *'Amidah*, ibn Shu'eib explains that reminding ourselves of the miracles God has done for us will intensify the *kavannah* with which we pray, and as a result He will hear our prayers.[123]

In other cases, the explanations are of a symbolic nature. Ibn Shu'eib relies on Rabbinic aggadot in explaining why the Ḥannukah candle is lit at the end

[117]See below pp. 115-116.

[118]63Ca. An allusion to the manna which was protected by dew. See Tosafot on Pesaḥim 100b.

[119]89Cb. Since Maimonides says the purpose of the shofar is to awaken a person from his sleep—ומכאן (!) כתבו בירו׳ שאסור לאדם שישן בראש השנה כדאמרינן התם בר נש דדמיך בריש שתא ועוסקים בדיניה לעיל שהוא מורה עצלה דכתיב מה לך נרדם.

[120]74Dc. While discussing the prohibition on uttering God's name in vain within the context of the laws of oaths and vows *(Matot—Mas'ei)* he includes needless blessings and chanting the reader's repetition of the *Amidah* with him.

[121]94D. Cf. *Tur, Oraḥ Ḥayyim* #551 who uses similar language, but then in his father's name disagrees with the opinion.

[122]Maimonides already characterizes it thus in M.T., *Issurei Bi'ah* 11:14-15.

[123]Cf. *Hamanhig, Ẓeror Haḥayim* and *Orḥot Ḥayyim*, where different explanations are offered for the halakhot.

of sunset[124] and why the shofar of Rosh Hashanah should be made from a ram's horn. With respect to the latter, he explains that, since the ram which served as a substitute for sacrificing Isaac was *"ne'eḥaz bisevakh,"* tangled in the brush (Gen 22:13), it symbolizes Israel who is tangled in sin.[125]

He also uses symbolic explanations similar to aggadic ones, such as: the shaking of the *lulav* as an act of rejoicing;[126] the *tum'ah* that devolves upon a woman who excretes unabsorbed semen is due to the fact that the semen could potentially have become life but did not;[127] the custom of praying in a bent over position all during Rosh Hashanah symbolizes the necessity of bending the heart on this day.[128]

R. Joshua's search for explanations of halakhot and *minhagim* led him naturally to Kabbalah, which attempts to interpret even the small details of the *miẓvot*. His use of Kabbalah in this area is limited, but it is significant in the way in which it is used. He mentions enough kabbalistic symbols that the initiated will understand and appreciate what he is doing. Thus in discussing the need for diluting concentrated wine for the Passover seder and the preference for red wine over white, ibn Shu'eib merely says that according to Kabbalah *('al derekh ha'emet)* one should use diluted, red wine.[129]

More detailed is his explanation of why the blessing of *Sheheḥeyanu* is not recited when counting the *'Omer*. The period of *'Omer*—the 49 days between Passover and Shavuot—ibn Shu'eib says, is associates with *Din*—God's stern justice—because the *'Omer* sacrifice, made on Passover, consists of barley, *se'orim*, related to the word *sa'arah*, wrath. It is therefore not a period of rejoicing and the blessing is not recited. The same explanation accounts for the mourning practices themselves which are observed during the period, such as not shaving and not scheduling marriages.[130]

The custom of observing these mourning practices only until the 33rd day, *Lag Ba'omer*, was one whose origin perplexed many interpreters of customs. Ibn Shu'eib's explanation, which was cited later by R. Joseph Caro in the *Beit Yosef* and the *Shulḥan Arukh,*[131] is as follows:

[124] 17Ac, in order to associate it with the pillar of fire in the desert which appeared only with the disappearance of the pillar of cloud; based on Shabbat 23b.

[125] 90B. See *Bereshit Rabbah* 56:9.

[126] 90Bc כמאן דנקיט רומחה ומנענה; 94BcCa כמאן דנטיל רומחא וסליק למגדלא ומנענע ואומר דין נצח; cf. Lev. R. 30:2 (ed. M. Margoliyot, p. 594).

[127] Thus it "died" and is *tamei*; 48Db.

[128] 90Ac.

[129] 40Bb. Red symbolizes *Din*, strict judgment; white symbolizes *Raḥamim,* mercy. Cf. Tishby, *M.H.*, I, p. 152.

[130] 41Dbc.

[131] *O.H.* 493. See S. Abramson, Introduction, p. 44.

I have not found any basis for the widespread custom to let the moustache grow only until *Lag Ba'omer*....I have heard that the Midrash says [that the students of R. Akiva died until] *pros ha'azeret* which means fifteen days before Azeret [Shavu'ot], just as *pros hapesah* and *pros hehag* mean fifteen days in Nisan and Tishri. Upon subtracting fifteen from 49, 34 are left which consist of 33 full days and part of the 34th, for part of the day is like the whole. According to this, the mourning practices cease on the 34th of the *'Omer* not the 33rd.[132]

Interesting and significant is his use of Kabbalah to decide an halakhic controversy. When reading the Torah during the morning services, the Cohen is called first to the Torah as a fulfillment of the Biblical verse *"vekidashto"*—"You shall consecrate him [the priest]" (Lev 21:8)—which requires that the Cohen take precedence in ritual matters. The Levite follows, but halakhic scholars disagree whether the sanctity of the Levite is derivative from the Cohen's—and therefore when the Cohen is absent the Levite should receive no special preferences and should not received the first *'Aliyah*—or whether the sanctity of the Levite is independent of the Cohen: if so the Levite may retain a privileged position and therefore receive the first *'Aliyah.* Ibn Shu'eib argues that the Cohen and the Levite are paired, one representing the powers of the "right," mercy, and the other the powers of the "left," strict judgment. Since they symbolize opposite powers, one cannot replace the other—which can be proven by the halakhot that it is prohibited for a non-Cohen to officiate in the Temple in place of the Cohen just as it is prohibited for a non-Levite to function in his place. Therefore, ibn Shu'eib concludes, the Levite may not be called first in the absence of the Cohen, for he would be taking the place of the Cohen, which is the equivalent of misarranging the powers of the *Sefirot.*[133]

One instance which requires a more detailed knowledge of kabbalistic symbolism to appreciate is ibn Shu'eib's explanation of the holiday of Ḥannukah, the menorah, the oil and the prohibition on deriving benefit from the oil. The eight days of Ḥannukah, the eight days of Sukkot, and the Ḥannukah menorah which has eight branches (unlike the menorah of the Temple which had only seven) symbolize the world to come, which will come after the conclusion of the cycle of seven *shemitot* or eons. Ibn Shu'eib then continues with an intricate kabbalistic explanation of the oil and the seven

[132] 41Dc. See now D. Sperber, "Minhagei Aveilut Bitekufat Sefirat Ha'omer," in Z. Malakhi ed., *Meḥkarim Betarbut Ha'ivrit...Lezekher A. M. Haberman* (Tel Aviv 1984), pp. 361-369.

[133] 53Db. Cf. 67Cb. The halakhic source for the problem is in Gittin 59b. The custom in Ashkenaz according to the *Agur* was not to substitute a Levi for a Cohen (*Agur* par. 183). The Sefirotic symbolism of the Cohen and Levi are Zoharic. See *Ozar Hazohar* s.v. *kohen.* I have not found a source for ibn Shu'eib's explanation.

branches of the menorah of the Temple, mentioned in Zechariah, which symbolize the 49 gates of *Binah.*[134]

The use of Kabbalah is important, for it shows ibn Shu'eib's attempt to relate the halakhah to metaphysical categories which involve the participant in a cosmic drama.[135] A receptive audience could only be strengthened in their observance of halakhah and *minhagim* by such interpretations.

In summary, one of ibn Shu'eib's central concerns was to motivate his listeners to careful observance of *miẓvot*. He felt that such motivation could be accomplished primarily by making *miẓvot* meaningful, and he therefore presents a wide range of types of reasons in his Derashot. Ultimately it is the kabbalistic *ta'amei hamiẓvot* which he considers the true explanations for the *miẓvot*. Kabbalah was well suited for that task since it interpreted *miẓvot* as the exclusive means for achieving certain goals; this eliminated one of the major problems of rational *ta'amei hamiẓvot*, the circumventing of *miẓvot* by achieving the alleged goals of the *miẓvot* through other means. For kabbalists the *miẓvah* was unique and hence irreplaceable; therefore, it was safeguarded.

[134] 17Ab; see 41Da where he explains why the *'Amidah* must be repeated if גשם is accidentally substituted for טל. *Geshem* is *Din* and *tal* is *Raḥamim*. Here Kabbalah is used to explain existing halakhot and not to determine what the halakhah should be.

[135] Concerning Ḥanukkah he also mentions kabbalistic criteria in connection with a halakhah, although it is not used as the basis of a decision (17Ac):
ומדליק ועולה כדרך מעלין בקודש ולא מורידין ואין הלכה כבית שמאי דאמר כנגד פרי החג ואע״פ שהוא מכוין ג״כ לסוד הענין יותר טוב הוא מעלין בקודש ולא מורידין.

Chapter VI

Prayer

Of particular interest are R. Joshua's discussions of prayer and synagogue ritual. He frequently addresses both the legal and the theoretical or theological aspects of prayer. The halakhot and customs of prayer, the text of the liturgy, synagogue attendance and decorum, and the meaning and purpose of prayer are all frequently mentioned throughout the Derashot.

The most systematic discussion of the laws of prayer is in the *derashah* to *Shmini*, where ibn Shu'eib uses a homiletic device rather than a conceptual focus for organizing the material.[1] After a discussion of the greatness and importance of prayer, he quotes a verse from Ecclesiastes (4:17), "Guard your feet when going to the House of the Lord." Ibn Shu'eib takes the word *raglekha*, your feet, as the key word in the verse, and connects it to seven central halakhot of prayer: a clean appearance; personal hygiene; posture; walking to and from the synagogue; avoidance of distraction in order to achieve proper *kavvanah*; bowing; and constant awareness of prayer.[2] Each

[1]44-45. The connection to the *parashah* is forced. From a discussion about the importance of abstaining from certain foods in order to promote *kedushah* (sanctity), he proceeds to discuss three aspects of *kedushah*, the last of which is קדושת המצות, כמו שדרשו בספרא והתקדשתם זו קדושת המצות (47Dab); two *mizvot* of great importance which lead to *kedushah* are the recitation of *Shema* and prayer which is supported by אמרו חכמים ז״ל והתקדשתם זו ק״ש והייתם קדושים זו תפלה.

The *derashah* קדושת המצות is attributed to the Sifra but does not appear there as quoted (see Sifra *Kedoshim*, ch. 10, halakhah 2, Lev. 20:7). It is found in *Sifri*, Numbers, 115 (ed. H. Horovitz, p. 127) והייתם קדושים לאלהיכם זו קדושת כל המצות. Quoted too in R. Ezra's commentary to *Shir Hashirim* (p. 529). The second *derashah*, זו תפלה, I have not found.

[2]All except the last are specific halakhic concerns. The last one, which refers to prayer in general, I shall discuss below.

halakhah ibn Shu'eib relates to the word *regel*; he sometimes adds an aggadic passage that would encourage and strengthen the observance of the quoted halakhah, or add an explanation for the halakhah. For example, prayer requires correct posture: one must stand with both feet together, to appear like the angels about whom it is said "their feet appear like a straight leg" (Ezek. 1:7). Ibn Shu'eib adds that this posture, with hands clasped, is a position of abandonment and resignation towards God.[3] Other halakhot which do not fit into this homiletic structure are also included in the *derashah*, such as the requirement of saying the prayers audibly and understanding their meaning.

Some of the halakhot of prayer that he discusses are: the manner in which one should put on the *talit*;[4] interruption in *Pesukei Dezimra*;[5] various laws concerning the recitation of the *Shema*, such as *kavvanah*[6] and extending the *dalet* in the first verse;[7] connecting the *Ge'ulah* blessing with the *'Amidah*;[8] the special *kavvanah* in the first three blessings of the *'Amidah*;[9] mistakes in the *'Amidah*;[10] laws of latecomers to the prayer service;[11] the one hundred daily

[3]45Ac.

[4]25B.
מימינם ומשמאלם מלאכי השרת אומרים לשר של מים אל תגע בהם מימנם כי תורה הם מקבלים דכתיב מימנו אש דת למו ומשמאלם תפילין לפניהם ברית מילה מאחוריהם טלית ועל כן משליכין קצת החכמים ציציותיהם לאחוריה'
I did not find this explanation in contemporary minhag literature such as *Hamanhig, Orḥot Ḥayyim*, Abudraham or *Ẓeror Haḥayyim*. See, however, *Tur, O.Ḥ.* #8 and *Beit Yosef* who cites a midrash as the source.

[5]28Aab. Cf. *Hamanhig*, ed. Y. Raphael (Jerusalem 1978), p. 43 and notes. No interruptions are permitted between *Barukh She'amar* and *Yishtabaḥ*. Between *Yishtabaḥ* and *Barkhu* one should also not speak, in accordance with a decision of Alfasi; however, he notes, most people are not careful about it. According to Kabbalah, he adds, it is important because the blessing of *Yishtabaḥ* mentions fifteen types of praises to God which is the numerical equivalent of *yod hay*. Since *Yishtabaḥ* alludes to God's name and in the *Kaddish* we pray for the incomplete name to be made great and then we pronounce it in *Barkhu*, there should be no interruptions. This is a good example of ibn Shu'eib's use of Kabbalah to explain halakhic details.

[6]44Db.

[7]79Ca. See below this chapter.

[8]24Da.

[9]79Bbc. See also discussion below.

[10]See 74Dc where he criticizes those who repeat the *'Amidah* with the *sheli'aḥ ẓibbur*. It is a mistake and people must be corrected, he says. See also 79Bc concerning other laws of the *'Amidah*.

[11]The halakhah quoted (in the name of Geonim) is that the latecomer may abbreviate the *Pesukei Dezimra* in order to be able to say the *'Amidah* with the congregation. The abbreviated form is *Barukh She'amar, Tehilah Ledavid, Halelu El*

blessings;[12] some laws relating to the Torah reading;[13] the *Kedushah* of *Musaf*;[14] the prayer at the end of the Sabbath[15] and the blessing of the moon;[16]

Bekodsho, Yishtabaḥ. If that is not possible, begin with the blessings of *Shema* and omit *Pesukei Dezimra*. All this is also cited by the *Tur* in the name of Natronai Gaon (*O.Ḥ.* 52). R. Joseph Karo comments that the advice of Natronai (like ibn Shu'eib's) not to recite the *Pesukei Dezimra* only applies to its recital with the blessings. Ibn Shu'eib's presentation of that halakhah tallies with R. Joseph Karo.

[12]80Cc. The Talmud (Menaḥot 43b) associates the requirement to pronounce 100 blessings daily with the verse in Deut. (10:12):

תניא היה רבי מאיר אומר חייב אדם לברך מאה ברכות בכל יום שנאמר ועתה ישראל מה ה׳ א׳ שואל מעמך.

Ibn Shu'eib's version is:

ורז״ל דרשו בברכות במלת מה אל תיקרי מה אלא מאה ודרשו מכאן ק׳ ברכות. וכן עולה מ״ה בא״ת ב״ש כי המ״ם הוא יו״ד והה״א צד״י ולכן הם ק׳ ברכות ולכן יש בזה הפסוק צ״ט אותיות וכשתקרי מה מאה הם ק׳ רמז למאה ברכות

See Rashi and Tosafot to this passage and *Dikdukei Sofrim*; *Sefer Hamanhig* (ed. Y. Raphael), p. 28 and notes. See R. Baḥya, Deut. 10:12, and Zohar III 179a; see *Niẓoẓei Zohar*, 10. Ibn Shu'eib likes to use gematrias and other kinds of letter combinations. See above, ch. II.

[13]53D, 87Cc, 96D.

[14]19Bc. He explains that ברוך שם כבוד מלכותו לעולם ועד is not recited after the verse of *Shema* in the *Kedushah* of *Musaf* because the *miẓvah* of קבלת עול מלכות שמים has already been fulfilled. The verse is read now only as הזכרה בלבד.

[15]35AB. See *She'iltot Derav Aḥai Ga'on, She'ilta* 1 (with commentary of Neẓiv, vol. 1, p. 9); *Tur O.H.* #295; Abudraham, p. 184. See also S. Abramson, "Mafteḥot Litshuvot hage'onim," *Wolfson Jubilee Volume* (Jerusalem 1965), Hebrew section, p. 6, and the sources cited in the notes. The custom of reciting the last verse of Psalms 90 and entire Psalm 91 after *Ma'ariv* on Saturday night is not mentioned in the Talmud but is mentioned often by the Ge'onim. The various explanations account for 1) extended prayer on Saturday night, 2) the verse ויהי נועם, and 3) the entire prayer. Ibn Shu'eib lists several explanations, most of which are found in other sources. 1) The verse ויהי נועם was recited by Moses at the time of the completion of the Tabernacle (thus we pray that מעשה ידינו should be blessed). See *Tur* and Abudraham. 2) The prayer with the repetition of the last verse—as is our custom—contains 129 words. For 129 years Adam produced demons and spirits until Seth was born in his 130th year. Psalm 91, known as שיר של פגעים, is recited to keep us from such a fate. This explanation is his own. See, however, Abudraham for a different numerology. Cf. *Tur* שע״י כן נשלם השם היוצא מהם. 3) The prayer does not contain the letter *zayin*; we pray to be saved from injury so that we will not need כלי זיין, armaments (thus in *Hamanhig* and Abudraham). 4) The absence of the *zayin* alludes to the seven times we do not recite ויהי נועם (i.e., whenever a holiday falls in midweek); see Abudraham. 5) The souls of sinners return to *Gehinom* on Saturday night after the conclusion of the Sabbath prayers; in order to delay their return, we sing and prolong the recital of these prayers (see *Tur* and Abudraham).

[16]24Bc and 34C; the matter is discussed frequently in contemporary kabbalistic literature.

the recitation of Hallel;[17] the dew blessing;[18] counting of the *'Omer*;[19] the special *Haftarot* preceding the Ninth of Av;[20] *Selihot*;[21] the laws of shofar;[22] the laws of *lulav*;[23] and the laws of Hanukkah.[24]

R. Joshua comments in other places in the Derashot on such central theoretical questions as the relative importance of prayer and sacrifices; the problematics as well as the crucial importance of verbal prayer; inwardness in prayer; the role of *devekut*; as well as some of the *sodot* or kabbalistic secrets of prayer. When pieced together, a fairly coherent theory of prayer emerges which combines elements from the aggadic, philosophic and kabbalistic traditions.

1. Prayer and Sacrifice

The question of whether prayer has independent importance or whether it serves only as a temporary replacement for sacrifices is alluded to in a passage

[17]Briefly, 94Dc. 95Aa.

[18]Ibn Shu'eib offers a kabbalistic explanation of the custom of beginning the recitation of מוריד הטל in the second blessing of the *'Amidah* at the beginning of Passover. טל symbolizes God's compassion, רחמים, like the maẓah.
ובעבור כי הטל הוא רחמים הצריכו חכמים ז"ל לחזור למי שטעה והזכיר גשם במקום טל. ובימות הגשמים אם הזכיר טל במקום גשם אינו חוזר.
This reason is not found in contemporary books of customs.

[19]41D. Ibn Shu'eib presents a thorough summary of the halakhic issues connected with the counting of the *'Omer* as well as many explanations for the customs connected with it. He deals with the time of counting (at night after the stars are out), the different opinions concerning one who forgot to count at night; the status of counting after the destruction of the Temple in the absence of the *'Omer* itself and the sacrifices. In connection with this last point he says תמימות are no longer necessary today because the counting nowadays is in joyful anticipation of the giving of the Torah: כי החשבון בזמן הזה הוא לשמחת נתינת התורה He then adds some explanations for customs of mourning during the *Sefirah* period (see below, this chapter).

[20]72Ba.

[21]See below, this chapter.

[22]90AB. The *derashah* includes other aspects of the Rosh Hashanah prayers.

[23]94D. He cites and discusses many halakhot and minhagim connected with *lulav*: the place in the prayers to shake the *lulav*; the directions of the shaking; the number of times and their symbolic and kabbalistic meaning; when to say the blessing, including a short discussion of ברכות עובר לעשייתן. According to Rashba, e.g., the principle of עובר לעשייתן is fulfilled as long as the blessing is recited before the completion of the *miẓvah*. Cf. Shakh, *Yoreh De'ah*, #19, par. 3 and the sources he cites.

[24]17AB. A number of halakhot are mentioned briefly in the *derashah* to *Vayigash* which is read around Ḥanukah time. 1) The time for lighting the candles; 2) the terminus ad quem for the *miẓvah* of Ḥanukah lights; 3) what to do if the lights are extinguished; 4) how many candles to light on each night; 5) which blessings to recite on which nights; and 6) the prohibition on fasting and eulogizing on these days.

in the Talmud (Berakhot 26b): two opinions are cited. According to one, "prayers were established by the Fathers"; according to another, "prayers were established in conformance with the regular sacrifices."[25] Although the Talmud harmonizes the two opinions, the notion that prayer originated independently of sacrifices and is perhaps superior to it is inherent in the former opinion.[26] And elsewhere the Talmud says explicitly "prayer is greater than the sacrifices" (Berakhot 32b).

This statement was taken quite literally in medieval Jewish philosophy, where the superiority of prayer over sacrifices was stressed, particularly by Maimonides and his followers. According to Maimonides, sacrifices are a "secondary intention" whose goal was to reorient the worship of the Israelites to the One God by using then-familiar modes of worship, whereas "crying out in prayer and similar acts of worship are closer to the first intention."[27] The post-Maimonidean acceptance of this notion is typified by Joseph ibn Caspi's statement in his commentary to the Torah:

> This *parashah* and the ones following it concern the *miẓvot* of sacrifices. It is known that Moses our Teacher was forced to include it in his book even though God does not want burnt offerings and sacrifices; it was out of necessity that he included it, for it was the custom of the nations to bring sacrifices. Since that is so, it is enough to know the words of these *parshiyot*—and if we do not know them there is no harm in it.[28]

This historical explanation of the origin of sacrifices was forcefully rejected by kabbalists who repeatedly stress the importance of and great secrets contained in the sacrifices. The sacrifices bring about a Divine harmony, and kabbalistic writings dwell on the importance and significance of the details of the sacrificial ritual.[29]

Like them, ibn Shu'eib rejects the historical explanation of the origin of sacrifices and attributes importance even to the details of the sacrifices;[30] yet at the same time he vigorously pursues the notion of the superiority of prayer.

[25]Berakhot 26b.

[26]Cf. Tishby, *M.H.*, 2, pp. 247-248. The Talmudic statement that prayer is greater than sacrifices (Berakhot 32b) was probably not meant literally. See Tosafot, ad loc., concerning the relationship of prayer and good deeds (i.e., that prayer with good deeds is greater than prayer alone). Their explanation probably would apply to prayer and sacrifices; this is supported by the following statements of R. Eleazar, the author of the former, concerning the status of prayer after the destruction of the Temple.

[27]Guide III,32.

[28]*Maẓref Lekesef* in *Mishneh Kessef*, 2 (Cracow 1906), p. 229.

[29]See, e.g., Naḥmanides, Lev. 1:9; Tishby, *M.H.*, 2, pp. 194-206.

[30]See *derashah* to *Vayikra*, p. 36.

> The matter of prayer is a very weighty one. The Rabbis of blessed memory have said "prayer is greater than all the sacrifices"[31] as it is written "even when you make many prayers I will not hear" (Is. 1:15).[32] This is not an exaggeration—it is firmly true in a literal sense that prayer is superior to sacrifice.[33]

He goes on to give two reasons for the superiority of prayer over sacrifices. First, "sacrifices may be the object of ridicule *(kintur)* when upon the table of the Lord one sees blood and fat. Self-doubt creeps in[34] and heretics are critical." None of this applies to prayer, the essence of which is the inner expression of man's soul. Furthermore, there are many limitations associated with sacrifices that restrict it as a medium of worship. They require many preparations, a specific place, specific times, special people to perform the sacrifice, and if any of these are missing then the sacrifice is unacceptable, whereas prayers can be said any place and any time, while the Temple is standing or after it is destroyed.[35]

Further proof of the superiority of prayer ibn Shu'eib finds in the Talmudic statement quoted earlier that the prayers were established by the Fathers:

> Even though sacrifices are to be praised, prayer is superior to them. It is for this reason that our holy Fathers, while knowing the greatness of sacrifices, passed down to us only prayer, as it is written: Abraham established the morning prayer, Isaac the afternoon prayer and Jacob the evening prayer. We see from all this that prayer is something superior and honorable.[36]

[31]גדולה תפלה יותר **מכל** הקרבנות. In our editions of the Talmud the reading is גדולה תפלה יותר מהקרבנות (Berakhot 32b). Ibn Shu'eib may have added כל as a rhetorical flourish. See *Dikdukei Sofrim* ad loc.

[32]In other words, not only will I ignore sacrifices but even prayers. Ibn Shu'eib is emphasizing the verse's use of the word "even."

[33]44Dc.

[34]יצר הרע מקטרג.

[35]44Dc-45Aa. It is interesting how ibn Shu'eib turns a Maimonidean passage concerning sacrifices to his own advantage. Maimonides in the Guide (III,32) in explaining the superiority of prayer over sacrifice notes that, although sacrifices are commanded in the Torah, they are of secondary intention, and in order to distinguish them from prayer special restrictions were placed on sacrifice rituals:
לא חייב עלינו כמו שהיה בתחלה ר״ל שנקריב בכל מקום ובכל זמן ולא שנעשה היכל באשר יזדמן ושיקריב מי שיזדמן החפץ ימלא את ידו, אבל נאסר כל זה עלינו והושם בית אחד אל המקום אשר יבחר ה׳ ואין מקריבין בזולתו...ולא יהיה כהן אלא זרע המיוחד. אבל התפלה והתחנה מותרת בכל מקום וכל מי שיזדמן.
Ibn Shu'eib ignores the context of the statement, i.e., that the restrictions were to modify the sacrificial ritual in order to eliminate its pagan associations, and uses the facts of limitation to demonstrate that prayer by virtue of its wider applicability is superior to sacrifices which are severely limited in their applicability.

[36]45Ac.

R. Joshua's insistence on the superiority of prayer may be explained both by his historical circumstances as a Jew in Christian Spain and by the overall structure of his beliefs. In a *derashah* to *Ẓav*, ibn Shu'eib says very explicitly:

> The intention of these verses is that one should not think that sacrifices were the original method intended by the Holy One Blessed be He to atone for the unwittingly sinning soul, and that without the institution of sacrifices, such as is the case now because of our sins, atonement is not possible, neither through prayer nor repentance nor good deeds. It is in this manner that the nations taunt us saying that, since we have no Temple, no priest and no sacrifice, our sins cannot be atoned for in any manner. This is not the case.[37]

Ibn Shu'eib goes on to show, following Maimonides, as proof that sacrifices were not God's first intention, that there is no mention of them at Mt. Sinai. It is clear from the above that R. Joshua is polemicizing strongly against Christian attacks upon Judaism, and this is certainly one reason for his repeated insistence upon the superiority of prayer over sacrifices.

But conceptually ibn Shu'eib provides the basis for this position as well. The nature of the superiority of prayer is rooted in a hierarchy of *miẓvot* established already by R. Baḥya ibn Pakuda in his *Ḥovot Halevavot.* According to R. Baḥya, there are three classes of *miẓvot*. The first is "the duties of the heart" to which he devotes the majority of the book. The second is "the duties that require physical movement, but are at the same time duties of the heart, such as the recital of prayers, study of the Torah, praise and laudation of God and study of science." The third class consists of duties that only involve physical activities and in which the heart has no part except the feeling of devotion to God when we begin to perform them.

[37] Jewish Theological Seminary MS R 1607, p. 225v.
שמעה עמי ואדברה ישראל ואעידה בך...לא על זבחיך אוכיחך. כוונת הפסוקים האלו להעיר האדם על כוונת הקרבנות שלא יחשוב האדם כי הקרבנות הם תחלת מחשבת הב״ה ית׳ לכפר על הנפש השוגגת. ואלמלא לא יהיה קרבן בעולם כמו בזמן הזה בעונותינו שלא יהיה לנו כפרה לא בתפלה ולא בתשובה ולא במעשים טובים **כמו שמלעיגים עלינו אומות העלם** ואומרים כי מאחר שאין לנו מקדש ולא כהן ולא קרבן שלא יהיה לנו כפרה בשום ענין אינו כן. ועל זה באו אלו הכתובים להודיענו כי אין הכוונה ראשונה של הב״ה להביא קרבן רק על הדרך שנאמר אחר זה, ובעבור זה אמר לא על זבחיך אוכיחך. והעד כי במעמד הר סיני הנכבד לא נצטוינו להקריב קרבן ועל זה אמר הנביא ירמיהו בזאת כי לא דברתי את אבותיכם ולא ציויתם ביום הוציאי אותם מארץ מצרים על דברי עולה וזבח כי אם את הדבר הזה ציויתי אותם לאמר שמעו בקולי רוצה בו כי הכוונה בבחירת השם בישראל הוא לשמוע בקולו ולקבל עליו עול מלכות שמים ולקראו באמת והוא שיצייר אדם בלב הדבר שיוציא מפיו מייחוד השם וממשלתו ושאר תפלותיו כמו שאמ׳ ישעיהו הנביא עם זו יצרתי לי תהילתי יספרו, ז״ו בגימטריא י״ג רמז אל הנער שהוא בר מצוה משיגיע לשלש עשרה שנה והיא העבודה השלמה כמו תפלה בכוונה וצדקה ומעשים טובים. ועל זה אמר משה רבינו ע״ה ומי יתן והיה לבבם זה להם ולא תהיו צריכים לעבוד אותו בדרך...
later on 226v, ועל דרך האמת התפלות וההודאות נכבדות מן הקרבן לפני השם כמו שהעיד על זה דוד ע״ה. The *derashah* is not included in the printed Derashot.

For R. Baḥya, therefore, although prayer includes an aspect of physical activity, it still shares the superior spiritual position of the duties of the heart. Prayer without *kavvanah* is unacceptable:

> The essence of prayer is the soul's longing for God, humbling itself in His presence, exalting its Creator, offering praises and thanksgiving to His name. Prayer consists of words and their meanings. Words need a subject of thought, but a subject of thought needs no speech if it is possible to set it in orderly fashion in the heart. The latter is the essence of our devotion *(kavvanah)* and the chief aim to which our attention should be directed.[38]

Thus prayer—whose essence is *kavvanah*—is ranked above all the other obligations of the limbs.

Ibn Shu'eib constructs a slightly different hierarchy of worship, but the result is similar.

> When a person pours out his soul before his Creator, praises Him Who is the Lord of humankind, and worships Him with his pure soul, he is worshipping in the most superior way, as they have said in the Sifra—"to worship Him with all your heart [Deut. 11:13]—that is prayer." There are three types of worship—with one's body, one's money and possessions, and with one's soul. Prayer requires body and soul—the *kavvanah* of the soul which is internal expression [*hahigayon hapenimi*] as well as speech, language and body movement.[39]
>
> Thus they have ordained to recite [before the *'Amidah*] the verse "O Lord open my lips" (Psalms 51:17) which alludes to the physical utterances [*hahigayon haḥiẓoni*] and at the end [of the *'Amidah*] "may the words of my mouth and prayer of my heart [*hegyon libi*] be acceptable to You" (Ps. 19:15) which alludes to the internal expression [*hahigayon hapenimi*].[40]

The notion that prayer is man's inner expression is more fully developed in another passage where ibn Shu'eib draws a parallel between the three types of *berakhot* (blessings) and the three parts of the human soul.[41] The three kinds

[38] *Ḥovot Halevavot, Sha'ar Ḥeshbon Hanefesh*, ch. 3, ninth item (trans. M. Hyamson [Jerusalem 1965]), vol. 2, pp. 205-207 and 211.

[39] 44Dc.

[40] 45Ba:
ועל זה תקנו בתחלת התפלה ה׳ שפתי תפתח ופי יגיד תהלתך שהוא ההגיון החצוני ולבסוף יהיו לרצון אמרי פי שהוא ההגיון הפנימי
This notion of internal and external expression is perhaps derived from Zohar I 169a:
ת״ח דוד מלכא אמר יהיו לרצון אמרי פי אלין מלין דאתפרשין. והגיון לבי אלין מלין דסתימין דלא יכיל ב״נ לפרשא לון בפומיה דא הוא הגיון דאיהו בלבא דלא יכיל לאתפרשא.
See Tishby, *M.H.*, 2, p. 258.

[41] The parts of the soul come up repeatedly in the Derashot. See 2C, 18D, 22A, 29A, 30B.

of *berakhot* are *birkot hanehenin*, blessings made for some pleasure derived, *birkot hashevaḥ*, blessings of praise, and *birkot hamiẓvot*, blessings made upon the fulfillment of *miẓvot*. The parts of the soul have their seat in different parts of the body: the *nefesh* which is the vegetative soul has its seat in the liver. It is the *nefesh* the source of man's physical being and pleasure and is the source of expression of *birkot hanehenin*, blessings for food and physical pleasure. The *ru'aḥ*, the vital or sensitive soul, resides in the heart and is the source of expression of blessings of praise, for praise comes from the heart "in the form of inner expression *(higayon penimi)* as it is said *vehegyon libi*, the expression of my heart, and from the tongue—the outer expression *(higayon hizoni).*"[42] Finally the *neshamah* or rational soul whose seat is in the mind is the source of expression for the *birkot hamiẓvot* for, just as the *neshamah* is the superior of the three souls, the *miẓvot* are part of the Divine Chariot.[43]

A corollary of the notion that prayer is an expression of man's inner self, that is, of his soul, is that prayer is the unique expression of man—and that by praying man demonstrates his uniqueness. "Mankind is worthy of its name and its [Divine] form only during times of prayer."[44] Prayer is an expression of the soul—and also, as R. Judah Halevi had already said before him, it is a source of its nourishment. "The wise man said that prayer feeds the soul just as food nourishes the body and just as the angels and the *ḥayyot hakodesh* are fed by supernal light."[45] Since prayer sustains the soul, it is proper for man to look forward with great anticipation to the times of prayer, which are times when "the soul secludes itself with its God...for the greatness of man is apparent only when he secludes himself with his Creator."[46]

Seclusion of the soul with God is an aspect of *devekut*, cleaving to God, a goal valued by Jewish thinkers within both the philosophical and the kabbalistic camps.[47] "The intention of prayer is to cleave to God as it is written 'and you shall cleave to Him' (Deut. 13:5). This is a stake upon which everything hangs."[48]

He does not define here the nature of this *devekut*, but in another place[49] in commenting on the same verse, "and you shall cleave to Him," he

[42]29Ab. The passage also appears in JTSA Ms., p. 224r. For another use of הגיון פנימי, see Isaac Polikar, *'Ezer Hadat*, ed. G. Belasco (London n.d.; Israel 1970), p. 86.

[43]29Ab.

[44]45Bb.

[45]Ibid. See *Cuzari* III,5: שכן תפלת אדם טובה לנפשו כשם שהמזון תועלת לגופו

[46]45Bb.

שימתין עתות התפלה כי האדם אינו נקרא אדם ואין לו צורה אלא בשעת התפלה שהוא עושה פעולה נכבדת והיא עבודת הנשמה שמתבודדת עם אלהיה כי בעתות ההנאות הן מעלה הבהמות וכל מעלת הגוף אינו נראה אלא כשהוא מתבודד עם בוראו והשכל פועל פעולתו שהוא תכלית הבריאה.

[47]See, e.g. *M.H.*, 2, pp. 284-293.

[48]45Ca.

[49]83Bb.

paraphrases Naḥmanides' definition of *devekut* (in his comment to Deut. 11:2), which explains it as an intense awareness of God while involved in mundane affairs; R. Joshua alludes as well to Maimonides' contemplative conception of *devekut* as described in the Guide.[50]

2. Prayer and the Philosophers

Given his understanding of the nature of prayer, it is natural for ibn Shu'eib to stress, as had halakhists, ethicists, philosophers and kabbalists before and after him, the importance of *kavvanah* in prayer[51] and to object to any interruptions or idle talk during the prayers. Ibn Shu'eib polemicizes in a number of places against abuses in prayer and synagogue ritual and these polemical statements may have had their conceptual origins in the following.

Jewish philosophers in the Middle Ages, and Maimonides in particular, found difficulty with the notion of verbal prayer, first, because by making positive statements about God one becomes involved in the problem of God's attributes, and also because the immutability of God's will would make any request to Him meaningless. As a result of these problems, Maimonides alludes to the possibility that silent prayer is theoretically preferable to verbal prayer[52] although in practice he never actually advocates such a position.[53]

The thirteenth century, however, did see advocates of just such a position. In a polemic by R. Jacob b. Sheshet in *Sha'ar Hashamayim* we learn of people who abandoned prayer on philosophic grounds. He cites those who say that:

> Prayer is only a consciousness in the mind. Let the living contemplate, for that is the first principle; there is no advantage to those who use their tongue; it is far more desirable not to utter a word. The pronouncing of prayers is foolishness; by speaking, one sins, by opening one's lips one insults....What benefit is there to one who rubs sleep from his eyes...going to his room to cry, getting up at midnight to pray and supplicate, to praise and glorify at great length?...He who cannot be conceived of by thought, how can He be described by words?[54]

[50] III, 54. See H. Huna, "Sod Hadevekut Eẓel Haramban," *Sinai* 11 (1942) 86-99.

[51] 79Ba.

[52] Guide III, 32.

[53] See Marvin Fox, "Hatefilah Bemaḥshavto Shel Harambam," in G. H. Cohn, ed., *Prayer in Judaism: Continuity and Change* (Jerusalem 1978), pp. 142-167. Fox deals with the tension in Maimonides between his philosophical position and his halakhic and personal commitments to prayer.

[54] R. Jacob b. Sheshet, *Oẓar Neḥmad*, vol. III, pp. 164-165.
וכן אמרו שאין התפלה רק להזכיר תמיד במחשבתו, והחי יתן אל לבו כי הוא היסוד הראשון. ואין יתרון לבעל הלשון ויותר נאה מקובל, רצוני כי אין מלה בלשונו וחתוך התפלה בשפתים כסל למו, חמאת פימו דבר שפתימו. וכל פוצה שפתיו נתן תפלה וכל פה דובר נבלה. החפץ לו באמרים וקול כסיל ברוב דברים, הלאל יסכון גבר בבקשתו, להציל לו מדעתו. ועל כן לא תועיל התפלה אשר עשה לתהלה עאכ"ו בקשות ותחנונים ולחשים העניים והאביונים מבקשים ולא ישאל החכם צרכיו רק מפני ההמון הסכל כי השקט לא

Ibn Shu'eib betrays an awareness of this problem, as he strongly rejects the practical implications of this situation: "Although He is perfect in the ultimate sense, still He is elevated and praised by our blessing."[55]

In light of the practical solutions given to the problem by certain followers of the philosophic position, perhaps we can understand ibn Shu'eib's particularly harsh language concerning violations in the prayer ritual. As a preacher, he may have taken language from polemical contexts dealing with those who repudiate prayers and applied it to violations as well. Thus he says:

> Whoever violates this *takkanah* throws off the yoke of Heaven and is a sinner and a rebel. There should have been no need to warn about this for it is obvious, but there are some who violate it and are neglectful.[56]

The synagogue, being a "miniature temple," requires us to "sit in [it] with fear as if we were sitting before the *Shekhinah*. We must therefore pray with *kavannah*."[57] And those "people who abandon the worship of God and their prayers, who rise early but come late for the worship of God, are worthless and empty."[58] R. Joshua does not indicate that there is any ideological basis for their neglect, but the existence of such contemporary attitudes as noted above may have encouraged this kind of language.

But while ibn Shu'eib rejects the philosophical reservations about prayer and their implications, he shares the concern for strict adherence to the very precisely formulated language of prayer shown by Maimonides and his followers as well as by the Ḥasidei Ashkenaz, each for different reasons. Frequently he discusses the correct reading of a prayer, often accompanied by an explanation.[59] Brevity and precision are two guiding principles in prayer.

יוכל ומה יתרון לגוזל שינה מעיניו ומעפעפיו תנומה ויבא החדרה ויבך שלה יקום בחצות הלילה להפיל תחנה ותפלה ולהרבות שברו ותהלה...אם יקראני לא יענה אם יצעק אליו לא יענה ומי שלא ישיגנו רעיון איך יתארהו ההגיון ואשר אינו גוף ולא כח בגוף איך נאמר לו עננו קומה והושענו

[55] 87Ac.

כי אם הוא ית׳ שלם בתכלית השלמות הוא מתעלה ומתקלס בברכותינו כמו שבאו מדרשים רבים על זה כמו שדרשו בפסו׳ ויהי בישורון מלך. ובפסוק נדיבי עם נאספו ובפסוק יונתי בחגוי הסלע ואמרו שכינה בישראל צורך גבוהה וכתיב ישראל אשר בך אתפאר וכתיב מה תעשה לשמך הגדול וכמ״ש הנהנה מן העה״ז בלא ברכה מעל שנ׳ גוזל אביו ואמו...ואמר ישמעאל בני ברכני וזה סוד שהקב״ה מניח תפילין וכמו שלמדו מזו הפרשה את ה׳ האמרת וגו׳ ולפי הדרך הפנימי פי׳ כבוד שבעבודתינו אנו מקריבין הכבוד אל ה׳ א׳ ובא השפע והטוב לעולם משובע דגן תירוש ויצהר וזהו ברוך כבוד ה׳ ממקומו.

[56] 44Db.

[57] 30Dc.

[58] 14Db.

[59] Ibn Shu'eib makes many references to the proper *nusaḥ* of the prayers, e.g., 3Bc
והגירסא 24Aa ;והראוי לומר בימים ההם בזמן הזה בלא וא״ו 17Ba ;וי״ג ראה והקטין צורת הלבנה
והמדקדקים אומר (!) בתפלת ליל שבת וינוחו בה ובוים 27Cb ;הנכונה אני ולא השליח בה״א הידיעה
זמן מתן תורתינו ולא יום 59Ca ;וחותם על הארץ ועל פרי הגפן והחותם על הגפן טועה 40Bc ;וינוחו בו
בגלל ז׳ בסיוון נתנה תורה

"Let your words be few" (Eccl. 5:1)—that means you should not extend the prayers but rather adhere to those prayers established by the earlier sages. Included in this is the warning to use only the prayers of those scholars who know how to please. This applies to *piyyutim* as well.[60]

To further emphasize the importance of precision and brevity he cites the Talmudic passage quoted by Maimonides in the Guide concerning the man who led prayers in the presence of R. Ḥanina and went on to praise God using a long string of descriptive epithets. R. Ḥanina responded with annoyance at this long list, "Have you mentioned *all* of His praises?" By listing God's praises one encounters the problem of praising Him improperly and insufficiently, and hence only those praises ordained by the Men of the Great Assembly may be uttered.[61] Maimonides uses this passage in the course of demonstrating that positive attributes cannot be predicated of God. R. Joshua ignores the philosophic problem confronting Maimonides and cites the Talmudic passage as an example of the importance of precision and brevity in prayer. This demonstrates once again ibn Shu'eib's familiarity with philosophic problems and the manner in which he changed and adapted philosophic sources to fit his needs as a darshan.

3. Prayer and the Kabbalists

The various aspects of prayer noted so far fall within the framework for which ibn Shu'eib uses the phrase *berakhot ẓorekh hedyot*, "prayers and blessings serve man's needs." Ibn Shu'eib uses that phrase in the context of a discussion of *birkot hanehenin*, blessings for some pleasure derived. *Birkot hanehenin* are obligatory, says ibn Shu'eib, because they serve as a permit to enjoy the pleasures of the world: for if one derives pleasure without acknowledging God's ownership, he is in effect denying God's providence.[62] Ibn Shu'eib would probably have classified the other explanations of the nature of prayer that we have discussed above as likewise reflecting *ẓorekh hedyot*, man's needs. But prayer has another function as well, for *berakhot ẓorekh gavo'ah*, "blessings are for God's benefit," as well. Drawing on kabbalistic interpretations of the nature and meaning of the *berakhah* starting from Sefer Habahir, continuing with R. Ezra,[63] R. Azriel,[64] Rashba,[65] R. Joseph

[60]45Cb. This theme originates with *Sefer Ḥasidim*; see p. 395, par. 1619-1621 in Wistinetsky's edition. See also Derashot 79Bc כי כל המלות יש להם ענין. Cf. the attitude of Me'iri in *Beit Habeḥirah*, Berakhot 11a (ed. S. Dickman [Jerusalem 1965]), p. 23.

[61]Guide I,59; Berakhot 33b.

[62]52Ab.

[63]Commentary to *Shir Hashirim, Kitvei Haramban*, 2, p. 526.

[64]G. Scholem, "Der Begriff der Kavvanah in dem alten Kabbalah," *MGWJ* (1934) 501 n.3; Tishby, *M.H.*, 2, p. 254.

[65]*Teshuvot*, vol. 5 #51. He alludes to the kabbalistic meaning of Berakhot 7a.

Gikitilia,[66] R. Baḥya b. Asher[67] and Recanati,[68] ibn Shu'eib first shows how both the Bible and the Talmud allude to God's need for man's blessings.[69] He cites passages such as the one in Berakhot (7a) in which God says "Ishmael my son, bless me" or (Yevamot 64a) "God desires the prayers of the righteous" and others.[70]

All of these raise the question: "if prayer were merely praise, why would He desire the prayers of the few righteous?"[71] R. Joshua concludes, therefore, that a *berakhah* brings about "addition and magnification; it is cognate to *bereikhah*, a pool which flows from the source."[72] *Berakhah-bereikhah* is a symbol of the last *Sefirah, Malkhut* (Kingdom).[73] Our blessings magnify this *Sefirah* which overflows with blessings for all of His creatures.[74] Like the other *miẓvot*, prayer affects not only man but the *Sefirot* above as well.

In many other passages ibn Shu'eib uses the notion of *berakhot ẓorekh gavo'ah*, showing how many prayers symbolically allude to the *Sefirot* and how their construction is modeled on the relationship of the *Sefirot*. For example, the eighteen times that the name of God appears in Psalm 29 symbolize the lower nine *Sefirot*; since each *Sefirah* has an aspect of *Din*, stern justice, and *Raḥamim*, compassion, there are in effect eighteen *Sefirot*; they are also symbolized in the 18 blessings of the *'Amidah*.[75] In a different passage, the first three blessings of the *'Amidah* are taken to symbolize the *Sefirot* of *Ḥesed, Gevurah* and *Tif'eret*.[76] The purpose of our worship, R. Joshua says in a summary statement, is to create unity within the Godhead. The result of that unity is the overflow of abundance to man.[77]

Ibn Shu'eib's theory of prayer is thus predominantly influenced by kabbalistic tradition. Although he utilizes and integrates ideas and

[66]*Sha'arei Orah*, ed. Y. Ben Shlomo (Jerusalem 1970), vol. 1, p. 8.

[67]*Shulḥan shel Arba'* in *Kitvei R. Baḥya*, pp. 488-489.

[68]Commentary on Deut. 8:10.

[69]52AB; see too 80Cc.

[70]Baba Meẓia 114a, Shabbat 89a.

[71]52Ba.

[72]Ibid.

[73]See *Sha'arei Orah*, vol. 1, pp. 58-60.

[74]See 87Ac. See also R. Baḥya, Deut. 8:10 (p. 300).

[75]26Dab; see Berakhot 28b.

[76]79Bb. Cf. *M.H.*, 2, p. 268, for kabbalistic references. Cf., too, Derashot 27B.

[77]87Ba. See also 79C on the symbolism of the letter *dalet* of *eḥad* in *Shema'*. Cf. *Be'ur Sodot Haramban* 32,D; Zohar I, 233a; G. Scholem, *Pirkei Yesod*, p. 125. Note ibn Shu'eib's opposition to moving the head in all directions as part of the recitation of the *Shema'*. See G. Scholem, *Ursprung und Anfange*, p. 275, where R. Meir b. Simon of Narbonne is cited. See now M. Idel, "Hasefirot Sheme'al Hasefirot," *Tarbiz* 51 (1982) 278.

interpretations which are derived from the philosophic tradition, they are usually ideas not incongruent with Kabbalah; in addition, he often ignores the original philosophic context of the idea and thereby transforms its significance. Thus while, as we have seen, he accepts quite literally the notion of the superiority of prayer over sacrifices, he bases himself on a Talmudic statement[78] and ignores Maimonides' historical explanations, preferring instead to emphasize the great mysteries of the sacrifices. Again, as we have seen, while opposing prolixity in prayer just as Maimonides did, he ignores the problem of attributes which was Maimonides' primary concern.

The ideas derived from Halevi, for example that prayer nourishes the soul, are combined with kabbalistic conceptions of the efficacy and need for prayer, and supplemented with a hint of a polemic against those who abandon prayer on philosophic grounds. All of this is in accord with the predominant place of Kabbalah in ibn Shu'eib's thought.

The elements of both systems seem to be characteristic of his thinking and preaching; it would seem, however, that the components of a clear system can be identified, a system rooted in the thought world of Kabbalah but comfortably adopting ideas and concepts from philosophic contexts. While one must always be on guard against over-systematizing the writings of a preacher, particularly one as eclectic as ibn Shu'eib, apparent eclecticism does not preclude systematic thought.[79]

[78]See Tishby, *M.H.*, 2, p. 247. The Zohar, however, sometimes agrees that prayer is greater than sacrifice; see Scholem, *Hakabbalah Bigeronah*, pp. 335ff. Ibn Shu'eib here does not follow the Gerona School.

[79]See H. A. Wolfson, *Philo*, vol. I, pp. 96-107, 113-115, particularly 114.

Chapter VII
Aggadah and Aggadic Commentary

One of the most striking features of the Derashot ʻal Hatorah is its extensive use of aggadah. Indeed there is not a single *derashah* in which ibn Shuʻeib did not incorporate a great deal of aggadic material. Ibn Shuʻeib interpreted, explained and expanded upon many of the aggadot which he utilized. In his use of aggadah we shall see that he did not lock himself into any unbending or unyielding system of interpretation whether it be philosophic or kabbalistic, literal or non-literal, allegorical or simple. Ibn Shuʻeib assembled aggadot and interpreted them, but the aggadah also served, alongside Scripture, as a medium through which he could express his ideas. Ibn Shuʻeib displays profound erudition in this realm—an erudition which, when placed in the hands of a skilled rhetorician like ibn Shuʻeib, made for a richly textured *derashah*. Analyzing his use of aggadah and his method of aggadic commentary will help us to understand the nature of the Derashot and ibn Shuʻeib's place in the history of aggadic use and interpretation.

In considering ibn Shuʻeib's use of and interpretation of aggadah, we must bear in mind the great variety of types of aggadah in the Talmud and the Midrashim.[1] There are aggadot that expand and dwell upon biblical narratives, embellishing and adding new stories to the old. There are aggadot that expound upon single verses, parts of verses, single words or sometimes even single letters. There are aggadot entirely unconnected with Scripture, which recount stories of the sages and ethical maxims. Some aggadot are clear and simple, others enigmatic; some present problems for the philosophically trained, others are theologically or philologically problematic. The

[1]See Isaak Heinemann, *Darkhei Ha'aggadah*[2] (Jerusalem 1954); Joseph Heinemann, *Aggadot Vetoldoteihem* (Jerusalem 1974).

problematics were not always apparent in Talmudic times, and the need for interpretation and explanation was not felt.[2]

In the early centuries of the Middle Ages, literary creativity in the field of aggadah centered around the expansion, editing and recording of the existing corpus of aggadah, written and oral. In that period, many of the aggadic midrashim we have today were written or edited. Thus Song of Songs Rabbah was compiled around the sixth century, Ecclesiastes Rabbah and the Tanhuma-Yelamdenu corpus around the eighth century, and Exodus and Numbers Rabbah in the eleventh and twelfth centuries. All these are examples of exegetical and homiletical midrashim, which both incorporate existing aggadic material as well as add more in the style of the original.[3]

Towards the end of the Geonic period, with the spread of philosophy in Babylonia and Spain, Jews who were exposed to philosophic thought began to examine aggadah in a different light.[4] Aggadic passages that discuss God in anthropomorphic terms, such as the Talmudic description of God wearing *tefilin* (Berakhot 6a), provoked puzzled questions to the Geonim.[5] Other aggadot that seemed to contradict reason, such as the existence of objects before creation, or that seemed to be gross exaggerations, or described startling miracles were all subject to question and rationalization.[6] Perhaps on this account, one finds among the Geonim a tendency to limit the authority of the aggadah severely.[7]

In twelfth-century Spain, problematic aggadot received the attention of R. Judah Halevi in the Cuzari,[8] and R. Abraham ibn Ezra.[9] Ibn Ezra, in the introduction to his commentary on the Torah, lists a number of categories of problematic aggadot: among them, aggadot that are contradictory, those that have allegorical meaning, those that should not be taken seriously because they were meant to entertain and comfort or were intended for the masses, and aggadot which are minority opinions and hence are not normative. Ibn Ezra sought to resolve these difficulties in aggadah by reinterpretation or rejection.

[2]Cf. J. Heinemann, *Aggadot Vetoldoteihem*, passim.

[3]See the various articles in EJ for recent statements on the state of scholarship as of 1969.

[4]See M. Saperstein, *Decoding*, ch. 1; B. Z. Dinur, *Yisrael Bagolah* I,4 (Jerusalem 1962), pp. 260-261 and 288 n.47.

[5]See *Oẓar Hage'onim, Berakhot*, pp. 12, 14.

[6]See below, this chapter, and the aggadot cited by R. Abraham Maimonides in his essay (n. 12).

[7]See above n.4.

[8]Cuzari III,73.

[9]In the standard editions of *Mikra'ot Gedolot.*

The proper interpretation of aggadah was a matter that concerned Maimonides, and he addressed the matter on several occasions. He was particularly concerned with the literalist reading of aggadah which, if believed, brings disrepute upon the Sages and, if denied, undermines their authority. Proper interpretation of aggadah and the discernment of non-normative aggadah[10]—and here Maimonides adheres to the Geonic distinction between Talmudic and Midrashic aggadah—are two important principles in Maimonides' aggadic interpretation.[11]

Maimonides' son, R. Abraham, goes into much greater detail in sorting out types of aggadot.[12] He distinguishes first between *derashot*, that is, exegetically based comments, and narratives. Within these two broad categories there are those whose manifest meaning—*peshat*—is to be accepted as is, although just what that *peshat* is is not always easy to discern. Some have both a hidden and a manifest meaning, others just a hidden meaning, and there are those which use poetic and literary license. In the narrative aggadot he again differentiates between stories that are literally true, those that are symbolically true, and didactic fictions. R. Abraham's typology of aggadah reflects great seriousness in its approach and does not seem to leave room for aggadot which are not in some way binding.[13]

Ashkenazic Jewry did not have to contend with the conflict between philosophic principles and aggadah, and hence we do not find the same attempts at classification and interpretation among Ashkenazic scholars. What is found among Ashkenazic scholars are compilations of aggadot such as the *Yalkut Shim'oni* of the thirteenth century and *derashot* that copy the old midrashic

[10]Normativity of course refers not to the realm of belief but to action. But even here Maimonides compares some aggadot to non-normative halakhic opinions. See the passages cited in the next note, particularly the "Letter on Astrology."

[11]See Maimonides, Introduction to his Commentary to the Mishnah (ed. Kafaḥ), p. 65; Introduction to Perek Ḥelek, p. 117; Guide, Introduction, I,71 and III, 43; and "Letter on Astrology," *HUCA* III (1926) 356.

[12]His *Ma'amar 'al odot Derashot Ḥazal* has been printed frequently. See R. Margaliyot, ed., *Milḥamot Hashem* (Jerusalem 1953); see too E. Hurvitz, "Derashot Ḥazal Lerabeinu Avraham ben Harambam," in S. B. Hoenig and L. D. Stitskin, eds., *Joshua Finkel Festschrift* (New York 1974), pp. 139-167.

[13]Cf. J. B. Sermonetta, ed., *Sefer Tagmulei Hanefesh* of Hillel of Verona (Jerusalem 1981), notes to pp. 180-191, esp. p. 188. R. Abraham's category of exaggerated language is not identical to R. Hillel's "amusing anecdotes" *(milta dibediḥuta)*. On the problem of seriousness in the aggadah, see I. Heinemann, *Darkhei Ha'aggadah*, pp. 186-195. Cf. the attitude of the Maharal of Prague; see Ya'akov Elbaum, "R. Judah Loew of Prague and His Attitude to the Aggadah," in *Scripta Hierosolymitana* 22 (1971) 28-47.

style.[14] Among the Tosafot, aggadot are often treated in the same manner as the halakhah; that is, contradictions are resolved using dialectic reasoning.[15]

A fierce defense of a literalistic understanding of aggadah is found in the work of R. Moses Taku, a thirteenth-century German Talmudist. He insists that anything the Sages have said must be accepted in its literal sense, although he too differentiates between the authoritative status of the Talmudic aggadah and the aggadah of the Midrash; the aggadot of the Talmud are unimpeachable, whereas the aggadot in extra-talmudic works could have been forged.[16]

In the thirteenth century we find examples of public disclaimers of the authority of aggadah during the public disputations in which Jews were forced to participate, such as the debate of R. Yehiel in Paris in 1242 and Naḥmanides in Barcelona in 1263. While the sincerity of the disclaimers may be open to question, they may very well reflect the real positions.[17]

A significant innovation in the realm of aggadic commentary occurred in philosophic circles in the thirteenth century. In the recently identified aggadic commentaries of R. Isaac b. Yedaiah[18] and those of R. Yedaiah Hapenini[19] we see philosophic ideas being propagated through interpretation of aggadot, aggadot that were not necessarily problematic. R. Isaac, for example, produced a systematic philosophic interpretation of aggadah in which specific words were assigned specific philosophic meanings.[20]

[14]See above, ch. II, pp. 22-23 and nn.23 and 24.

[15]See E. Urbach, *Ba'alei Hatosafot* (Jerusalem 1955), pp. 551-553.

[16]Moses Taku, "Ketav Tamim," in R. Kircheim, ed., *Oẓar Neḥmad*, pp. 62-64.

[17]See "Vikuaḥ Rabeinu Yeḥiel Miparis," in J. D. Eisenstein, ed., *Oẓar Vikuḥim* (Israel 1969), p. 82; "Vikuaḥ Haramban" in C. D. Chavel, ed., *Kitvei Rabeinu Mosheh ben Nahman* (Jerusalem 1963), p. 308. See now the new translations and summary of scholarship in H. Maccoby, *Judaism on Trial. Jewish-Christian Disputations in the Middle Ages* (East Brunswick 1982). Concerning Naḥmanides' attitude to aggadah, see B. Septimus, "'Open Rebuke and Concealed Love': Naḥmanides and the Andalusian Tradition," in I. Twersky, ed., *Rabbi Moses Nahmanides (Ramban): Explorations in His Religious and Literary Virtuosity* (Cambridge MA 1983), pp. 15-22. Concerning R. Ḥayyim ibn Mussa, see M. Pachter, *Homiletic and Ethical Literature*, p. 11, n.29.

[18]See Saperstein, *Decoding*, particularly ch. 7.

[19]See I. Twersky, "R. Yedayah Hapenini Uferusho La'aggadah," in S. Stein and R. Loewe, eds., *Studies in Jewish Religious and Intellectual History Presented to Alexander Altmann* (Alabama 1980), Hebrew section, pp. 63-82; M. Saperstein, "Selected Passages from Yedaiah Bedersi's Commentary on the Midrashim," in I. Twersky, ed., *Studies in Medieval Jewish History and Literature* II (Cambridge MA 1984), pp. 423-440.

[20]See Saperstein, *Decoding*, ch. 3.

Similar in method was what kabbalists were doing with aggadah in the same century. For them, there were whole groups of aggadot that had special kabbalistic meaning, and in aggadic commentaries such as R. Ezra's and R. Azriel's, as well as in systematic works such as *Sha'arei Orah* and *Ma'arekhet Ha'elohut* and particularly in the Zohar, the mystical side of aggadah is emphasized and expounded upon.[21]

Aggadah was used not only in ideological contexts. It was used by medieval exegetes to varying degrees in their Scriptural commentaries, as the commentaries of Rashi, R. David Kimhi and Ramban illustrate. Ethical works such as *Sha'arei Teshuvah* of R. Jonah of Gerona and *Kad Hakemaḥ* of R. Baḥya b. Asher and books of customs such as the *Sefer Hamanhig* of R. Abraham b. Nathan Hayarḥi use aggadot extensively as exempla and precedents. It is in the perspective of all of these different uses that ibn Shu'eib's use of aggadah should be viewed.

Ibn Shu'eib does not spell out his methodology, nor would it be expected in the context of weekly sermons. The following statement, however, does tell us something of the kind of selectivity of aggadic material ibn Shu'eib intended at least for one of his *derashot*:

> I will explain the words of the Sages as they appear in their diverse and divergent homilies on the *Song of Songs*. I will select from their homilies only those whose approach is best and cite them concisely. I will deal with major themes and their verses for I cannot explain every single verse. This would extend the homily and make it unbearable.[22]

The above statement is made by way of introduction to his commentary to the *Song of Songs* in a *derashah* for the last day of Passover. What is important is the very explicit awareness of his role as an interpreter of aggadah. What the criteria are for the "best approach" is not clear here, but he does inded cite the aggadot concisely in this *derashah*.

A principle of selectivity is given in the *derashah* to *Teẓaveh*, which contains in it a *derashah* for Purim:

> I will not bother to write the aggadah which is found in its regular place. I will merely allude to it—for why should I exert myself to rewrite it? But new matters that are not explained in the aggadah, but which I gathered from the Midrash and from the commentators of blessed memory —those I will write. The rest will just be alluded to.[23]

Here his criterion for selection is clearer. But he does not apply this principle in all of his *derashot*: he generally utilizes aggadot from all sources, Talmudic and Midrashic, familiar and unfamiliar.

[21] See Y. Tishby, ed., *Perush Ha'aggadot Lerabi Azriel* (Jerusalem 1945); G. Scholem, *Major Trends*, pp. 31-32; above, ch. I, pp. 14-15.

[22] 42Bc.

[23] 31Ca.

As one would expect of a darshan who quotes aggadot extensively, ibn Shu'eib gives great weight to the authority of the aggadah. It is a repository of authentic and correct interpretation of Divine truths, for the aggadah was part of the tradition revealed to Moses at Sinai. This emerges from his comments on the Talmudic description of the range of R. Yohanan b. Zakkai's knowledge. We have discussed this passage above. The Talmud (Sukkah 28a) presents a long list of R. Yohanan's accomplishments which begins with "Scripture, Mishnah and Gemara" and ends with "great matters and small matters." "Great matters," explains the Talmud, refers to "*ma'aseh merkavah*, the Work of the Chariot; small matters, the questions of Abbaye and Rava." As we have said, the problematics of such a statement are immediately obvious.[24] The Talmud is ranking "the Work of the Chariot"—apparently an extra-halakhic matter, however one defines it—as a matter of greater importance than the discussions of Abbaye and Rava, the great majority of which are halakhic discussions. The passage therefore became an important prooftext for medieval scholars—halakhists, philosophers and kabbalists alike—in their discussions of the relative value of halakhah versus philosophy or kabbalah. Differing views called forth different definitions of the "Work of the Chariot" and "the questions of Abbaye and Rava."

Maimonides identified *ma'aseh merkavah* with metaphysics and interpreted the statement literally—i.e., that metaphysics is superior to halakhah axiologically.[25] This position was not easily accepted by opponents of philosophical study or by some kabbalists, for it posited the superiority of a system outside of halakhah and foreign to it and set the stage for antinomian positions.

Ritva,[26] for example, seems to understand *ma'aseh merkavah* as kabbalistic theory, whereas "the questions of Abbaye and Rava" refer not to the realm of halakhah in its entirety but to specific inferences that they drew. The Talmud

[24]Cf. above, p. 107. See I. Twersky, "Some Non-Halakhic Aspects of the Mishneh Torah," in A. Altmann, ed., *Jewish Medieval and Renaissance Studies* (Cambridge MA 1967), pp. 111-113; idem, "Religion and Law," in S. D. Goitein, ed., *Religion in a Religious Age* (Cambridge MA 1974), pp. 73-74; idem, *Introduction to the Code of Maimonides (Mishneh Torah)* (New Haven, 1980), pp. 366, 500; idem, "Berur Divrei Harambam Hilkhot Me'ilah, Perek Shemoneh Halakhah Shemoneh—Lefarashat Ta'amei Hamiẓvot Larambam," in J. Salmon, ed., *Perakim Betoldot Haḥevrah Hayehudit Biyemei Habeinayim Uva'eit Haḥadashah* (Jerusalem 1980), pp. 32-33; H. A. Davidson, "Philosophy as a Religious Obligation," in S. Goitein, ed., *Religion in a Religious Age*, pp. 63-64; J. Katz, "Halakhah Vekabalah Kenos'ei Limud Mitḥarim," *Da'at* 7 (1981) 40-43.

[25]See Mishneh Torah, *Yesodei Hatorah* 4:13.

[26]*Ḥiddushim*, Sukkah 28a.

and its study retain preeminence, and no foreign body of knowledge takes precedence.

Me'iri,[27] an older contemporary of ibn Shu'eib, solves the problem in the opposite manner by admitting physics and metaphysics as part of the definition of "great matters" but then continuing "even the minor inferences in these disciplines [i.e., physics and metaphysics] which will be inferred in future generations...were known by R. Yohanan." Presumably for him these latter are "the questions of Abbaye and Rava," that is, neither the "large matters" nor the "small matters" in the passage are halakhic matters.

Rashba, however, in a letter which apparently served as a basis for part of ibn Shu'eib's discussion, takes both "large" and "small" to be halakhic matters. Rashba says that *ma'aseh merkavah* refers to the reasons for the laws discussed by Abbaye and Rava and compares it to theoretical foundation of medicine: its understanding is crucial but, unless the medicine is mixed properly and taken, the theory is ineffectual. This explanation solves the problem of the hierarchical relationship of halakhah and *ma'aseh merkavah* while retaining the primacy of the fulfillment of *mizvot*.

Ibn Shu'eib adopts Rashba's position, but he does not seem comfortable with calling anything halakhic a minor matter. Therefore in a manner similar to Hame'iri he redefines "the questions of Abbaye and Rava" not as halakhic discussions, but as "the inferences of Abbaye and Rava in aggadah, which the Holy One blessed be He revealed to Moses, including even the novellae which a student presents to his teacher."[29]

For our discussion of the status of aggadah, it is the end of this statement that is crucial, for it accords aggadah the status of an authoritative interpreter of Scripture, having been revealed at Sinai. Indeed ibn Shu'eib is profuse in his use of aggadah as interpretation of Scripture, with every page of the Derashot filled with aggadic interpretation of Scripture. But ibn Shu'eib does not seem to mean here that literally all aggadah was revealed to Moses at Sinai. Such a position was indeed advocated by a younger contemporary, R. Meir Aldabi, in *Shevilei Emunah*,[30] but, as we shall see below, ibn Shu'eib frequently modified and even rejected aggadic statements. Rather, he is saying here that in the same manner in which halakhah is said to have been

[27]*Beit Habeḥirah*, Sukkah 28a, ed. D. Liss (Jerusalem 1966), p. 91.

[28]The letter was cited by A. Frumkin in his edition of *Siddur R. Amram Gaon*, p. 40. See too *'Ein Ya'akov*, Sukkah 28a.

[29]See Y. Peah 2:4 and the parallel sources; Y. Hagigah 1:8, Lev. R. 22:1. Cf. Berakhot 5a and Megillah 19b.

[30]See *Shevilei Emunah* (Warsaw 1887), p. 161. See too A. Heschel, *Torah Min Hashamayim Be'aspaklariyah Shel Hadorot*, II (New York 1965), pp. 234-237, for the midrashic sources that attribute aggadah to Sinaitic revelation.

revealed at Sinai down to every future novella, although halakhic creativity is not stifled, the aggadah was also revealed at Sinai.

Aggadah as legitimate or authoritative interpretation of Scripture underlies the method of works such as *Yalkut Shim'oni*, which arrange aggadic comments according to the order of the biblical verses they explain,[31] and at times ibn Shu'eib virtually imitates their method, as in his midrashic-style commentaries to the book of Esther[32] and the Song of Songs,[33] which are incorporated into the *derashot* for the appropriate Sabbaths. But ibn Shu'eib also takes the stance of a commentator on aggadah; here he shows his clear understanding of the method of the aggadah. He will at times comment on what brought the Sages to deviate from the simple meaning of Scripture. For example, when he presents the midrashic account of the judgment of Solomon in the case of the two harlots contesting parenthood of a child (I King 3:16-28), ibn Shu'eib explains why the Sages say that they were spirits imitating harlots or that they were *yevamot*—widows with no children:

> A harlot would not want someone else's child—on the contrary she would kill her own; therefore Rav said they were spirits imitating harlots, and the Rabbis say that they were *yevamot*, for *yevamot* would want a son in order to free themselves from the necessity of levirate marriage.[34]

Here his explanation reveals both contemporary medieval conceptions and real exegetical insight.

Sometimes the midrash itself cites its exegetical basis, as in the case of the midrashic explanation of the appearance of a man to the lost Joseph in search of his brothers (Gen. 37:15-17). There, the midrash (B.R. 84:24) explains that not one but three angels met him, since the word "man" appears three times in the story: "a man found him," "the man sent him," "the man said." Ibn Shu'eib cites this[35] and comments parenthetically that even though the definite article is used the second two times *(ha'ish)*, implying that it is still the first "man," the midrash must suppose that to Joseph they all looked the same but they came in succession, one at a time. Thus he defends and explains the midrash's own basis for its homily.

Ibn Shu'eib sometimes reproduces aggadot passively, but often he takes a more dynamic approach. He not only joins aggadot from various sources,

[31] See Y. Elbaum, "Shalosh Derashot Ashkenaziyot," *Kiryat Sefer* 48 (1973) 340-347.

[32] 31B-32A.

[33] 42A-44A.

[34] 28Cc. See Song of Songs Rabbah 1:10; Midrash Tehilim 72:2; Ginzberg, *Legends*, VI, 284, n.26. In a manner characteristic of his treatment of such matters, ibn Shu'eib continues with some halakhic aspects of levirate marriage.

[35] 15Bb.

something we find done by the later editors of the Mirashim and by authors of ethical works that compile rabbinic sayings on specific topics, such as the fourteenth-century work, *Menorat Hama'or*,[36] but he elaborates upon, expands, and develops existing aggadot. An example of a simple compilation is the *derashah* for *Naso*[37] where ibn Shu'eib strings together a series of aggadic statements on modesty. But in other places he adopts the aggadic method himself, adding new proofs from Scripture, deriving conclusions from these verses, and clarifying and establishing the meaning of the aggadah by interpolating explanatory phrases. There are two aspects to ibn Shu'eib's use of aggadah. He both continues in its original manner and stands outside of the aggadah in an interpretative relationship as well.

The *derashah* for the last day of Passover, for example, includes a homiletical commentary on the Song of Songs, where ibn Shu'eib starts out with some existing midrashic explanations to which he adds and expands.

> "Let Him kiss me with the kisses of His mouth" [Song 1:2]—this refers to Abraham our father, may he rest in peace, who was the first to cleave to God and observed the laws of the Torah [which he knew] through the Holy Spirit as it is written "since Abraham listened to My voice" [Gen. 26:5].[38]

The notion of Abraham as lover of God already appears in the midrash, but its elaboration in this manner is a result of ibn Shu'eib's own gathering of sources.[39]

Ibn Shu'eib frequently uses aggadot to explain other aggadot. In his *derashah* on *Ki Tisa*, ibn Shu'eib deals with the problem of Moses' request to see God's face and God's response, "You cannot see My face, for man may not see Me and live" (Ex. 33:20). "They have said in the Midrash, no one can

[36]Actually both books by that name—by Al-Nakawa and by Aboab. The relationship between aggadah and its interpretation in these books is a matter that needs clarification.

[37]60D. Cf. *Kad Hakemaḥ* of R. Baḥya b. Asher, s.v. *ga'avah* (pp. 103ff.). Ibn Shu'eib and Baḥya differ in their evaluation of the extremist position of Maimonides (*De'ot* 2:3). Concerning pride, Maimonides says that one must go to the extreme away from pride and towards humility. Ibn Shu'eib explains (61A) that Maimonides favors the position of Sotah 5a that says that not even a bit of pride is permitted and that he is opposed to the opinion that states that a *talmid ḥakham* should possess a small amount of pride; Baḥya (pp. 108-109) says that Maimonides agrees with this second position.

[38]42Bc.

[39]Kissing as a symbol of *devekut* is alluded to in the Midrash (Song of Songs R. 1:16) and in both philosophic and kabbalistic commentaries (see, e.g., Maimonides M.T. *Teshuvah* 10:3, the commentaries of R. Moses ibn Tibbon and R. Ezra of Gerona). Here ibn Shu'eib merges it with the historical interpretation of the Song of Songs.

see God while alive but one can see Him in death."[40] Ibn Shu'eib continues and asks what does "in death" *(bemitatan)* mean? Is the soul given a special vision at the moment of death, or is it after death that the soul is specially granted unique powers? He assembles Scriptural verses and aggadic statements that support both opinions.

In this last example we see ibn Shu'eib standing in a conscious interpretive relationship to the Midrash. In the same manner that Scripture must be interpreted and explained, so must aggadah be explained and expounded upon. The same types of questions and problems that the *derashah* poses to Scripture are posed to aggadah, and the two provide the infrastructure of the *derashah*.

A good example of the reflective expansive approach to aggadah is ibn Shu'eib's exposition of the aggadah.

> Said a certain Galilean—blessed is the Merciful One Who gave a three-fold Torah to a three-fold nation through a third on the third day in the third month."[41]

Ibn Shu'eib asks the obvious questions—what is meant by a three-fold Torah, a three-fold Israel, etc.? He first presents Rashi's explanations for each unit, such as that the three-fold Torah consists of Pentateuch, Prophets and Writings. But then he adds some alternate and added explanations.[42] Thus he suggests that the three-fold nature of the Torah is that it consists of three parts—narrative, commandments and the secrets of creation and the Chariot. These in turn parallel (as we have discussed above) the three souls—*neshamah, ruah* and *nefesh*, and *sefer, sefor* and *sippur*, as well as *hokhmah, tevunah* and *da'at*, through which the world, the Tabernacle and the Temple were created. "Through a third" means Moses, who was the third born after Aaron and Miriam. This is Rashi's explanation; but ibn Shu'eib then draws a parallel between Moses and Jacob, who was the third of the fathers and whose symbol is Truth, *emet*, as is Moses'. Alternately, Moses was hidden for three months and finally—"Moses was the third of the prophets; Adam and Noah prophesied in one fashion and Moses in another. He is therefore praised in three places in the Torah."[43]

[40]32Bb; Num. R. 14:22
וכן אמרו במדרש בחייהן אינן רואים אבל במיתתן רואין. ויש בזה ב׳ פירושים. הא׳ לאחר מיתתן ממש...והפירוש השני לאחר פטירתן סמוך למיתתן.
In our version of the midrash we read בחייהם אינם רואים אבל רואים **בשעת** מיתתן. Cf. Zohar I, 218b; *Mishnat Hazohar* II, 149.

[41]26D-27A; Shabbat 88a.

[42]Cf. *Pirkei Derav Kahanah*, ed. Buber, p. 105 (ed. Mandelbaum, p. 213); *Tanhuma, Yitro* 10; *Midrash 'Asseret Hadibrot* in A. Jellinek, ed., *Beit Hamidrash* I, 67.

[43]I did not find a parallel to this in any of the midrashim that deal with this theme. See L. Ginzberg, *Legends* V, p. 83, n.30.

"On the third day" provides ibn Shu'eib with an opportunity to deal at length with the chronology of the giving of the Torah. He brings logical and Scriptural proofs for the proper chronology, discusses the three "crowns" given to Israel and their parallel in the three important vessels in the Tabernacle, and clarifies the meaning of some of the verses connected with the giving of the Torah. Finally, the symbolism of the third day is played out to match the third millennium, the time of the theophany, and the third day of creation during which the waters gathered; water is a symbol of Torah.

"In the third month" suggests to ibn Shu'eib the parallel between Abraham, Isaac and Jacob, and the Hebrew months Nissan, Iyyar and Sivan: Nissan, the month of the Exodus, an act of *ḥesed*, the quality of Abraham; Iyyar, the month of complaints and the attack of Amalek, symbolized by the quality of Isaac, stern justice; Sivan is the month of truth, *emet*, Jacob's quality.

We have seen how ibn Shu'eib takes a suggestive aggadah and creates a homily based on the blending of interpretation and creative expansion of the aggadah.

Ibn Shu'eib's interpretation of the Talmudic saying that the "merit of the fathers has ceased" is another instance of his expanding on aggadah, although this time he displays some independence of Rabbinic explanation, something we will pay attention to in greater detail below.

> The Rabbis of blessed memory said, "In the days of Hosea, the merit of the fathers was exhausted" [Shabbat 55a]. However, we are left with the merit of the Holy One, Blessed be He. This is what is meant by the verse "The virgin of Israel is fallen. She shall no more arise"[Amos 5:2]. And although in the west [the land of Israel] they have interpreted the verse to read "She shall fall not again; arise o virgin of Israel," the conclusion of the verse indicates otherwise, as it says, 'She is cast down upon her land, there is none to raise her up,' and this is not consolation. Furthermore in the preceding verse the prophet says, 'Hear ye this word which I take up for a *lamentation* over you, O house of Israel.' The real meaning of the verse is, 'She shall rise no more by virtue of her own merit, for the merit of the fathers has ceased and no one can raise her. But the Lord can raise her....[44]

The fusing of the verse from Amos with the aggadah in tractate Shabbat is ibn Shu'eib's innovation. What is interesting here is that in ibn Shu'eib's use of the verse he deviates from the Rabbinic interpretation of the verse, or

[44]24Cb; cf. 58Db. Cf. Naḥmanides' Commentary to the Torah, Lev. 32:26. See Shabbat 55a and Tosafot, s.v. *Zekhut Avot*. Interesting is ibn Shu'eib's passing comment that "we are left with the merit of the Holy One be He" ונשאר זכות הקב״ה. See S. Schechter, *Some Aspects of Rabbinic Theology* (New York 1910), pp. 177-181.

rather rejects it outright. From here and other places,[45] it is clear that one cannot take literally ibn Shu'eib's statement above, that all aggadic interpretations were given to Moses at Sinai.

Let me stress again that ibn Shu'eib was not a philosophical rationalist. Thus for example, miraculous events do not cause him discomfort. On the contrary—ibn Shu'eib polemicizes several times against the rationalizing attempts of the philosophers, as we saw above in ch. IV in the case of the aggadah concerning the prophetic powers of fetuses at the parting of the Red Sea. He strongly objects to "those who say that the words of the Rabbis were not intended literally. Why should we turn the aggadot into allegories and metaphors and interpret the words of the Torah in a non-literal manner? If God bestowed gifts and abundant grace in order that they may merit prophetic vision, why should we reject this?"[46]

In a similar manner ibn Shu'eib objects to Maimonides' interpretation of the theophany. According to the Talmud, the verse "Moses commanded us Torah" (Deut. 33:4) teaches us that it was Moses who informed the Israelites of 611 out of the 613 commandments—611 is the numerical value of the word *Torah.* The remaining two, the first two commandments of the Decalogue, "the Israelites heard from the All-powerful *(Gevurah)* Himself" (Makkot 23b-24a). Maimonides, whose theory of prophecy precludes the possibility of direct revelation to the masses, because of their inadequate intellectual preparation, says that the Israelites heard only an undifferentiated sound which Moses interpreted for them. The Talmudic passage cited above, Maimonides says, means that "these two principles, I mean the existence of the Deity and His being one, are knowable by human speculation. Thus these two principles are not known through prophecy alone."[47]

However, ibn Shu'eib says:

> The opinion of the Sages is decisive, for Torah was commanded to us by Moses; Torah adds up to 611 in *Gematria*, leaving only the remaining two which were in fact transmitted from the mouth of the Almighty.[48]

One suspects that ibn Shu'eib protests so adamantly here against non-literalist interpretation because these were issues that became the hallmarks of rationalist controversy. In the same way, later in the fourteenth century, Shem Tov ibn Shem Tov in his *Sefer Emunot* protests against Maimonides' rationalistic modification of the Rabbinic statement.[49] Ibn Shu'eib therefore felt it necessary to respond forcefully to Maimonides' position.

[45]See, e.g., 70Cb where ibn Shu'eib prefers דרך הפשט of Scripture in opposition to Rabbinic interpretation. Ibn Shu'eib clearly differentiates between the two.

[46]25CD.

[47]Guide II,33; tr. Pines, p. 364.

[48]27D.

[49]Part II, ch. I of *Sefer Ha'emunot* (Ferrara 1556; repr. Westmead UK 1969).

It is not, however, only in a polemical context that ibn Shu'eib insists on literalness. There are many instances where he opts for literal interpretations of miraculous events in a non-polemical context as well. He does not flinch for a moment when he describes the aggadic comment on the verse from Ezekiel (16:7).

> 'I made you thrive [lit. I made you multiply 10,000 fold] like the plants of the field.' This should be understood in the manner in which the Sages of blessed memory used it in Tractate Sotah, to explain how the Israelites [in Egypt] increased in number from seventy souls to six hundred thousand. The words 'plants of the field' should be understood to allude to the fact that women gave birth in the fields out of fear of [Pharaoh's] decree against the newborn male children. The mothers would leave the infants in the field to be swallowed up by the earth. But the Holy One, blessed be He, placed by them two dishes, one of milk and the other of honey (as it says in Sotah) and eventually they would spring up like the grass of the field.[50]

There is no attempt here to interpret metaphorically or allegorically, nothing that would indicate the slightest sign of discomfort with the literal meaning of the aggadah.[51]

Most significant is ibn Shu'eib's interpretation of a mishnah in tractate Rosh Hashanah. The Mishnah asks,[52] concerning Exodus 17:11, "Whenever Moses held up his hand, Israel prevailed; and whenever he lowered his hand, Amalek prevailed." But "could the hands of Moses promote the battle or hinder the battle?" The Mishnah responds, "It is rather to teach you that such time as the Israelites directed their thoughts on high and kept their hearts in subjection to their Father in Heaven, they prevailed; otherwise they suffered defeat." Here the Mishnah plays down the miraculous aspect of the story. Ibn Shu'eib, to the contrary, says:

> [Moses] had to raise his hands, for when he lowered them, Amalek would prevail; and when his hands did battle on high, [the Israelites] would be victorious below. Setting his hands down caused the Prince of Amalek above to be victorious and below Amalek would also win.[53]

Miraculous happenings were completely within the course of events for ibn Shu'eib. One is surprised therefore that, when he comes to deal with the aggadah that each plague in Egypt consisted of four or five plagues, he explains that it is not literally so but rather that each plague involved each of

[50] 23D based on Sotah 11b.

[51] See also 33Bc on the special clothing of the Israelites.

[52] Mishnah R.H. 3:8, tr. Danby (Oxford 1933), p. 192.

[53] 26Ba.

the elements.[54] One could certainly not claim that this is a rationalization, but it does reflect a more naturalistic view of the miracle of the plagues.

In truth, however, rational and non-rational are not the proper categories when dealing with ibn Shu'eib's approach to his aggadic sources, for rhetorical considerations rather than theological ones are often the determining factors for the good darshan. The preacher knows that at times it is by demystifying and rationalizing that his listeners can be convinced and impressed, while at other times it is by purposely emphasizing the mystical or non-rational component that the audience's imagination will be captured. We can understand therefore why the miraculous is not a category which forces ibn Shu'eib into interpretive exercises, particularly when the aggadah is one that expands upon the biblical narrative.

What then were the motivating factors that caused ibn Shu'eib to interpret aggadot rather than simply to present them as they are? Two factors were operative. First, ibn Shu'eib shared the widely held belief that aggadah is the repository of ancient Jewish knowledge. Maimonides' statement is representative:

> Do not think that the *derashot* [i.e., the aggadah] found in the Talmud are of no significance or of little value. They have an important purpose: they contain deep allusions and great matters. When one examines the *derashot* very closely one may understand from them matters that are truly valuable in the highest degree, for in them are revealed Divine matters and true matters which men of wisdom tried to hide and not reveal, as well as all the truths of the philosophers through the ages.[55]

In a similar manner kabbalists interpreted aggadah to show how kabbalistic ideas are hidden in rabbinic aggadah. We find this approach already in the Sefer Habahir and also in the commentary of R. Azriel, the Zohar and later kabbalistic literature.

Ibn Shu'eib shared the assumption that there are aggadot that have an inner meaning, and it is this desire to explicate the ideas hidden in the aggadah that motivates ibn Shu'eib's interpretative attempts. Now although he believed in Kabbalah as the true explanation of reality, this belief did not exclude the use of philosophical-allegorical interpretations as well. The use of multiple levels of interpretation was in vogue at the beginning of the fourteenth century, as we see from the commentaries of R. Baḥya b. Asher.

But it is not only the attempt to uncover the hidden doctrinal meanings that motivated ibn Shu'eib. The aggadah is a challenge for any homilist or exegete,

[54] 23B. See M. Kasher, *Haggadah Shleimah* (Jerusalem 1961), p. 53 of the text, commentary par. 290 and nn.575 and 576. Ibn Shu'eib's sources seem to be Rashbam and Ritva.

[55] Maimonides, Introduction to the Commentary to the Mishnah (trans Y. Kafaḥ, 3 vols. [Jerusalem 1963], vol. 1, p. 19). Cf. Guide I,71.

bristling as it is with logical, theological and philological problems. It is these two factors together that undoubtedly goaded ibn Shu'eib into frequent aggadic commentary.

Ibn Shu'eib's kabbalistic interpretations of aggadah will be discussed below in the context of his Kabbalah generally. Nevertheless at this point it is important to note that he did not pass up the opportunities that aggadah afforded for bolstering and supporting kabbalistic notions. Although ibn Shu'eib's use of Kabbalah is usually connected with verses from Scripture, he will often weave an aggadic allusion into the discussion. At other times he will offer a variety of explanations for an aggadah, as we will see below, one of them being the kabbalistic explanation. Often the kabbalistic explanation is alluded to or stated in terms that are not transparently kabbalistic and only those so trained would recognize the kabbalistic allusions.

Here are two examples of ibn Shu'eib's kabbalistic interpretation of aggadah.

In the *derashah* to *Vayeḥi*,[56] discussing Genesis 49:1, ibn Shu'eib introduces an aggadah from Pesaḥim 56a concerning Jacob's desire to reveal the end of days. The aggadah tells that the Holy Spirit departed from Jacob, rendering him incapable of revealing the end of days. Jacob suspected that this was a sign that his children were sinners. Thereupon his children responded "Hear O Israel, the Lord is our God, the Lord is One. Just as you believe in one God, so do we." At that moment Jacob said "Blessed be the name of His glorious kingdom forever." The Talmud then asks whether this last verse should be recited when reciting the *Shema*, for it does not appear in the Torah, but Jacob did pronounce it. The conclusion of the Talmud is that it should be read quietly, based on the following parable:

> The matter may be compared to the daughter of a king who smelled cooking spices. If she requests them, she would suffer disgrace; if she does not request them she will suffer. So her servants began to bring her the spices secretly.

This aggadah is cited as the basis for the recital of "Blessed be the name of His glorious kingdom forever and ever" with the *Shema*, as well as the basis for its being recited in a whisper.[57] It became a popular text among kabbalists in the thirteenth century and is commented on extensively, particularly in the various commentaries of students of Rashba on Naḥmanides.[58] Ibn Shu'eib says:

[56] 19B.

[57] See M.T. *Keri'at Shema* 1:4 (Maimonides omits mention of its being recited in a whisper); *Hamanhig* (ed. Raphael), p. 76; Me'iri, Pesaḥim 56a.

[58] See Naḥmanides, Recanati: R. Baḥya b. Asher (but cf. *Kad Hakemaḥ*, s.v. *Yiḥud*, p. 199) *Be'ur Sodot Haramban, Keter Shem Tov* and *Me'irat 'Einayim* to Deut. 6:4; cf.

This matter is of great weight and is hidden away for those who know its secret. It is known that cooking spices are things that flavor the pot, as it says in tractate Yoma [75a] "'they cooked it in a pot' [Num. 11:8] from here we learn that cooking spices descended with the manna." The Rabbis' parable in this matter is apt for, just as the pot [of manna] was lacking nothing, similarly the verse of *Shema* was explicit enough for those who understand. The long *dalet* teaches us by allusion about the absolute unity and we should not need more than that. However, since it is not as explicit as the verse 'Blessed be the name of His glorious kingdom forever,' for it is made clearer there when His kingdom is alluded to in the verse that teaches His unity, we therefore must say it secretly so as not to have sorrow or degradation. The "daughter of the king" refers to *knesset Israel* [the tenth Sefirah, *Malkhut*]. "Should she say 'blessed etc.' she will be degraded," for Moses the greatest of the prophets did not say it. Not saying it will bring her sorrow, for the unity is not explicit in Moses' words, for he was great and understood the matter on his own; but what was clear to him is sealed to us. Therefore Israel His servants are accustomed to say it secretly out of respect for the honor of Moses who did not recite it.[59]

The king's daughter, *knesset Yisrael*, which is the last of the Sefirot, *Malkhut*, Kingdom, must unite with the upper Sefirot in order to bring the blessings of the upper worlds, the "cooking spices," to the lower worlds. This union is alluded to in the letter *dalet* of *eḥad* (one), but is it made explicit in the declaration of "Blessed be the name of His glorious kingdom for ever and ever." By reciting it aloud, it is as if the *Shekhinah* is lacking in the *Shema*; by not reciting it at all it appears as if the unity is lacking; therefore it is said silently.[60]

A second example of ibn Shu'eib's kabbalistic interpretation of aggadah is in his *derashah* to *'Ekev*.[61] He poses the following question: the Torah promises material reward for the fulfillment of *mizvot:* children, longevity and sustenance, as it says (Deut. 7:13-15), "He will bless the issue of your womb and the produce of your soil, your new grain and wine, and oil....The Lord will ward off from you all sickness." If so, how could Rava say (Mo'ed Katan

Oẓar Hakavod to b. Pesahim 56a; *Ha'emunah Vehabitaḥon* ch. 3 (p. 360), *Tikunei Zohar, Tikuna 'Asira'a* (25a); *Tikunei Zohar Ḥadash*, 110c; *Shoshan Sodot* (Korets 1784; repr. Israel 1970), p. 8; *Meẓudat Ẓion* of Radbaz 2A.

[59]19B.

[60]Ibn Shu'eib then adds a different kabbalistic explanation of the aggadah in the name of R. Ezra which says that "Blessed be..." is the part that is the real expression of unity. Its omission by Moses is due to the fact that Moses states the commandment of the recital of Shema, but does not affirm there the acceptance of the yoke of heaven.

[61]81A.

28a) that "[the blessings of] long life, children, and sustenance are not dependent upon merit but upon the stars [*mazal*]." The passage is one that is extensively dealt with in medieval Jewish literature because of its clearly implied determinism.[62] Many Rishonim modify the statement in various ways. Rashba, who is cited by ibn Shu'eib,[63] says that the *mazal* determines the individual but not the community, who are rewarded according to their merit. R. Jacob b. Sheshet in his *Meshiv Devarim Nekhoḥim*[64] suggests that *bemazal talya* means that the righteous person cannot by his own merit determine the outcome of the three items—but as a result of prayer and intense personal concern, God may change the heavenly *mazal* to bring reward for the righteous. R. Menahem Hame'iri in the *Beit Habehirah* to Mo'ed Katan rejects the statement as nonauthoritative without any attempt to resolve the difficulty. "It is only the opinion of an individual and it is untenable to religion."[65]

After offering Rashba's explanation, ibn Shu'eib gives a kabbalistic explanation, one which completely reinterprets the word *mazal*. It is derived, he suggests, from the word *nzl*, to flow, as in the verse "Let water flow *(yizal)* from his pail" (Num. 24:7). The implication is that *mazal* represents a *Sefirah* higher than *Zekhut*, perhaps *Keter*. As proof ibn Shu'eib cites three verses, one for each of the three items—children, long life and sustenance—which show that those who prayed for them prayed to the highest *Sefirah*. For example, Hannah, who prayed for children, prayed *'al Hashem* (1 Sam. 1:10)—not *el Hashem*, to God, but *'al*, above, God, as it were, that is, to the highest *Sefirah*.[66]

[62]See B. Z. Benedict, "Mezonei Bemazala Talya," *Torah Shebe'al Peh* 19 (1977) 223-246, reprinted now in his *Merkaz Hatorah Biprovence* (Jerusalem 1985), pp. 243-268.

[63]81A; Rashba, Responsa I,148. Cf. R. Baḥya b. Asher to Deut. 8:18 (p. 301).

[64]Ed. G. Vajda (Jerusalem 1968), pp. 88-89. Cf. Baḥya b. Asher, Deut. 31:14 (pp. 449-450).

[65]M.K. 28a. See Benedict, "Mezonei," pp. 232f. See Maimonides, "Letter on Astrology," pp. 349-356. Cf. Me'iri to Sotah 2a (ed. A. Liss [Jerusalem 1967], p. 7) where predetermination is characterized as **כפי המקרה או מערכת התולדה**. Me'iri deals with the statement that forty days before the birth of a child his mate is decreed. While solving the conflict between this statement and another which clearly states that one's mate is based on merit, Me'iri allows for the possibility that one's first mate is determined כפי המקרה או מערכת התולדה. Thus he does not reject out of hand the possibility of predetermination.

[66]See R. Isaac of Acco, *Me'irat 'Einayim, Vayeira*, ed. C. Erlanger (Jerusalem 1975), p. 69; *Sha'arei Orah*, ch. I; Recanati, *Toldot*; and *Zohar Hadash* 36B, which is almost the verbatim source for ibn Shu'eib. The interpretation of בני חיי ומזוני in kabbalistic literature deserves special treatment: it is cited widely. See all of its uses in the Zohar collected by R. Margaliyot in his edition of *Zohar Ḥadash*, p. 125a.

But it is not only kabbalistic ideas that ibn Shu'eib sought to propagate through aggadic interpretation. Occasionally, he engaged in metaphorical or even allegorical interpretation without any reference to Kabbalah. The discussion of the aggadah of the jewel tied around Abraham's neck, cited above in chapter II,[67] is a very clear example of allegory. The jewel around the neck stands for principles that heal the incorrect opinions that are the sickness of the soul, and its placement in the solar sphere is a symbol of God's unity.[68]

A similar approach is taken in the following:

> [The Sages] therefore said that it is forbidden to derive pleasure from this world without a blessing, And they said that it is as if one is stealing from the Holy One, Blessed be He, and from Knesset Israel, as it is written, "He who robs his father or his mother and says there is no transgression is the companion of a man who destroys" (Prov. 28:24; Berakhot 35b). The simple meaning [*peshat*] of this aggadah is that, by omitting the blessing, one in effect denies His providence, acting as if we do not believe that all our livelihood is from Him but rather from the Princes and the planets.[69]

Here again the allegorical method is clearly at work. The simple meaning of "stealing" in the aggadah should be that the person is deriving pleasure illicitly. Ibn Shu'eib, however, claims that the simple meaning *(peshat)* is that the person is denying providence. This is a rather startling assertion, particularly in light of the fact that ibn Shu'eib usually differentiates clearly between the realm of the literal and non-literal. But his desire to propagate his views through the vehicle of aggadah coupled with the preacher's propensity to convince himself that the clever non-literal interpretation, developed to fit a midrashic saying into a homiletic context, is actually the simple meaning, explains the claim to *peshat* here.[70]

In a similar manner, ibn Shu'eib uses his interpretive skills, this time in a moral allegory, to explain the fate of those who dispose of their nail clippings

[67]P. 30. See too R. Moses Almosnino, *Me'ameẓ Koaḥ* (Venice 1588), 199b-200a, who cites the kabbalistic explanation—but then seeks rationalist explanations.

[68]Ibn Shu'eib follows the view attributed to Rashba—see *Ein Ya'akov* to BB 16a. Ibn Shu'eib's formulation of the idea is original. The view attributed to Rashba does not appear in most manuscripts of Rashba's aggadic commentaries, and not in early editions of *Ein Ya'akov*. It does appear in MS Bodleian 2282/6 attributed to Abraham of Rome.

[69]52Ac; Berakhot 35b and Rashba ad loc. See R. Baḥya b. Asher, "Shulkḥan Shel Arba'" in C. Chavel, ed., *Kitvei R. Baḥya b. Asher*, p. 488.

[70]It may be that ibn Shu'eib's insistence that this interpretaiton is *peshat* is in order to contrast it with the kabbalistic interpretation to which he does not allude but is found in kabbalistic sources such as *Ma'arekhet Ha'elohut*, p. 129b. It should be noted here that ibn Shu'eib clearly delineates beween the halakhah itself, its aggadic explanation and his interpretation of the aggadah.

improperly. The Talmud says[71] that he who throws away nail clippings is wicked, he who burns them is saintly *(ḥasid)* and he who buries them is righteous *(ẓaddik)*. Ibn Shu'eib says that the nail clippings stand for the "sect of cursed scorners" and therefore:

> He who leaves them be and throws them away from the others is wicked. He who burns them is a *ḥasid* for he thus utterly wipes them out so that no memory of them is left. He who buries them, that is reprimands them and hides them in prison where they will not be seen, is righteous *(ẓaddik)*.[72]

Here ibn Shu'eib is interpreting a halakhic matter, treated as halakhah by many Rishonim, although not codified in most halakhic codes.[73] He certainly does not claim that his explanation is *peshat*, and he clearly emphasizes the allegorical character of his interpretation. But it is significant that ibn Shu'eib will utilize the very method that he condemns in other contexts. Here he follows the path of the philosophic commentators in subjecting even halakhic matters to metaphorical explanation.[74] Thus we see that, when allegory or metaphor serve the purpose of his sermon, ibn Shu'eib does not hesitate to make use of them and even to apply them to halakhot.

Nevertheless, allegory and metaphor are not the major feature of ibn Shu'eib's aggadic exegesis, nor is the desire to propagate his ideas his only motive for non-literal interpretation. As we have noted above, the literature of aggadah is filled with puzzling and challenging aggadot. The good darshan would want to challenge his audience with these passages, as well as demonstrate his ability and ingenuity in interpreting them.

We have noted above that the miraculous is not a category which sends ibn Shu'eib into interpretive exercise. However, logical and theological contradictions and problems often do elicit explanation and even extensive commentary from him. For example:

> "There existed ordered events [*seder zemanim*] previous to creation." Their intention in this statement is not to imply a doctrine of non-creation [*kadmut*] God forbid...for this is why they said 'ordered events' and did not say that 'time existed previously' [*shehayu zemanim*], in order to emphasize that all was planned out.[75]

The possibility of an eternal world is unthinkable for ibn Shu'eib, for it would contradict the plain meaning of Scripture—hence he interprets *seder zemanim* in the way he does.

[71]Niddah 17a. Cf. with Ibn Shu'eib's order in the next note.
[72]53Bb. See above, p. 53.
[73]E.g., Naḥmanides in his *Ḥidushim* to Niddah 17a.
[74]See I. Twersky, "R. Yedaiah Hapenini Uferusho La'agadah."
[75]22Cb based on B.R. 3:7.

In another cosmological statement of the Sages, ibn Shu'eib finds a logical difficulty.[76] When the Sages speak of seven things which preceded Creation,[77] ibn Shu'eib concludes that the statement has a secret meaning, arguing as did many before him[78] that before Creation there existed neither time nor place; therefore where or when could things be? Ibn Shu'eib's solution is two-fold: there is a hidden, kabbalistic meaning to the statement, but there is a manifest *(nigleh)* meaning as well. The seven items did not actually precede Creation but were part of a master plan for Creation, and ibn Shu'eib goes into great detail, bringing Scriptural, aggadic and logical proofs to show how each item was a necessary part of Creation and was therefore included in the master scheme.[79] After concluding this exposition,[80] ibn Shu'eib then explains that the seven items actually stand for the seven *Sefirot* (or *middot*),[81] which leads our darshan into a discussion of the symbols of the number seven in Creation and in the universe.

Here we see how on the one hand the logical difficulties force ibn Shu'eib to change the literal meaning of the passage, while the kabbalistic possibilities open for him another channel of interpretation. The two approaches complement one another rather than contradict.

Another example of a theological problem is the one ibn Shu'eib finds in the famous story of the stove of Akhnai, the story of how all the miracles performed by R. Eliezer were unable to convince the Rabbis that a decision rendered by majority vote should be changed.[82] Ibn Shu'eib's problem is: how can God authorize miracles in support of a position that will be defeated? Or, in other words, how can He lose?![83]

Ibn Shu'eib explains that indeed all the miracles did occur as described,[84] but they were intended as a test from God to see whether the Sages would remain steadfast to the principle of majority rule. But what of the response of the Holy One, Blessed be He, to this "defeat"? The story has Him say "My

[76] 59AB, 91A.

[77] Nedarim 39b; Pesahim 54a.

[78] See, e.g., R. Abraham ibn Ezra, Introduction to Commentary on the Torah.

[79] Cf. Cuzari III,73.

[80] See Rashba's Commentary to the Aggadot (ed. S. Weinberger) Nedarim 39b and ed. L. A. Feldman in *Hagut 'Ivrit Ba'america* 1 (Tel Aviv 1972), pp. 421-423; cf. R. Judah of Barcelona, *Perush Sefer Yeẓirah* (Berlin 1885), pp. 88-89; *Ran*, Nedarim 39b; Introd. of R. Jacob ibn Habib to *'Ein Ya'akov.*

[81] Cf. Zohar III 34b; A. J. Heschel, *Torah Min Hashamayim*, vol. II, p. 32 and nn.31-34.

[82] 28Bc. B.M 59b.

[83] See the history of the interpretation of the story by I. Engelard, "Tanur Shel 'Akhnai—Peirusheha Shel Aggadah," *Shenaton Hamishpat Ha'ivri* 1 (1974) 45-56.

[84] This is not universally accepted. See Engelard, p. 54, n.44.

sons have defeated Me *(niẓḥuni banai).*" Here ibn Shu'eib suggests an original interpretation:[85] the word *niẓḥuni* is related to *lamenaẓe'aḥ*—meaning praise—they praise Me by standing by the principles of established revelation. The miraculous is not a problem; the theological difficulty is.

Ibn Shu'eib addresses himself to the theological problems inherent in the aggadah which states (Shabbat 88a) that, when the Torah was given at Sinai, the mountain was suspended over the heads of the Israelites with the threat that if they did not accept the Torah they would be buried under the mountain. The Talmud suggests that this act of coercion undermines the validity of the binding authority of the Torah. Now although the Talmud states that the Torah was later willingly accepted, ibn Shu'eib[86] refuses to admit that indeed the Torah's authority is undermined. He argues that the statement was made only by those who would seek to challenge the Torah, for in truth the authority of the Torah is based on the Divine Will that it be accepted and furthermore, an act, even if coerced, is legally valid. Ibn Shu'eib deviates from the plain meaning of the aggadah which sees the forced nature of its acceptance as a challenge, in order to avoid its theologically unacceptable consequences.

Not only aggadot with theological difficulties call forth Ibn Shu'eib's interpretive talents. He excels in the careful exegesis of other difficult aggadic texts where the methods of philological exegesis—clarifying basic terms, unraveling seeming inconsistencies, uncovering the Scriptural basis for aggadic statements, in a word, full explication of text—join with homiletic expertise. Let us examine some of the evidence for his skill as explicator.

Seeking out the Scriptural basis of an aggadah is an important element in aggadic exegesis, and ibn Shu'eib pays careful attention to this relationship between aggadah and Scripture. Thus concerning the verse "on the first tablets, which you shattered *(asher shibbarta)*" (Ex. 34:1)—he cites[87] the response that the Sage put in God's mouth—"may your strength be increased for breaking them *(yiyeshar koḥakha sheshibarta)*"[88] and explains that the Talmud is not interpreting the word *asher* to mean *yiyeshar koḥakha*, for then the verse "who made the calf" *(asher asu et ha'egel)* (Ex. 32:35) might equally well indicate approval of the Golden Calf. Instead ibn Shu'eib suggests that the sages deduce God's positive assessment of Moses' act by virtue of the fact

[85]This interpretation also appears in the *Sefer Hapeliah*; see Engelard, p. 56; *Sefer Hakaneh* (Korets 1784), pp. 79ff = *Sefer Hapeliah* (Israel n.d.) part II, p. 30c. The Derashot were written before *Sefer Hapeliah*, but there is no evidence of influence in this instance. See the literature cited above, ch. III, nn.149, 152.

[86]26CD. Cf. Rashba in *'Ein Ya'akov* to Shabbat 88a.

[87]33Ab.

[88]Shabbat 87a. Ibn Shu'eib's explanation is cited by ibn Ḥabib in his commentary to *'Ein Ya'akov* ad loc. in the name of Rashba.

that He commanded that the broken tablets be placed in the Ark; if the tablets were the remnants of unacceptable action by Moses then they would not have been placed there. Ibn Shu'eib's assumption here that rabbinic biblical interpretation must be consistent leads him to find a new Scriptural source.

But his talents in aggadic exegesis go beyond *quellensforschung*. The following example shows his thoughtful sensitivity to the dynamics of aggadic interpretation.

> The sages have explained...that the phrase "to do justly" (Micah 6:8) refers to the laws; "to love mercy" *(ḥesed)* refers to acts of lovingkindness *(gemilat ḥesed)*; what then does "to walk humbly" mean? It refers to raising money for the bride and burying the dead. For there is an argument a fortiori. Since it says 'to walk humbly' with respect to matters which one ordinarily does publicly, how much more so does it apply to matters which one ordinarily does in private. The intention of the Sages was to say that the words 'walk humbly' modify 'mercy and justice' *(ḥesed umishpat)* and are not a separate command—the meaning is that one should do acts of *ḥesed* and the *miẓvot* in a modest manner, for the sake of Heaven and not to glorify oneself.[89]

Ibn Shu'eib understood clearly the lack of parallel between the three phrases of the verse, justice, mercy and walking humbly, and particularly the lack of parallel in the Sages' interpretation. The first two, law and acts of lovingkindness, are broad categories, whereas the two examples for walking humbly are specific *miẓvot*. He therefore emphasizes that "walking humbly" modifies the other two. It describes the method of fulfillment and does not constitute a separate category. Ibn Shu'eib clarifies the content of the aggadah by carefully paying attention to its structure and meaning.

A particularly enigmatic midrash brings forth an ingenious solution based on both halakhic and semi-halakhic texts. There exist a number of discrepancies between the two versions of the Decalogue, and one of the most well-known variations is the change in the commandment to observe the Sabbath from "remember" *(zakhor)* (Ex. 20:8) to "guard" (or "observe," *shamor*) (Deut. 5:12). Many explanations were offered by the Sages, and ibn Shu'eib addresses himself to one of them.

> They have said in the Midrash, *zakhor*—on the sea, *shamor*—on land. The explanation of this is that at sea everything is bright, for there are no separations nor any trees. As a result one might think that there is still plenty of time until sunset and forget to inaugurate the Sabbath while still light, because it seems that the day is still strong and there is still plenty of time for its inauguration; therefore the Torah says

[89]36Ac. See Sukkah 49b; Makkot 24a.

> *zakhor*—remember while it is still daylight—to inaugurate the Sabbath. The meaning of "*shamor*—on land" is as follows: on land there are shadows from the houses, the hills and the trees. It therefore seems to be night and people depart from the Sabbath before the proper time. This is the reason for *shamor* 'guard' on land. This correlates with what the Sages have said 'Let my lot be with those who inaugurate the Sabbath in Tiberias and with those who usher it out in Sepphoris.' Tiberias is low and darkness comes early, and as a result Sabbath is inaugurated when it is really day; in Sepphoris, which is high up like a bird, daylight lingers and Sabbath is ushered out only when it is indeed dark.[90]

By turning "sea" and "land" into halakhic symbols and bringing support from related aggadic-halakhic sources, ibn Shu'eib succeeds in rendering this enigmatic passage intelligible and halakhicly significant.

Ibn Shu'eib's most spectacular performance as aggadic commentator is when he applies several different methodologies all to the same aggadah. For example, the Talmud (Berakhot 3a) describes the three parts of the night, each marked off from the other by certain phenomena. "In the first watch the donkey stirs; the second, dogs yell; in the third watch, the infant nurses from his mother's breast and the woman speaks with her husband...."

Ibn Shu'eib presents no less than five different interpretations of this aggadah.[91]

> According to the simple meaning, these responses are similar to the *Pirkei Shirah* [hymns of the animals];[92] or else the living things are

[90] 50Bc. I have not located the source for the statement. However, the connection of *zakhor* and *shamor* with the anticipation and delaying of the Sabbath is already found in *Midrash Tana'im*, ed. D. Hoffman (Berlin 1908), p. 21. See too *Midrash Hagadol* Deut. 5:14 (ed. S. Fish [Jerusalem 1972]), p. 113.

[91] 24B.

[92]

ולפי פשט הדברים הוא כמו פרק שירה, או שבעלי חיים נתן להם התעוררות בזה שכוחותיהם עושים זה כמו שאמרו ז"ל אין לך עשב מלמטה שאין לו מזל מלמעלה ומכה אותו על קדקדו ואומר לו גדל

Cf. *derashah* to *Shoftim* 83Cb.

ורז"ל תקנו פרק שירה שמשבחים לבוראם או שרים שלהם וכוחותיהם שמשבחים לשם כי כל בריה ואף לעשבים יש כחות בשמים.

I translated the passage in the text so as to be consistent with the passage just cited in *Shoftim*. Malachi Beit-Aryei in "Perek Shirah, Introductions and Critical Edition" (Ph.D. thesis, Hebrew University 1966), pp. 15-16, feels that ibn Shu'eib suggests only one interpretation of *Perek Shirah*, namely, that the animals have corresponding angelic powers above who sing hymns. Actually, from the correlation of both of the passages in the Derashot concerning *Perek Shirah* we see that ibn Shu'eib considers two possible interpretations of *Perek Shirah*. The first is that creatures themselves literally praise God שמשבחים בוראם and the alternative is "או שרים שלהם"—their corresponding "princes" or angelic powers. Cf. *derashah* to *Shoftim:* או שבעלי חיים נתן

aroused by the actions of their corresponding powers above. As the Sages of blessed memory have said, "Every blade of grass below has a planet above which hits it on its head and instructs it to grow [B.R. 10:6].

There are those who interpret it in a different manner. These things symbolize man's powers, for during the first watch man's digestive system is at work, which is symbolized by the donkey carrying its load. During the second, the limbs which serve men's lusts receive their due and shout (again?); during the third all the organs have fulfilled their tasks and the wife speaks with her husband, arranging the home and ordering their needs.

Others explain otherwise...that the donkey braying alludes to the necessity of man being awake studying the Torah during the first watch, just as the donkey is awake, as it is written (Lament 2:19) "Arise and cry out in the night at the beginning of the watches"; that means the beginning of the first watch. During the second watch, dogs cry out—the second watch symbolizes sleep; man should sleep during the second watch to give his body its due so that it may be nourished and do its job. During the third watch he speaks with the members of his household and prays early.

According to the inner meaning[93] [the three watches] allude to the two doorposts and the lintel.[94] The "donkey brays" should be understood as an allusion[95] to the verse "and Abraham arose early and saddled his

להם התעוררות בזה שכוחותיהם עושים זה Cf. R. Moses Taku, *Ketav Tamim* (n.16), p. 63 who doubts the authenticity of *Perek Shirah.*

93

ועל דרך הפנימי הוא רומז למזוזות ולמשקוף חמור נוער דכתיב וישכם אברהם בבקר ויחבוש את חמורו והוא ברוגז רחם תזכור והוא רמ״ח איברים. וכן כתיב בפנחס ויקח רומח בידו, ובמלך המשיח רוכב על חמור, ובמשה וירכבם על החמור בה״ה הידיעה. ודרשו ז״ל שהוא החמור של משיח ושל אברהם ואין ספק שאותו חמור יחיה עד המשיח. וכלבים צועקים פחד יצחק ואמרו ביבמות כלבים צועקים מלאך המות בא לעיר, וזהו ולכל בני ישראל לא יחרץ כלב לשונו — כי משם הקטיגור והדם והחרב. ואשה ספרת עם בעלה רומז לאשת חיל. ותקם בעוד לילה ותתן טרף לביתה וגו׳ כי מקבלת פרס מבעלה והיא עת דודים והיא שעמדה לאבותינו ולנו. והתינוק היונק רמז לשר העולם מטטרון כמו שאמר נער הייתי וגו׳ פסוק זה שר העולם אמרו. For parallels see *Oẓar Hakavod* Berakhot 3a; *Ma'arekhet Ha'elohut* p. 173 (and commentary of R. Judah Ḥayyat ad loc.); *Shoshan Sodot* 51b; *Meshiv Devarim Nekhoḥim* ch. 29.

[94]Earlier, ibn Shu'eib said that the two doorposts symbolize Abraham and Isaac, or the Sefirot of *Ḥesed* and *Gevurah*, and the lintel symbolizes Jacob, the median.

[95]Cf. *derashah* to *Pinḥas* 73Bb
ובמדרש כ׳ נזדמן לו (לפנחס) רמ״ח כנגד רמ״ח איברים שנזדרז לכבוד השם בכל איבריו ושם נפשו בכפו ולא ירא מן הארבעה ועשרים אלף מישראל שהיו שומרים אותו ועוד כנגד רח״ם תזכור שבטח בחסד אלקים ובמדת אברהם.

donkey *(ḥmr)*";[96] also "he will be compassionate *(rḥm)* even in anger" (Hab. 3:2); also this alludes to the two hundred and forty-eight *(rmḥ)* limbs; also there is an allusion in the verse "and Phineas took the sword *(rmḥ)* in his hand" (Num. 25:7); the King Messiah will ride on a donkey *(ḥmr)* and with respect to Moses too it says he saddled them on the donkey *(ḥmr)*; note the definite article—for the Sages have expounded that the donkey of the Messiah and of Abraham are identical. There is no doubt that that very donkey will live until the time of the Messiah. The howling of dogs symbolizes the Fear of Isaac. They have said in Yevamot "when dogs howl, the Angel of Death is in town."[97] This is the meaning of "not a dog shall bark at any of the Israelites" (Ex 11:7); there [on the Left side] the Sefirah of Gevurah is the Accuser, Blood and Sword. "A woman speaks with her husband" alludes to the Woman of Valor, as it says "She arises when it is yet dark and provides food for her household, etc." (Prov. 31:15). She receives the reward from her husband[98] for it is a time for lovers. It is this which has sustained us and our fathers. The suckling infant alludes to the Prince of the World, Metatron,[99] as it is said "I have been young, etc." (Ps. 37:25): this verse was said by the Prince of the world.[100]

Thus in a masterful feat of exegesis, ibn Shu'eib presents two literal interpretations, two metaphorical explanations, one psychological, the other practical-religious, and finally a kabbalistic explanation which is the reason for introducing the aggadah in the first place, i.e., in order to illustrate the notion of the two doorposts as symbols of Abraham = *Ḥesed* and Isaac = *Din* and the lintel as symbol of Jacob = *Tif'eret.*

To sum up: we have seen all the various ways in which ibn Shu'eib employs aggadah in the Derashot. He extensively uses aggadot that extend and expand upon the biblical narrative, often accepting the aggadic explanations as fact, although he was certainly aware that the Sages themselves were not dogmatic in their historical aggadot and often present options or alternate opinions.

Beyond this ibn Shu'eib uses aggadah as the basis for his own aggadic creativity. He starts with an aggadah and, employing its methodology of expounding Scripture, he continues the process. Sometimes in the process of

[96]See *Ma'arekhet Ha'elohut* p. 173, who explains that the first donkey in the Torah is mentioned in connection with Abraham. Hence *ḥamor* became the symbol of *ḥesed. Ḥmr* and *Avraham* also have the same numerical value *(gematria)*, namely 248.

[97]B.K 60b.

[98]This is an allusion to the unification of the Sefirah of *Tif'eret* and *Malkhut.* See *Ma'arekhet* 172b.

[99]Metatron represents the Sefirah of *Malkhut*; see, e.g., *Ma'arekhet* 72b; see R. Margaliyot, *Mal'akhei 'Elyon* (Jerusalem 1964), p. 79.

[100]Yevamot 16b.

expansion and development of aggadic themes he proceeds differently, taking the conscious stance of a commentator and exegete of the aggadah itself. As a commentator he is sensitive to nuances of expression and is able to suggest original explanations of aggadot. He displays understanding of the logical, theological, and philological problems in the aggadot and offers solutions which sometimes fit the simple meaning of the aggadah, but often constitute a homily upon a homily. He does not hesitate to employ metaphor or allegory, but this is done not out of rational objections to the miraculous, but as an attempt to make sense of enigmatic aggadic passages and as a way of using aggadah as the basis for propagating ideas and moral lessons that he wants to further. Kabbalistic ideas are developed from many aggadot. Above all, ibn Shu'eib is serious in his approach to aggadah. While many aggadot are accepted at face value or are expanded upon and others receive novel interpretations, all are considered important. Flexibility in use and interpretation are the characteristic features of ibn Shu'eib's use of and interpretation of aggadah.

Chapter VIII
Kabbalah

Above in the first chapter we took note of the intensification of kabbalistic activity in thirteenth-century Spain and the variety of literary forms which the kabbalists used to convey their ideas. The literary *derashah*, we said, was little used as a medium of kabbalistic expression. Despite the gradual emergence of Kabbalah from small scholarly circles to wider audiences through its use in works of exegesis, it still remained an esoteric doctrine and was not considered appropriate for popular discourses. There was, in fact, vocal opposition to the public teaching of Kabbalah in the thirteenth century.[1] Although there are kabbalistic allusions in the *derashot* of Ramban[2] and in R. Baḥya ben Asher's *Kad Hakemaḥ,*[3] there is very much less Kabbalah in them than in those authors' Torah commentaries. Thus to our knowledge, ibn Shu'eib is the first darshan to use Kabbalah extensively in the *derashah*.

Ibn Shu'eib was thoroughly familiar with the kabbalistic literature of his day. He drew on the works of R. Ezra,[4] whom he quotes many times in the Derashot, and on R. Azriel's[5] commentary to the Aggadot. He was familiar

[1]E.g., R. Meir b. Simon of Narbonne. See G. Scholem, "Te'udah Ḥadashah Letoldot Reshit Hakabbalah," in Y. Fichman, ed., *Sefer Bialik* (1934).

[2]Naḥmanides' *Derashah Leḥatunah* is exceptional and may not have been a public lecture. Concerning kabbalistic ideas in his "Torat Hashem Temimah," see, e.g., pp. 167 and 174 in C. Chavel, ed., *Kitvei Haramban.* On Naḥmanides' self-imposed limitations in kabbalistic writing, see M. Idel, "'We Have No Kabbalistic Tradition on This'," in I. Twersky, ed., *Rabbi Moses Naḥmanides (Ramban),* pp. 51-74

[3]See E. Gottlieb, *Hakabbalah Bekhitvei Rabeinu Baḥya b. Asher*, pp. 25-27 and index of sources, s.v. *Kad Hakemaḥ*, p. 287.

[4]On R. Ezra, see S. Abramson, Introduction, p. 20 and below, n.52.

[5]See below, n.20.

with the Kabbalah of R. Moses of Burgos as well.[6] Needless to say, like the other students of Rashba, he was familiar with Naḥmanides' commentary to the Torah, which he uses countless times in the Derashot, including the *sodot*, the kabbalistic secrets in the commentary. Indeed, as mentioned above, the *Be'ur Sodot Haramban* may very well be a reworking of a commentary that ibn Shu'eib himself wrote.[7]

Ibn Shu'eib quotes the Zohar several times in the Derashot, referring to it as "Midrash R. Shim'on bar Yoḥai,"[8] but, like the other students of Rashba,[9] he does not rely heavily on it. There are as well unattributed passages whose source is in the Zohar.[10] In addition, there is a great deal of material for which there are parallels in the works of ibn Shu'eib's colleagues such as R. Baḥya, R. Shem Tov ibn Gaon, R. Isaac of Acco, in the *Be'ur Sodot Haramban*, and in Recanati's commentary to the Torah.

1. Kabbalistic Interpretation of Scripture

Ibn Shu'eib's use of Kabbalah in the Derashot is founded on the axiom that the Torah has more than one layer of meaning and more specifically that it has an inner meaning, which is its kabbalistic meaning. The notion of the manifold meaning of the Torah has a long history. There is a midrashic statement that there are "seventy faces to the Torah,"[11] and the medieval Jewish philosophers approached Scripture with the assumption that it has both an outer meaning and an inner, philosophical or allegorical meaning.[12] Among the kabbalists, the notion of the multiple meanings of the Torah was developed and in the thirteenth century took the form of a fourfold exegesis to the Torah. The four modes of exegesis, which are used explicitly and methodically, for example, in R. Baḥya b. Asher's commentary to the Torah,

[6]See below, this chapter.

[7]The work attributed to ibn Shu'eib's student R. Meir ibn Sahula is also attributed in some manuscripts to R. Joshua ibn Shu'eib. See below, Appendix, n.12. For some parallels and divergences between the Derashot and ibn Sahula, see Gottlieb, *Hakabbalah*, p. 175 n.20 and p. 214 n.1. Some additional parallels are (Derashot:*Be'ur Sodot*) 21Ac:*Bo*; 24Aa-b:*Bo*; 68Cc:*Ḥukkat*; 79Ca:*Va'etḥanan* (and cf. Derashot 19Bb); 90Aa:*Shemot*.

[8]11Ba; 18Aa; 33Cb; 60Aa; 67Cb; 69Ac; 71Ac; 75Cb. See Abramson, Introduction, p. 15. Not all of ibn Shu'eib's citations from "Midrash R. Shim'on bar Yoḥai" can be located in the Zohar.

[9]G. Scholem, *Kabbalah*, p. 236; M. Idel, "An Unknown Commentary on Naḥmanides' Mystic Doctrines" (Hebrew), *Da'at* 2-3 (1978-9) 121-122 and n.6.

[10]24Ca; 27Bc; 45Ba.

[11]See *Numbers Rabbah* 13:15; G. Scholem, *On the Kabbalah and its Symbolism* (New York 1965), p. 62.

[12]See S. Rosenberg, "'Al Parshanut Hamikra Besefer Hamoreh," *Jerusalem Studies in Jewish Thought* 1 (1981) 85-157 and the literature cited there.

are *peshat*—the simple or contextual meaning of the verse; *sekhel*—allegory; *midrash*; and *sod*—kabbalistic interpretation.[13] Ibn Shu'eib uses these same four modes, although not always on the same verse. When he refers explicitly to different exegetical approaches he refers only to a threefold approach: "these verses can be understood using *three* methods, *peshat, sikhli* and *midrash*."[14] He often mentions, however, that there is a *sod* or kabbalistic explanation of particular verse and then spells out the *sod* in explicit terms.

In one passage, to which we have already made reference, the *sodot* of the works of Creation and the works of the Chariot—*ma'aseh bereshit* and *ma'aseh merkavah*—become one of three parts of the Torah:

> Some say that the Torah itself is divided into three sections: narratives, laws, and the secrets of the works of Creation and the works of the Chariot. This in turn parallels the tripartite division of the soul—*neshamah, ruaḥ* and *nefesh*.[15]

Here *sodot* are not one layer of meaning of the Torah, that is, part of an exegetical methodology, but are one of the three divisions of the text of the Torah. Elsewhere, however, ibn Shu'eib says that he adopts Naḥmanides' principles of exegesis, which he characterizes as follows: there are three methods of exegesis, based on three possible ways of dividing up the letters of the Torah. The present arrangement of the letters of the Torah, the present division into words, creates a text of narrative and commandment. But one may divide it differently so that it explicates the names of God, or alternatively so that it explicates the "fifty gates of wisdom," which include all branches of knowledge, even those such as chiromancy and physiognomy, as well as the works of Creation and the Chariot.[16] The assumption that all wisdom is contained in the Torah is not new in itself and easily serves as the theoretical basis for a wide-ranging kind of exegesis.[17]

[13]See P. Sandler, "Live'ayat Pardes Vehashitah Hameruba'at," *Sefer Urbach, Haḥevrah Leḥeker Hamikra* (1955), pp. 222-235; G. Scholem, *On the Kabbalah and its Symbolism*, pp. 32-86; Y. Tishby, *Mishnat Hazohar* vol. 2, pp. 363-398.

[14]17Ca; 20Ca; 21Db. In these three instances he refers specifically to the interpretation of the book of Proverbs, but he is consistent in applying his exegetical methodology to all of Scripture.

[15]26Dc. ויש מפרשים, התורה עצמה נחלקת לשלשה חלקים, סיפורים, וסודות מעשה בראשית והמרכבה כנגד שלשה נפשות, נשמה, ורוח, ונפש. Cf. a similar triad on p. 59Cc, משפטים, חוקים, ומ״ב ומ״מ. Cf. too *Zohar Ḥadash* 83a: אף דברי תורה אית בה מעשה מדרש והגדה וסוד. See *M.H.* vol. 2, p. 366, and Zohar III 152a. On the correspondence to the parts of the soul see 17Ca: ובפסוקים הללו ישים אלו השלשה דרכים פשט כמו הנפש, השכלי כמו הרוח, השמעי כמו הנשמה

[16] 59A. Naḥmanides, Introduction to the *Commentary on the Torah* (ed. Chavel), pp. 4 and 6. See M. Idel, "The Concept of the Torah in Heikhalot Literature and Kabbalah" (Hebrew), *Jerusalem Studies in Jewish Thought* 1 (1981) 49-58.

[17]See, e.g., H. A. Wolfson, *Philo* I, pp. 155-163 and his sources.

According to the approach of redivision of the letters of the Torah, the secrets are in all parts of the Torah, and one must only know how to redivide or rearrange the letters properly. According to the other viewpoint, only certain parts of the Torah have mystical meaning, i.e., those designated as *ma'aseh bereshit* and *ma'aseh merkavah.* In practice, however, ibn Shu'eib, like other kabbalists, finds *sodot* in all parts of the Torah as presently constituted, in the narrative and legal portions as well as specifically mystical portions. Indeed, according to one passage in the Derashot, when the angels desired to receive the Torah in place of the Israelites "not in order to know the laws of slaughtering, *terefot* or eating of *maẓah*, but rather to know the secrets such as *ma'aseh merkavah* which are alluded to in the Torah," they were denied that opportunity because the *sodot* can be comprehended only through the performance of the commandments.[18]

One particularly rich source of *sodot* is the Song of Songs, which was interpreted by kabbalists and mystics as a song of mystic love. Ibn Shu'eib, in a *derashah* which is actually a running midrashic commentary to the Song of Songs, does not cite many kabbalistic interpretations but does assert that "all the words [of the Song of Songs] are hidden [secrets] of the Chariot and the names of the Holy One Blessed be He."[19]

This inner meaning, the *sod*, was esoteric knowledge, and ibn Shu'eib followed established tradition in reiterating the difficulty in attaining and comprehending it and the importance of keeping this knowledge secret. The difficulties are twofold: first of all, the secrets of the Torah can only be attained by Israel; secondly, even among Israel not everyone should try to comprehend these secrets, for not everyone is capable of it. Only Israelites possess the special "emanated prophetic intellect," and therefore only they can attain esoteric knowledge; but even among them not every individual is capable of exercising the prophetic or gracious intellect.[20] Concluding a discussion in which he finds kabbalistic allusions in some biblical verses, he says

> There is no doubt that these are very deep matters and cannot be comprehended by any mind with the exception of those few whom God calls and the prophets who have the strength to stand in the palace of the King.[21]

[18] 39Cc. See Shabbat 88b-89a; M. Idel (n.16), pp. 23ff. For literature, see his n.6.

[19] 42Ba. See S. Lieberman, "Mishnat Shir Hashirim,"in G. Scholem, *Jewish Gnosticism, Merkabah Mysticism, and Talmudic Tradition* (New York 1965), p. 125.

[20] 47Ab. See above, ch. IV, p. 82, and ch. V, p. 98. See Y. Tishby, ed., *Commentary of R. Azriel to the Aggadot*, p. 54, ll.14-15:
ארומם אותך במחשבתי עד תחלת גבול המחשבה המתעלית בכל כחה עד מקורה מן המקור ההוא מביע ברכה כבריכת מים הנובעת בלי הפסק

[21] 3Bc.

In describing the dangers involved in trying to comprehend secrets that one is not able to grasp, ibn Shu'eib draws on the Talmudic tale, frequently cited in philosophic and kabbalistic literature, of the four who entered *Pardes*, the garden of esoteric knowledge, of whom only R. Akiva survived. "Whoever recklessly speculates beyond his power to comprehend, not only does he not understand, but he loses all that he has learned."[22] In addition, there are matters which one may not think about at all, for they are beyond human comprehension. Thus, after presenting a midrashic interpretation of a verse in Song of Songs, ibn Shu'eib says

> According to Kabbalah there are hidden matters which one may not even think about, for the verses describe the higher chariot which is above the chariot of Ezekiel; they are the Sefirot.[23]

Thus there are matters accessible only to Israel; there are matters which not all of Israel can attain and are limited to unique individuals and prophets; and, finally, above these there are secrets which no one may think about at all and hence are inaccessible until messianic times. This last category is alluded to in the parable of

> a king who accumulated a treasure which was superior to the treasure of all kings and divided it into three parts, each part superior to the other. The least important he distributed to all the inhabitants of the kingdom; the second part he gave to his family servants and obedient followers; the third, the best, he hid away as a treasure for himself. Similarly, the Holy One Blessed be He divided wisdom into three parts: He gave intelligence *(sekhel)* to the nations of the world; He gave the Torah, which is the off-shoot *(novlot)* of His wisdom, to Israel; the rest he stored away for the future, when "the earth shall be filled with wisdom" (Is. 11:9).[24]

The notion that there is Divine wisdom not revealed in this world is alluded to in two other passages in the Derashot. The first is ibn Shu'eib's explanation of the significance of the verses in Numbers 10:35-36, which are set off in the Torah scroll by reversed *nuns.*

> There is one view that this section...is surrounded by special signs in order to tell us that it is an independent book. This is why the verse "She [wisdom] has hewn her seven pillars" (Proverbs 2:1) is significant, for it informs us that, although the Torah appears to us as five books, that is only generally true; when broken down into their parts, they are seven, as is evident to one who know to what the numbers five and seven

[22] 45Da. See Ḥagigah 14b.
[23] 43Bc.
[24] 47Ac.

> allude. The Torah alludes here to the future, when the power of the Torah will expand and we shall see all seven books.[25]

The books of Numbers will in the future consist of three books: the part until the *nuns*, the two verses between the *nuns*, which will expand, and the end of the book. In the same vein, ibn Shu'eib alludes to the expansion of the Torah in his *derashah* for *Shavu'ot* where he discusses the idea, mentioned above, of different possible divisions of the letters of the Torah.

> It is concerning this notion that the Sages said "these are the *mizvot*; a prophet may not innovate anything now *(me'atah)*." The word *me'atah* alludes to a great thing, to the coming *shemittot*. Examine carefully and you will see.[26]

The doctrine of *shemittot* that ibn Shu'eib is referring to is a doctrine developed in *Sefer Hatemunah*, and also alluded to frequently by Naḥmanides and his commentators,[27] according to which the world functions in cycles of seven thousand years called *shemittot*. At the end of seven such cycles will be the great Jubilee, when all things return to their source. Each *shemittah* is governed by a different Sefirah, and the Torah is therefore read differently in each *shemittah*, in accord with the Sefirah governing that *shemittah*, be it *Ḥesed*, grace, *Din*, judgment or *Raḥamim*, mercy. Thus, the Torah, which now instructs us as to what is permitted and what is prohibited, will be read differently in a *shemittah* where there is no evil desire and hence would not include prohibitions. Ibn Shu'eib emphasizes the statement that "a prophet may not innovate anything *now*," by which he wishes to stress that innovations or changes in the character of the Torah in another *shemittah* are possible.

The eschatological changes in the laws of the Torah are referred to in another context in the Derashot. Ibn Shu'eib cites the famous saying concerning the ultimate permissibility of the *ḥazir*, the pig, a saying which has a long history in Jewish literature.[28]

> I have seen in the Midrash of R. Shim'on ben Yoḥai a reason similar to Naḥmanides', that everything in the time of creation was pure, there being no impurity in the world, neither in man nor in animals. This is the meaning of the verse "and behold it was very good" (Genesis 1:31). It was the Snake who injected filth into the world and its creatures, and as a result everything was defiled. In the future everything will become

[25] 63Ba. See Shabbat 116a, Lev.R. 11:3. See G. Scholem, *On the Kabbalah*, pp. 79-82; idem, *Ursprung und Anfange*, p. 418.

[26] 59Ab.

[27] Concerning the dating of *Sefer Hatemunah*, Moshe Idel in a forthcoming article contends that it was written in the fourteenth century.

[28] See the article by S. Abramson in *Molad* 27 (1971) 424.

pure when the filth will cease, as they have said, "it is called *ḥazir* because it will return to Israel in the future *('atid laḥazor leyisrael)*.[29]

But regardless of what secrets of the Torah will be revealed in Messianic times or in other *shemittot* and what the nature of the Torah will be then, the Torah as it is written now with its stories and its laws yields many secrets, and ibn Shu'eib provides us with kabbalistic exegesis of many of them.[30] Two examples will suggest the nature of this kind of exegesis.

In *parashat Vayeẓei,*[31] ibn Shu'eib discusses the relationship between Jacob and his wives and particularly Leah's eagerness to bear Jacob children. He first explains the story according to its simple meaning—*derekh hanigleh.* Jacob made it known to his wives that God had told him that he would father twelve tribes. All the wives were eager to be the mothers of his sons, but Leah was more eager than the others, because she knew that she was hated by Jacob (Gen. 29:31), perhaps as a result of her father's act of deception. She was eager, therefore, to have children to prevent Jacob from divorcing her, something which she particularly feared because she, as the first born daughter of Laban, would be given in marriage to Esau, Rebecca's first-born son.

The hidden meaning, however, interprets Leah's and Jacob's actions in accordance with the Sefirot which they symbolize. Leah knew that Rachel was Jacob's true mate since Jacob had the quality of compassion *(darom=raḥamim)* which Rachel also possessed. Leah, however, who had the quality of Strict Judgment *(smol)*, thought that by bearing many sons she would approach Jacob's quality and as a result tried to have as many children by Jacob as possible.

Similarly in R. Joshua's interpretation of the story of Judah and Tamar (Gen. 38),[32] Judah is taken to symbolize the foot of the Throne, that is the Sefirah of *Malkhut*, and the progenitor of the Messiah. The children whom Tamar bears for him symbolize the Sefirot of *Tiferet* and *Malkhut.*

The symbols of the various Sefirot are central to ibn Shu'eib's kabbalistic comments in the Derashot, and it is to this aspect of Kabbalah and ibn Shu'eib's use of it that we now turn.

2. The World of the Sefirot

The central doctrine of Spanish Kabbalah was the system of Sefirot. As. R. Meir ibn Sahula in his commentary to *Sefer Yeẓirah* says: "What is known as

[29]75C. Cf. Ritva to *Kiddushin* 49b.

[30]For his kabbalistic treatment of *miẓvot*, see ch. V above on the Reasons for the Commandments.

[31]12Bc. Cf. Ramban Gen. 30:9 and Bereshit Rabbah 70:17.

[32]15C-D. See below.

Kabbalah is the wisdom of the ten Sefirot and the explanations of some of the *mizvot*."[33]

Throughout the Derashot, ibn Shu'eib interprets biblical verses as well as aggadic and halakhic passages in terms of the symbolism of the Sefirot, drawing on the rich imagery already developed in twelfth- and thirteenth-century kabbalistic works, such as *Sefer Habahir*, the works of R. Ezra and R. Azriel, and the Zohar. Catching ibn Shu'eib's allusions presupposes a familiarity with this symbolism (which implies incidentally that among his audience were those with such knowledge). While ibn Shu'eib does not indulge in any full-fledged discussion of the theoretical aspects of Sefirot, there is enough material in the Derashot to identify his ideas about the Sefirot and the important symbols used.

Although the term "Sefirot" does appear in the Derashot,[34] ibn Shu'eib does not use it often. Some of the terms he uses are *middah—middot* ("Ways");[35] *havvayot* ("Existences");[36] *ma'amarot* ("Sayings");[37] *yamim elyonim* ("Supernal Days");[38] and *aspaklaryot* ("Mirrors").[39] The number ten, the number of the Sefirot, figures prominently in ibn Shu'eib's homilies.[40] Whenever he can, he will point out a correlation to the various groups of ten found in the Torah and the Talmud and Midrash. The ten trials of Abraham stand for the ten *aspaklaryot.*[41] Abraham's age of 100 years at the time of the revelation to him of the birth of Isaac reflects the perfection inherent in that number, for each of the ten Sefirot has itself ten aspects.[42] The ten plagues, the ten commandments, and the ten names of God all allude to the ten Sefirot.[43] The Sefirot are divided in two different ways in the Derashot. Most often ibn Shu'eib refers to the upper three Sefirot and the lower seven, a division commonly found among kabbalists. But he refers to another division as well, the division of the Sefirot into five upper ones and five below them.[44] The statement appears in a homiletical context, and he does not expand on this assertion.

[33]Cited by G. Scholem, "Hatḥalot Hakabbalah," *Knesset* (1945) 185, from Angelica Library MS p. 2b.

[34]E.g., 26Da, 59Da, 66Cb.

[35]12Db, 58Db, 59Bb.

[36]6Dc.

[37]46Ab.

[38]59Bb.

[39]5Cc, 24Ac, 46Ab.

[40]See above, ch. II, p. 31; ch. V, p. 93.

[41]5Cc.

[42]6Dc.

[43]23Bc, 28Aab.

[44]59Db. Cf. Zohar II, 90a and b. See R. Baḥya to Gen. 28:13, p. 24.

One of the fundamental problems that kabbalists dealt with concerning the Sefirot was the relationship between *Ein-Sof* (the Infinite), *Keter* (Crown), which is the first of the Sefirot, and the other Sefirot. In early Kabbalah, *Ein-Sof* was not a Sefirah; it represented that aspect of the Godhead which embodies absolute perfection, in which no distinctions and differentiations are made, that which is absolutely hidden and unknowable. Only God in His manifestation through the Sefirot is knowable and reachable. This approach seemed to opponents of Kabbalah such as R. Meir b. Simon of Narbonne dangerously close to dualism.[45] However, some kabbalists developed an alternative system in which *Ein-Sof* was identical with the first Sefirah, *Keter.*[46] Indeed *Ein-Sof-Keter* remained above human comprehension, but at least it was within the Godhead and not separate or detached. But because of the hidden nature of *Keter*, we find some kabbalists inserting a Sefirah called *Da'at* to fill the count of ten.[47]

Ibn Shu'eib follows this second system of identifying *Ein-Sof* with *Keter*. In the *derashah* to *Yitro* he explains that both with respect to the ten sayings with which God created the world and the ten commandments, the first of each set is hidden.

> This Psalm [Psalm 29] mentions God's name eighteen times, standing for the 18,000 worlds that emerged from the nine Divine sayings *(ma'amarim)* explicitly mentioned in the Works of Creation, for the tenth is hidden in the word *bereshit*....For it too is a *ma'amar*. In this *parashah* too there are nine commandments but the tenth is hidden, for there are no words or commands....The command of *anokhi* is hidden just like *bereshit*....There is an important reason why they are hidden—because each set of commands stands for the ten Sefirot and the tenth is the Holy of Holies. Even thinking about it is forbidden, as the rabbi of blessed memory [Naḥmanides] alludes to in his commentary to Genesis. From the nine revealed *ma'amarot*, eighteen were extended, for each included *Din* and *Raḥamim*....[48]

Similarly in the *derashah* to *Vayakhel* he says "the saying *(ma'amar)* '*bereshit*' is hidden and has no emanation."[49] This lack of direct connection of

[45]See G. Scholem in *Sefer Bialik*, pp. 148-149.

[46]See Y. Tishby, *M.H.*, vol. 1, pp. 107ff.

[47]See G. Scholem, *Kabbalah*, p. 107.

[48]26Da. See Naḥmanides, Commentary to Genesis 1:1 (Chavel, p. 11).

[49]34Ba: המאמר בראשית סתום הוא ואין בו התפשטות See too 6Dc:
ולכן באו אותיותיו עשרה כנגד עשרה הויות שמהם י׳ נסיונות צדיק כנגד תשעים שנה של שרה שהם ט׳ עשריות ט׳ מאמרות כי העשירי נעלם במלת בראשית
Cf., however, 59Dc where he says י׳ מאמרות כנגד י׳ דברות דבור אנוכי כנגד יהי אור Cf. *Sha'arei Orah*, beginning of the second *Sha'ar*, for a different approach and R. Baḥya to Gen. 1:2 (p. 21) who insists on keeping *Keter* within the 10 Sefirot, which are distinct from the *'ilat ha'ilot*—the Final Cause.

the first Sefirah with the process of emanation accords with the doctrine of the identity of *Keter* as *Ein-Sof.*

Following the kabbalists who identify *Keter* and *Ein-Sof*, ibn Shu'eib too inserts the Sefirah of *Da'at* after *Ḥokhmah* and *Binah.*

> It says *Ḥokhmot* [wisdoms] to symbolize *Ḥokhmah, Tevunah*, and *Da'at*; it is with these that He created that which is above and that which is below. "She [Wisdom] has hewn her seven pillars" (Prov. 9:1)—refers to the seven Supernal Days of creation which cannot be measured by time but which are alluded to by all the sets of seven.[50]

The nature of *Da'at* ("Knowledge") is not spelled out by ibn Shu'eib, but in one place he says that "sexual union in a holy manner is honorable and contains within it the secret of *Da'at*."[51] Ibn Shu'eib is reflecting the *Iggeret Hakodesh*, a thirteenth-century work attributed to Naḥmanides, which says:

> the secret of knowledge that I am alluding to is the secret of man being included in the secret of *Ḥokhmah, Tevunah*, and *Da'at*. Man symbolizes the secret of *Ḥokhmah*, woman the secret of *Tevunah* and the pure union contains the secret of *Da'at* which is the secret of man and wife.[52]

Ḥokhmah, Tevunah, and *Da'at* are the sources for the emanation of the lower seven Sefirot, as we saw in the passage above.[53] In *Ḥokhmah* lies the very first traces of the Sefirot in their pristine state before becoming individuated. Creation in potentia is in *Ḥokhmah*.

> Symbolizing the first thought of the Creator to create this world is the verse "He will build His house with wisdom [*Ḥokhmah*]" (Prov. 24:3) for the very first thought connects with the final action.[54]

However, *Ḥokhmah* is minute and undifferentiated; and hence it is compared to *Terumah*, the priestly tithe, which has no minimum requirement and hence only a minute amount is required to fulfill one's obligation. *Ḥokhmah* is also symbolized by the first *heh* of the Tetragrammaton.[55]

The third Sefirah, *Binah* (understanding) emanating from *Ḥokhmah*, is the Sefirah in which distinction and differentiation take place: "Symbolizing differentiation and inference is the verse '...and it will be established through

[50]29Da. See R. Ezra's Commentary to the Song of Songs, p. 495.

[51]48Dc. According to some kabbalists, *Da'at* and *Tiferet* are identical. See *Ma'arekhet Ha'elohut*, 63a; *Sha'arei Orah, Sha'ar* 5.

[52]See *Iggeret Hakodesh* in *Kitvei Haramban*, vol. 2, p. 324. S. Abramson, *Sinai* 90 (1982) 232ff., speculates that, since the above citation (n. 51) is contained in a section introduced and concluded by attribution to R. Ezra and a great deal of the material in the section is found in the *Iggeret Hakodesh*, the real author of the *Iggeret* may be R. Ezra.

[53]29A.

[54]29Db.

[55]30A, 54Ab, 22B, 17Ac.

understanding' [*tevunah*]."[56] The great tree of life is a symbol of *Binah* from which "everything emanates."[57] *Bikkurim*, the first fruits which are brought from the seven fruits of the Land of Israel, are symbols of *Binah*; the seven days of creation, the seven sabbatical years, and all groups of seven, such as the seven commandments of the sons of Noah and the seven things that existed before creation—all these symbolize the seven Sefirot which emanate from, and hence are included in, *Binah.*[58]

Whereas the first three Sefirot are hidden (just as "the first three of Abraham's trials are not written in the Torah—but seven [trials] are explicit"),[59] the symbols of the lower seven Sefirot are manifest in the Torah.[60] Of these lower seven Sefirot, ibn Shu'eib most often mentions the Sefirot of *Ḥesed* ("Compassion"), *Gevurah* ("Might"), *Tiferet* ("Beauty") and *Malkhut* ("Kingdom"). The most frequent connection that ibn Shu'eib makes, a commonplace in kabbalistic literature, is the connection between Abraham and *Ḥesed*, Isaac and *Gevurah*, and Jacob and *Tiferet.*[61] This identification is a development of the Talmudic saying that "the Fathers are the *Merkavah*, the Divine Chariot," to which ibn Shu'eib adds "Abraham is on the Right and Isaac is on the Left. The first is compassion and the second is justice...and Jacob encompasses both. For this reason Jacob was born with a perfect balance of his fathers' powers." As *Da'at* is the conjunction of *Ḥokhmah* and *Binah*, so is *Tiferet* the union of *Ḥesed* and *Gevurah.*[62]

In another homily, ibn Shu'eib explains that the word *kol*—a voice—appears in Psalm 29 many times. The first three times it appears—"the voice of the Lord peals across the waters...the voice of the Lord is mighty; the voice of the Lord is full of majesty"—are linked by ibn Shu'eib with the Sefirot of *Ḥesed, Gevurah*, and *Tiferet*. Water is a symbol of compassion and stands for *Ḥesed*, might *(koaḥ)* is Isaac, and majesty *(hadar)* is Jacob.[63]

Among the seven lower Sefirot, *Tiferet* occupies a central position. Jacob's image, that is, *Tiferet*, is engraved on the Throne of Glory.[64] The centrality of *Tiferet* is represented in its harmonization of *Ḥesed* and *Gevurah*. "Jacob

[56]29Db.

[57]59Cc.

[58]See 30Ab, 87Bc.

[59]5Cc.

[60]Ibn Shu'eib here seems to equate the upper three as equally hidden, as opposed to his comment above. Cf. R. Baḥya b. Asher, Commentary to Avot in C. Chavel, ed., *Kitvei R. Baḥya*, pp. 617-618.

[61]E.g., 12Db, 14Aa, 27Ba, 90Aa, and many others.

[62]11Aa, 15Cb, 54Ab. See *Be'ur Sodot Haramban*, beginning of *Beshalaḥ*; R. Baḥya b. Asher, Gen. 48:22. Cf. n.51 above.

[63]27Ba.

[64]15Cb. See above, n.62.

encompasses justice and compassion, that is, Abraham and Isaac."[65] In addition, Jacob as the third of the Fathers is associated with the third month Sivan, the month of the giving of the Torah, which is also associated with *Tiferet.*[66]

The last Sefirah, *Malkhut* or *Shekhinah*, is the fourth foot of the Divine Chariot or Throne.[67] *Malkhut*, symbolized by King David,[68] is passive; it is compared to the moon which receives its light from the sun, *Tiferet*. The relationship between *Tiferet* and *Malkhut* is referred to in many different ways. "The wife confers with her husband": the husband is *Tiferet* and the wife is *Malkhut,*[69] or "*Mishpat* and *Ẓedakah* are in complete union," *Mishpat* referring to *Tiferet* and *Ẓedakah* referring to *Malkhut.*[70]

Ibn Shu'eib also points to the symbolism in the *me'orot*, the lights created on the fourth day of Creation, which parallel Judah, the fourth son, who is the father of royalty—*malkhut.*[71] The children of Judah, Zeraḥ and Pereẓ, are also symbols of *Tiferet* and *Malkhut.*[72]

From all of the above we see that ibn Shu'eib possessed extensive, thorough and detailed knowledge of Kabbalah. Here in this chapter we have seen its use in ibn Shu'eib's Scriptural exegesis, and we have seen generally how the symbolism of the Sefirot is resorted to in many different contexts. It is clear that the world of the Sefirot lay at the foundation of ibn Shu'eib's world outlook. As in other areas he is eclectic and, since he is primarily a darshan, not all of his sources harmonize. But what is evident is his distinct talent in using kabbalistic ideas in a popular homiletic framework. As we have said, one of the important accomplishments of the Derashot is the integration of Kabbalah with popular religion by weaving it into the fabric of the popular sermon.

[65]43Aa.

[66]96Aa. Cf. 26Dc.

[67]15Cc; see Zohar II 107a.

[68]5Bc.

[69]24Bb.

[70]23Da. *Mishpat* in the Zohar refers to *Tiferet*—see Zohar III 40b and I 193b. According to ibn Shu'eib, *Mishpat* may refer to *Ḥesed*. See 24Ab where the discussion ends with a note on the connection between Abraham and David.

[71]15Cc. See Zohar III 275b; R. Moses de Leon, *Shoshan Edut* in *Koveẓ al Yad* 8 (1977) 367-368.

[72]15Dc, based on Ramban Gen. 38:29. Ibn Shu'eib interprets Ramban as meaning that Zeraḥ should really be considered the eldest. The *Be'ur Sodot Haramban* explicitly disagrees:

"והוא הבכור בכח עליון" ראיתי מי שמפרש בו ש"הוא" חוזר לזרח הנותן יד...וזה לא נראה למורי נ"ר אלא
"והוא בכור בכח עליון" חוזר לפרץ

See E. Gottlieb, *The Kabbalah in the Writings of R. Baḥya ben Asher*, p. 214, n.1; see too R. Baḥya, Gen. 38:29.

Chapter IX
Evil, Exile and Redemption

1. The Problem of Evil

The problem of evil has been a central preoccupation of religious thought throughout its history. If God is good, how can there be evil in the world that He created? Medieval Jewish philosophy tried to solve the problem along Neoplatonic lines; God is not the source of evil, but rather it is a necessary product of the matter out of which the world is constituted. Evil is only the absence of good; there is no reality to evil—it is only negation.[1]

Ibn Shu'eib categorically rejects this solution. Wholeheartedly he adopts the kabbalistic position, which stresses the reality of evil in the world but assigns its ultimate source to powers within the Godhead which are not intrinsically evil. As in other topics, ibn Shu'eib draws on the writings of kabbalists who preceded him, including the Zohar.[2] Ibn Shu'eib is quite adamant in his rejection of the philosophic interpretation of evil. Quoting Naḥmanides' commentary to Job, ibn Shu'eib says:

> Satan is an angel created to cause evil and to injure, for the word "satan" is derived from *sitnah*, enmity. He is indeed an angel, not "nature" and not "potentia." Similarly, the Angel of Death is an angel created to cause death, for death is not negation *(afisah)* in the living

[1] See H. Blumberg, "Theories of Evil in Medieval Jewish Philosophy," *HUCA* 43 (1972) 149ff. and the literature cited. For the kabbalistic background, see I. Tishby, *M.H.* vol. I, pp. 285-307; G. Scholem, *Pirkei Yesod*, pp. 187-207. See too K. Bland, "Neoplatonic and Gnostic Themes in R. Moses Cordevero's Doctrine of Evil," *Bulletin of the Institute of Jewish Studies* 3 (1975) 103-129.

[2] Although there are no explicit attributions to the Zohar on this topic, he seems to have drawn on the Zohar on this point. See below, n.12.

being, but it is produced by the Angel of Death, who removes man's intellectual faculties, the soul which is not material.[3]

All of this, he says, is in opposition to Maimonides' view that Satan and the Angel of Death are powers inherent in matter itself. The ultimate source of evil, says ibn Shu'eib, is the primeval snake,

for they [Satan, the Angel of Death and the evil impulse] are distinct forces which come from the snake that seduced Eve, and from it comes the power of Samael who is mentioned by the Rabbis of the Talmud.

The snake is the source of the evil spirits called *shedim* as well as the source of impurity in the world.[4] This snake, ibn Shu'eib tells us in a *derashah* dealing with the staff of Moses which turned into a snake, is an evil emanation derived from the primeval snake whose symbols are *paḥad Yiẓḥak* and the Left side.[5] The Left side and Isaac are symbols of a holy power, the Sefirah of *Din* or strict justice.[6] Evil was brought into the world by the snake, who owes its metaphysical origin to the Sefirah of *Din* or justice, a notion which is found among the Gerona kabbalists.[7]

In the same *derashah*, ibn Shu'eib refers to the "names of impurity which come from the snake on the rock, from the Left side, outside the structure."[8] The last phrase is a clear allusion to the doctrine of the Castilian kabbalists such as R. Moses of Burgos who described the powers of evil as a system of the Sefirot outside and parallel to the ten Sefirot of the Godhead itself.[9] The *sitra aḥra*[10] is quite literally "the other side" and is the source of evil, although it may be ultimately derived from *Din*. Concerning the ultimate source of evil, ibn Shu'eib says in another place:

There is a place in the upper spheres to which the performer of *miẓvot* is bound, and this is the meaning of the Rabbinic saying "the reward of a

[3]68Da. Ibn Shu'eib abbreviates Ramban's discussion—see *Kitvei Haramban*, pp. 24-25.

[4]Ibn Shu'eib is emphatic in his assertion that these are three separate forces—against Maimonides' claim that (in ibn Shu'eib's words based on Guide II,6): הכל אחד עושה אלו הפעולות כמו שאמרו עולה ומסטין יורד ומתעה נוטל רשות ונוטל נשמה Derashot 68Db. See too Guide III,22. The personification of evil by the kabbalists is the basis of his insistence on three individual forces. See 22Db: וזהו נחש עלי צור כי כל אלו השדים באים ממנו ומכחו וממנו כח פרעה; and 68Db: מכל זה תדע שטמאתו אינה מצד עצמו כמו שרץ ונבלה אלא מצד הנחש. See too 47Ca and *M.H.* vol. I, pp. 304-307.

[5]22Db. ואמר עלי צור כי הוא מן הצור פחד יצחק צד שמאל

[6]11Ac. אברהם ימין יצחק שמאל זה רחמים וזה דין

[7]G. Scholem, *Kabbalah*, p. 123.

[8]22Dc. ויש מהם בסקילה והוא העושה מעשה על ידי השבעת שמות הטומאה הבאים מהנחש עלי צור מצד שמאל **חוץ לבנין**

[9]See G. Scholem, *Leḥeker Kabbalat R. Yizḥak Hakohen* (Jerusalem 1934), particularly pp. 146-164.

[10]The term itself does not appear in the Derashot.

mizvah is a *mizvah*"—the performer of the *mizvah* is bound to the [supernal] *mizvah* itself, which is the name of the Holy One Blessed Be He, for his soul is bound there. This is the true meaning of the word *mizvah*, as it is derived from *zvt* [bound]. The same applies to transgression, for there is a supernal place to which the defiled poison which emerges from the transgressions performed below passes; that place is called *nehar di nur*. It becomes entangled in the elemental fire and then descends to *Gehinom.*[11]

Now *nehar di nur*—the river of fire—mentioned here by ibn Shu'eib has been identified by some kabbalists as the Sefirah of strict Justice[12] and by others as the emanation of the Left.[13] It thus remains difficult to establish ibn Shu'eib's view concerning the ultimate source of evil.

But whatever the source of evil is, there seems to be no question that evil, or at least the powers that produce it, are a necessary part of creation. This idea is propounded in the Derashot in several places. In one passage, ibn Shu'eib says that Moses could not keep his hands raised continuously during the battle with Amalek because through his hands a Divine influx flows upon all of existence, preventing the "powers of accusation" from acting.[14] Since God did not create anything that is valueless and "it is not proper to eliminate the powers of accusation," Moses would rest his hands occasionally.[15]

In man, the "powers of accusation" and the "dregs of wine" manifest themselves as the *yezer hara'*, the evil inclination. It may indeed mislead, but

[11]86Dc.
כי המצות והעבירות יש בעולם העליון מקום שנקשר בו עושה מצוה, וזהו שכר מצוה מצוה, שנקשר במצוה עצמה שהיא שמו של הקב״ה שהוא תמיד נפשו שם צרורה מלשון צות. וכן בעבירות יש מקום עליוני שחמת טמא למטא בעבירה עובר למעלה באותו מקום שנקרא נהר די נור ומתגלגל ביסוד האש ויורד לגיהנם דכתי׳ עוברי בעמק הבכא וזה נמשך מצד שמאל
See G. Scholem, *Hakabbalah Begeronah*, p. 327; Commentary of R. Ezra to Song of Songs, p. 528.

[12]See, e.g., *Shoshan Sodot* 37a. נהר די נור מ״ה הקשה

[13]G. Scholem, *Leheker Kabbalat R. Yizhak Hakohen*, p. 149. אצילות זה השמאל נרמז סוד נהר די נור אשר בו נדונים כל הבאים להתלבן ולהתברר ולהצטרף במצרף הליבון והטהרה; ibid., p. 150 מאצילות יד המלחמה אשר מתוך ממשלתה מתגלגלין ובאים כל ההפכים והתמורות והקטרוגים והנגעים והחרבן See the quotation from *Sefer Ta'amei Hamizvot B* in A. Altmann, "Lish'eilat Ba'aluto Shel Sefer Ta'amei Hamizvot," *Kiryat Sefer* 40 (1965): אבר מחזיק אבר בהיות האדם מקיים התורה והמצוה נותן חיזוק ואומץ בכל אברי המרכבה כמו שאמרו ז״ל אבר מחזיק אבר Prof. A. Altmann helped clarify some of the terms in this discussion.

[14]26Bb.

[15]Ibid. וכתב החכם ר׳ אברהם בן עזרא כי כשהיה נושא י׳ אצבעותיו היה השפע בא Cf. R. Bahya b. Asher, Exodus 17:12; *Be'ur Sodot Haramban*, end of *Beshalah*; Zohar III 63a; Recanati and *Me'irat Einayim*, ad loc. S. Abramson in his introduction to the Derashot corrects the text to read R. Ezra. E. Gottlieb in his *Hakabbalah Bekhitvei R. Bahya* (p. 39), says that in all the parallel texts this idea is never quoted in the name of R. Ezra.

> as they said [B.R. 9:7] "Behold it is very good" (Gen. 1:31)—this refers to the *yeẓer hara'*, for were it not for the *yeẓer hara'*, a man would not build a house or marry a woman....The *yeẓer hara'* is an important matter and greatly needed by the world.[16]

The copper snake that Moses held up (Num. 21:9) symbolizes the dual nature of the evil *yeẓer*. The snake which generally kills is here being used as a symbol of saving, "just as the *yeẓer* kills and brings life."[17] It is like leaven which when used in excess spoils and destroys.[18] Man can and should use these powers for good.

The powers that can cause evil are not only an anthropological necessity, but a metaphysical one as well. In one homily we are told that Esau, who is the essence of Isaac, i.e., the power of strict Judgment or *Din*, accompanies Jacob in this world because "the wine needs its dregs and wheat its chaff until it becomes ripe."[19] Thus the existence of evil, termed the "dregs of wine," the waste products of *Din*, a possible reference to the Zohar's doctrine on the matter,[20] is necessary for the ultimate perfection of creation, mundane and Divine. Analagous to this is the following:

> They are the impudent ones of the generations from whom stem all the ills that descend upon Israel in every generation. It is on their account that the destruction of the first and second Temples came about. The *mystery of creation required their creation*, the same mystery which required the creation of Satan, the *yeẓer hara'*, the Angel of Death and all the other accusers.[21]

Death too is not necessarily a manifestation of evil. The midrash already proposed that the words ***hinei tov me'od*** in Genesis 1:31, "it was very good," should be read ***hinei tov mot***—"behold death is good."[22] Ibn Shu'eib adds that death enables a person to comprehend matters that he never could while alive, and agrees with the "Wise man who said that death brings ultimate perfection, not like the student who said death is a defect and is bad for man."[23]

[16] 69Ac.

[17] Ibid.

[18] 68Dc. כי השאור בינוני מתקן, וכשהוא יותר מן הראוי מקלקלן וזהו מסודות הבריאה. See 86B,C כוונת הענין שימשול האדם ביצרו כל מה שיוכל להרחיק מן העבירות These are two different ideas: the first, sublimation; the second, harnassing and controlling evil instincts.

[19] 11Aa. ועשו מתמציתו של יצחק וזרע יעקב צריך לעשו עד שיגיעו הימים ויתבשלו הפירות כי היין צריך לשמריו והחטה לקשו עד שיתבשל

[20] Zohar I 148a מגו דתוקפא דטיהרא דיצחק מגו דורדיא דחמרא נפק. See Gottlieb, *Baḥya*, p. 239.

[21] 88Ac.

[22] *Bereshit Rabbah* 9:5.

[23] 86Ca. See Tishby, *M.H.* vol. II, p. 151.

Tum'ah, defilement, is caused by death, ibn Shu'eib adds, only when death is a result of sin, a result of the filth that was injected into Eve by the snake who tempted her.[24] However, those who die by a kiss, that is to say, not as a result of sin, like Moses, Aaron or Miram, engender no defilement.[25]

2. *Galut*: Israel and the Nations of the World

The difficulties, the suffering, the oppression and the burdens of life in exile were a constant reality to medieval Jews; we find this theme expressed repeatedly in their exegesis, their preaching and their ethical works.[26] Ibn Shu'eib's own views on *galut* (exile) and redemption and his attitudes towards non-Jews are built on classical Jewish attitudes but also adumbrate some opinions we find articulated in later centuries. Just as we saw above that, while admitting the reality of evil, he still stresses its ultimate necessity and purposefulness, so does he stress both the reality and the ultimate purposefulness of *galut.*

Galut is a very bitter and oppressive reality for ibn Shu'eib: "the torn olive branch which is in the mouth of the dove is symbolic of our exile and the derision and shame we endure to earn a living."[27] It was the uncertainty of the Jews' political status that soured their experience in thirteenth- and fourteenth-century Spain, despite a relatively sound economic position. Ramban, in Gerona a little earlier, expressed this notion in interpreting the phrase, "Your life shall hang in doubt before you" (Deut. 28:66): "because of our fear in exile among the nations who constantly issue decrees against us"; this despite economic prosperity which is "equal or better to the residents of this country."[28] The psychological burden of this uncertainty was seen as an even greater punishment than economic oppression.

But there were also economic difficulties. The heavy tax burden of which ibn Shu'eib complains[29] was a reality in Tudela and was an added difficulty to the life of the Jew. We know from many sources how heavy and oppressive

[24]Shabbat 146a; Derashot 69Bc; Tishby, *M.H.* vol. II, pp. 149-150.

[25]The very fact that human death engenders *tum'ah* was problematic for ibn Shu'eib. If the human body is a reflection of the Sefirot, how can it result in *tum'ah*? The answer was that it came from the Snake. See 2C:

והודיענו בזה הכתוב מעלת בריאת גופו וצורת איבריו בצלם ובדמות מעלתו גדולה מאוד. ויש ביצירתו ובציור איברינו...עינים נכבדים גדולים

Also 2B הוא עיקר הבריאה כלולה לפי דעת חכמי תורתינו

[26]See, e.g., Radak's response to *galut* in F. Talmage, *David Kimḥi, The Man and the Commentaries* (Cambridge MA 1975), pp. 43-53.

[27]4Dc.

[28]Commentary to Deut. 28:42 (ed. Chavel, p. 474).

[29]9Ba. See Radak to Psalms 26:6.

taxes were in thirteenth- and fourteenth-century Navarre.[30] "Israel's strength almost fails from oppression and suffering."[31]

The reason that Israel is in exile now, says R. Joshua, is the same reason as that of past exiles, the sins of the Jewish people.[32] Since *galut* is retribution for sin, we have no alternative but to accept God's decree and to justify His actions. Just as Jacob our father submitted himself to Esau, so must we submit ourselves to our masters. All the things that befell Jacob, his trials and tribulations, prefigure ours; we should follow his path and suffer the trials just as he did and we act as he did towards his brother when he saw himself in danger. Just as he submitted himself to Esau, addressing him as master, and commanded his messengers to say to Esau "'thus says your servant Jacob':—we too are summoned to subject ourselves in exile to Esau's sons and call them our master."[33]

But while ibn Shu'eib defends the justice of *galut*, he also attempts to see purposefulness in *galut* itself. First of all, he says, it has a purging cathartic effect upon the Jewish people. Suffering purifies and elevates and indeed can bring us closer to God than ease and comfort can.[34] Similarly, it intensifies our commitment and loyalty to Torah. The Torah already hints to the fact that, when the Jews are in exile, amidst suffering and troubles, they hold on to their beliefs and intentions much more strongly than in time of ease.[35]

Secondly, *galut* itself paradoxically demonstrates God's providence:

> Exile and trouble prove our religion! For were it not for the abundance of God's graciousness, neither a memorial nor a remnant would be left of us because of the magnitude of our dispersion and the hatred of the nations for us.[36]

[30]See, e.g., R. Samuel b. Joseph ibn Sasson in *Avnei Shoham* (cited by Y. Baer in *Minḥah Ledavid* [Jerusalem 1935], p. 199): כי גברו מאד המסים והנוגשים אצים, והמס היה לאלפים ולמאות וידל ישואל מאד; Dinur, *Yisrael Bagolah* II, 1, p. 170.

[31]10Ba.

[32]While the reason for this *galut* is obvious—our sins—ibn Shu'eib puzzles over the reason for the first *galut*—to Egypt. One answer he suggests was that it was in order to atone for the accidental sins of the fathers. The other reason, he says, is a *sod*, that is, there is a kabbalistic explanation which he does not spell out. Cf. R. Jacob Anatoli who explains that the purpose of the first *galut* was to prepare Israel to receive the Torah together as they left Egypt. Also, having seen His miracles, Israel would believe in God and His prophets. Thus the first *galut* was not intended as punishment—it was to form Israel into a nation (*Malmad Hatalmidim* [Lyck 1866], *Ẓav*, 96b-97A).

[33]13Da.

[34]97A, 4Db—thus in *Malmad* (above, n.32).

[35]4Db.

[36]37Ca. The awareness of the trials and tribulations of *galut* is a pervasive theme in Jewish literature. Halevi, to whom the quotation in the text is attributed, does discuss

Indeed the very manner of the dispersion is for ibn Shu'eib another proof of God's providence over us during *galut*.

> The descendants of Esau will never wipe us out, for they will do evil with only part of us; while one king issues decrees in his land affecting our money or our bodies, another king pities us and saves the refugees.[37]

Missing is the notion that Israel has a mission in *galut*, which we do find, for example, in ibn Shu'eib's contemporary, R. Baḥya b. Asher:

> There are two reasons for the dispersion, in my opinion; the first was in order for Israel to spread out in all directions among nations who have no understanding, in order to teach them the belief in the existence of God and His providence which flows upon humanity.[38]

The need to find meaning in the trials and tribulations of *galut* and to seek comfort in consolation and redemption made these pervasive themes in Jewish literature. Thus Abraham ibn Daud concludes his history with "the trustworthiness of the Divine consolation."[39] Maimonides too in his *Epistle to Yemen* discusses, as Twersky says, the "phenomenology of persecutions of the Jews, the theory of suffering which is a constant of Jewish reality and the promise of eternity which sustains this reality."[40]

Rabbi Joshua's student, Menaḥem ben Zeraḥ, continues this concern when he attempts to "clear up the great confusion which has entered the hearts of people as a result of the length of the *galut*, for the nations say that the punishment of *galut* has been inflicted upon us because of His hatred of us and that because of His love for the nations He gave them political power."[41]

Fourteenth-century Spain was a time which required a defensive response on the part of Judaism and perhaps even an aggressive attack against

the impact of *galut* on Israel, although not with the same emphasis. In *Cuzari*, II,44, he says

והצרות המוצאות אותנו סבה לתקנת תורתנו ובר הבר ממנו ויציאת הסיגים מתוכינו. [תרגום אבן שמואל:
— אבל המכאובים הבאים עלינו משמשים יסוד לחזוק אמונתינו להזככות הטהורים בתוכינו ולדחיית
הסייגים מקרבנו]

(see also *Cuzari* I,12, II,29-44, IV,21-23).

Halevi speaks here not only of purification as the result of *galut*, perhaps the only positive thing he does see in *galut* (see I. Heinemann, "Temunat hahistoryah shel RYHL," *Zion* 9 (1945) 172, n.4) but also how *galut* testifies to the veracity of God's providence.

See also Rambam, *Mishneh Torah, Issurei Bi'ah*, 14:1.

[37] 13Dc. See also 14Bc.

[38] *Kad Hakemaḥ* in C. Chavel, ed., *Kitvei Rabbenu Baḥya* (Jerusalem 1969), s.v. *ge'ulah* I (p. 115).

[39] G. Cohen, ed., *Sefer Haqabbalah* (Philadelphia 1967), p. 214.

[40] I. Twersky, *A Maimonides Reader* (New York 1972), p. 437. See A. Halkin, ed., *Iggeret Teman*, (New York 1952), pp. 79-81.

[41] Cf. *Ẓedah Laderekh* (Warsaw 1880), pp. 295-298.

Christianity as well. We know for example that Christian preachers would come into the synagogue and preach their sermons to a captive Jewish audience. Thus for example James II of Aragon decreed in 1299 that Raymon Lull was allowed to enter the synagogue and preach. It would not be surprising if in Tudela the situation was similar; and, if so, one would almost certainly expect a response, directly or indirectly, on the part of ibn Shu'eib. And indeed we hear him characterize the Gentile polemic in concise and precise terms:

> All the nations boast of their religions, each one taking pride in his own belief and wisdom and arguing that truth lies with them. Some boast of great wisdom, others take pride in strength and success, thinking that their success is proof of the truth of their religion. Worse—they falsify the works of our Torah, tearing it to shreds. In truth they are but images of men carved in wood or stone.[42]

Ibn Shu'eib responds here to both Christian and Moslem polemics against the Jews. The Christian argument that the success of the Christian religion is a proof of its truth was used repeatedly against the Jews. Similarly the accusation that the Jews falsified the Torah is repeated in Moslem polemics such as the *Silencing of the Jews* by Samu'al al-Maghribi;[43] ibn Shu'eib here makes the same accusation against the Gentiles.

The fact that the Jews were exiled from their land was frequently adduced as a Christian argument to prove God's rejection of the Jews.[44] Ibn Shu'eib reverses that argument, as we saw above, by emphasizing the providential nature of *galut*. One question still remained for ibn Shu'eib: how does one explain our suffering in the face of the undeniable success of the Gentiles? His answer lies in the qualitative difference between Israel and the nations.

> A small stain on an expensive garment makes a greater impression than a large stain on some other garment...a small fly in refined oil is more obvious than a large insect in thick dark oil.[45]

[42]Paris ms. #237, pp. 84D-85A; #238, p. 76.
כי כל האומות כלם מתפארות באמונתם וכל אחד מתפארת באמנתה ובחכמתה וטוענת שעתה האמת. יש מתפאר ברוב חכמה ויש מתפאר בגבורה ובהצלחה וסוברים שהצלחתם אות על אמונת אמתתם ולא עוד אלא שמזייפות דברי תורתנו עם השיריים שעושים בהם. ועל דרך האמת אין דמיונם אצלינו אלא כדמות צורת האדם המציירת באבן או בעץ
The passage is from his *derashah* to *Vayakhel* and is missing from the printed editions.

[43]See *PAAJR* 32 (1964) 33, 53ff.; Rashba, *Ma'amar 'al Yishmael*, in Perles, *R. Salomo*, Hebrew Section, p. 2.

[44]See David Berger, *The Jewish-Christian Debate in the High Middle Ages:* A critical edition of the *Niẓẓaḥon Vetus*, with an introduction, translation and commentary (Philadelphia 1979), text pp. 226-27 and notes as well as notes on p. 270 for parallel sources and arguments.

[45]33Db.

Israel is the beloved son whose father, out of love, disciplines him strictly.[46]

Sometimes, however, the Gentile polemic is absorbed into the Jewish counter-argument. In the following passage, ibn Shu'eib acknowledges the stultifying effects of *galut* upon the Jewish people, following an idea of R. Judah Halevi. But ibn Shu'eib goes beyond Halevi:

> A wise man and his student were walking along, and they found a cross of gold and a human bone. The wise man bent down and took the dry bone while the student took the cross. The wise man kissed the bone and buried it, covering it in fine cloth. The student said to him: "Why did you leave the gold and take the dry bone? Is not the former preferable to the latter?" Answered the wise man: "This bone is worthy of honor and respectful burial for it was once part of a wise and honorable man who possessed wisdom; this cross possesses no qualities whatsoever. It is covered with silver or gold, but its essence is vacuous, always was and always will be. Something which once was of the living and of the wise will return perhaps to its former greatness. Indeed, according to our belief, that dry bone will return to its former state at the time of resurrection.[47]

The parable presents the wide chasm that separates the Gentile and the Jew. Ibn Shu'eib again follows Halevi when he describes the qualitative differences that exist between Jew and Gentile. "Just as God chose humanity over all other living creatures, he chose one nation above all others."[48] Indeed, the idea of Israel preceded creation; the world was created for Israel, which is the essence of humanity.[49] God's love for us is like the love of a father for a beloved son, but the nations of the world are like a despised son; they receive their rewards in this world so that they will not have any merits for the world to come.[50]

The position of the non-Jew is not only metaphysically inferior but in addition his metaphysical source lies in the "left side," as the kabbalists called

[46] 87Dc.

[47] 37Bc. This striking expansion of Halevi's idea of Israel in *galut* as dried out bones is repeated almost verbatim without attribution 200 years later by R. Isaac Caro in *Toldot Yiẓhak* parashat *Vayikra* (Amsterdam 1708), p. 80A. H. H. Ben-Sasson quotes this passage from Caro in his "Galut uge'ulah Be'einav Shel Dor Golei Sefarad," *Sefer Yovel Leyiẓhak Baer* (Jerusalem 1961), p. 219, to demonstrate the impact of the Christian anti-Jewish polemics on the Jews. According to this, the impact predates the expulsion by some two hundred years. See also A. S. Halkin, ed., *Iggeret Teman* (Epistle to Yemen) (New York 1952), pp. 14-15 of Hebrew text.

[48] 66Da.

[49] 94Bb.

[50] 78Aa. See to 48Bb: "The soul of Israel is more sacred than that of the nations of the world."

the source of evil. "When the Lord is pleased with a man's conduct, He may turn his enemies into allies" (Prov. 16:2) R. Akiva expounded: ["His enemies"] refers to the snake.

> ...There are those who say that the snake refers to the Prince [i.e., the guardian angel] of Esau, since it alludes to the primeval snake. And this is the profound meaning of Azazel, as explained in *Pirkei Derabi Eliezer* concerning Samael, who is from the Left. "Evil will come from the North" (Jer. 1:14) also refers to the Prince of Edom. It is for this reason that they write from the left, for their roots and strength are there. Thus they write from left to right for the evil instinct is there.[51]

Empirically as well they are a corrupt people.

> ...We see the nations performing major transgressions. There is not a single one among them who does good. They do not fulfill even one of the seven *mizvot* which they were commanded and they anger God daily.[52]

The feeling towards Gentiles seems to be mutual.

> In this time God does great and awesome things by sustaining us among enemies who hate and utterly detest us, as the wise man said "there is no hatred greater than the hatred of the nations [for Israel]." We loathe and abominate their belief and reject their religion.[53]

Thus a deep hatred towards the Gentiles emerges from ibn Shu'eib, a hatred nourished by mutual antagonism.[54] Kabbalists of ibn Shu'eib's time shared this hostility towards the Gentile world. But ibn Shu'eib did not need Kabbalah to sustain his feelings. There would in any case have been sufficient material in aggadic literature and in the classic medieval thinkers such as Halevi and Maimonides to bolster such attitudes.

[51] 51Db. This passage is a good example of the way ibn Shu'eib assembles midrashic texts from various sources to create a new midrashic entity. The explanation of "enemies" as the "snake" appears a number of times in midrashic literature but never attributed to R. Akiva as ibn Shu'eib attributes it. See, e.g., *Yerushalmi*, Terumot 8:3; *Bereshit Rabbah* 54:1; *Pesikta Derav Kahana*, 11 (Mandelbaum, p. 175).

The interpretation of "enemies" from the verse in Proverbs as referring to the prince of Esau is ibn Shu'eib's own manipulation of a midrashic and Zoharic theme. In the *Tanḥuma (Vayishlaḥ* 8) Samael is identified as the Prince of Esau. The Zohar (I,144b) links this identification with the verse from Proverbs. Ibn Shu'eib turns it around, by linking the verse directly with the Prince of Esau which in turn alludes to the primeval serpent and from there to Azazel and then to Samael.

See too *Pirkei Derabi Eliezer*, chs. 13, 14 and Ramban, Leviticus 16:8.

[52] 33Db.

[53] 37Cb.

[54] To be sure, it is tempered by some pragmatism. See 85Cb on the prohibition against lying and misleading Gentiles.

3. Redemption

For ibn Shu'eib, we have said, *galut* displays the providential character of Jewish history. But beyond that, its existence is also an assurance that we will be redeemed.

> Our very dispersion is proof of the veracity of the promises. As all the exiles and all the curses have come about, so are we assured that all the great predictions and promises will likewise be fulfilled.[55]

Galut prepares us for the rewards of wisdom, prophecy and political power in Messianic times and great reward in the world to come.[56] Subjugation will be rewarded by greatness: just as, in aggadic tradition, the sun was rewarded for its modesty when challenged by the moon by being made the sole ruler of the day.[57]

There is no indication in the Derashot of active Messianic expectation. Only once does ibn Shu'eib cite a Messianic date: it was about 150 years away.[58] The Messianic coming is never spoken of in imminent terms; rather, we find pious expressions of hope for the coming of messianic times.[59] But that hope is ever present, and, indeed, as we have noticed, ibn Shu'eib ends each sermon with a formulaic expression of messianic expectation or hope.[60]

And though the expression was formulaic, the hope was not. Eschatologically, ibn Shu'eib believed, not only will the Jews be returned to their land and given political power; even the *yeẓer hara'* and death itself will disappear. "The goal of creation is to live forever and to be like the angels without an evil *yeẓer.*"[61] The very source of defilement, *tum'ah*, will disappear, for the filth which the Snake instilled in the world will be cut off, and all will be purified, "as it is said, the pig *(ḥazir)* will return *(yaḥzor)* to Israel."[62] We have also noted above the eschatological changes that ibn Shu'eib expects in the nature and meaning of the Torah itself, and the levels of meaning, now hidden, that will then be revealed.[63]

[55]94Bb. The source is Makkot 4a, which ibn Shu'eib quotes and interprets in this manner on p. 87D.

[56]14B-C.

[57]62Dc.

[58]43Dc. See A. H. Silver, *A History of Messianic Speculation in Israel* (Boston 1959), p. 98. My thanks to Dr. Marc Saperstein for this reference.

[59]See 59Ba, where Messianic times are described as the times of intellectual and moral perfection.

[60]See above, ch. II, p. 29.

[61]3Aa.

[62]75C. For further eschatological themes in ibn Shu'eib, see 34Ab on the elimination of the need for the red heifer, and 42A on the restoration of the world to its original pristine state. Cf. the discussion of *shemittot*, above, pp. 164-165.

[63]See above, pp. 163-164.

Such hopes sustained ibn Shu'eib's faith, and with them he hoped to sustain the faith of his listeners and readers. The exile may be long and bitter, he says, and its oppression may weigh on us heavily, but the end is always in sight; for all things return to their source, and the source of all things is in God.

Once again, we see that ibn Shu'eib develops aggadic themes within a worldview shaped by Kabbalah; its presentation in a manner that is popular and easily accessible is one of the great achievements of the Derashot.

Appendix
The Derashot and Modern Scholarship

The *Derashot 'al Hatorah*, although not infrequently cited and utilized by scholars during the last century, has not yet been the subject of a thorough analysis.

The only early treatment of ibn Shu'eib and the Derashot is by Alfredo Freimann who included in his article on Menaḥem b. Zeraḥ a short, perceptive and accurate sketch of the Derashot. Freimann correctly identified ibn Shu'eib's residence, listed many of his sources, and pointed to some of the salient features of the Derashot: their use of philosophic and kabbalistic sources, their frequent references to halakhot and minhagim, their wide range of sources and the social reality which they reflect.[1]

Neither of the two major histories of the Jews in Spain, Neumann's or Baer's, uses the Derashot as a historical source. Neither have students of the *derashah* literature dwelt on ibn Shu'eib's Derashot. In his classic work on the history of the Jewish sermon, L. Zunz dealt in one chapter with the early medieval *derashah*. His emphasis was more on the institution of the *derashah* than on its content. In summary fashion he presents a composite picture of 500 years of medieval *derashot* in rich bibliographical detail; but, as in any composite picture encompassing such a large chronological and geographical span, individual features are blurred.[2] In his fleeting reference to ibn Shu'eib's Derashot he classifies them as exegetical.[3]

Two important works on the *derashah* literature do not deal with ibn Shu'eib at all. The first is Israel Bettan's *Studies in Jewish Preaching, Middle Ages,*[4] in which he proposed "to reproduce the salient features of the sermon by portraying the character, the aims and achievements of the most important figures in the pulpit in the Middle Ages."[5] With the savor and zest of a preacher, Bettan characterizes seven important darshanim—R. Jacob Anatoli, R. Baḥya b. Asher, R. Isaac Arama, R. Judah Moscato, R. Azariah Figo, and R. Jonathan Eybeshitz—and summarizes their important ideas.

[1]Freimann, "Menaḥem b. Zeraḥ," pp. 149-152.

[2]*Haderashot Beyisra'el*, chapter 22, "The Derashah in the First Rabbinic Period."

[3]Ibid., pp. 196 and 518 n.47; see also p. 519 n.59.

[4]Cincinnati 1939.

[5]Bettan, preface p. x.

The book is prefaced by a useful survey of preaching in Talmudic times in which he discusses homiletic methodology, that is, the types of texts used for homilies and the various kinds of illustrative material, and emphasizes as well the underlying spirituality of rabbinic sermons. Although he did not treat the *Derashot* of ibn Shu'eib, certain of his insights into other preachers hold good for ibn Shu'eib as well.

The other is Prof. Joseph Dan's *Sifrut Hamusar Vehaderush,*[6] a survey of ethical and homiletic literature which is particularly valuable because it pays attention to the literary and aesthetic side of homiletic literature. Especially important is chapter two, which discusses the tension between the aesthetic and didactic elements in the *derashah*. Dan claims that, when the ideological tension between preacher and audience is great—when the darshan is introducing new ideas which might meet with some resistance from the audience—the didactic element in the *derashah* is greater than aesthetic elements such as rhetorical beauty and homiletic devices. When there is "cultural intimacy" between preacher and audience, the aesthetic element predominates.[7] While this may be true of certain darshanim, such as R. Jacob Anatoli on the one hand and some Renaissance preachers such as R. Judah Messer Leon on the other, the thesis is yet to be conclusively demonstated. In ibn Shu'eib, for example, there appears to be a careful balance between aesthetic and didactic. As we saw above (chapter II), ibn Shu'eib carefully cultivates the aesthetic aspect. On the other hand, the didactic element is also strong, and it is difficult to determine the degree of cultural intimacy that exists.

To complete the picture of preaching in medieval Spain, we are still in need of analyses of R. Nissim Gerondi,[8] R. Joseph ibn Shem Tov, R. Shem Tov b. Joseph ibn Shem Tov, and R. Joel ibn Shu'eib. The *'Ein Hakoreh* of R. Joseph is the first *ars praedicandi* in Hebrew literature, and the *'Olat Shabbat* of R. Joel ibn Shu'eib contains many important comments on the method and theory of the Hebrew sermon.[9]

[6]Jerusalem 1975.

[7]See pp. 26-46. The chapter originally appeared in *Hasifrut* 3 (Sept. 1972) 558-567.

[8]The bibliographical doubts concerning the *Derashot Haran* to which Dan alludes (p. 276 n.8) seem to have been adequately removed by Leon Feldman in his edition of those *Derashot* (Jerusalem 1974), introduction pp. 5-8, which shows convincingly that the author is R. Nissim b. Reuven Gerondi, teacher of R. Hasdai Crescas.

[9]See *'Olat Shabbat* (Venice 1577), p. 1b. The *'Ein Hakore* has never been printed.

Two other books, popular in nature, do deal with ibn Shu'eib. S. Glicksberg in *Haderashah Beyisrael*(Tel Aviv 1944) has a brief bibliographical reference to ibn Shu'eib (p. 112). Glicksberg expanded the notion of the *derashah* to include almost any non-halakhic work and thereby lessened the usefulness of his survey.

H. R. Rabinowitz, who was himself a rabbi and preacher in Iowa, shows a keen appreciation for the popular nature of ibn Shu'eib's Derashot, and in his *Diyokna'ot*

Many scholars in other areas, however, have utilized the Derashot extensively, and two of the most important are Louis Ginzberg and Gershom Scholem.

The Derashot are a rich source of midrashim, and Louis Ginzberg could and did mine the *Derashot 'al Hatorah* for its wealth of unknown midrashic traditions, as well as for variations of more familiar midrashim. In virtually every *derashah* Ginzberg found important and unique midrashic traditions extending over the entire range of biblical narrative, from *Bereshit* until the end of *Ketuvim*. But since Ginzberg was interested primarily in aggadot related to the biblical narrative, he did not deal with the many other midrashim cited by ibn Shu'eib.[10]

Gershom Scholem repeatedly discussed bibliographical problems related to ibn Shu'eib and combed the Derashot for its kabbalistic traditions. The bibliographical problems concern the authorship of the *Be'ur Sodot Haramban*, attributed in its printed edition to ibn Shu'eib's student R. Meir ibn Sahula. In Scholem's earlier writings, he cited manuscripts that attributed the *Be'ur* to ibn Shu'eib and pointed to citations in kabbalistic literature affirming that attribution.[11] Later Scholem suggested that the printed *Be'ur* is ibn Sahula's reworking of ibn Shu'eib's original commentary.[12] The style of the Derashot is certainly quite different from that of the *Be'ur*, but that does not preclude common authorship. Thus there remains a strong possibility that ibn Shu'eib also wrote the *Be'ur* on the Ramban.

The kabbalistic traditions in the Derashot themselves have been cited by Scholem in many of his books and articles.[13]

shel Darshanim (Jerusalem 1967) he presents a brief survey of interesting interpretations of verses by ibn Shu'eib. The book is lacking, however, a critical historical perspective (Joseph Albo is cited as a source for ibn Shu'eib) and does not employ any coherent analytic categories, either in the structure of the book or in the analysis of the darshanim.

[10]The Index volume to the *Legends of the Jews* (vol. 7) contains a list of most of Ginzberg's citations from ibn Shu'eib, except in the few cases where Ginzberg himself did not indicate the page in the Derashot to which he was referring.

[11]See, e.g., "Kabbalat R. Ya'akov Verabi Yiẓhak," *Mada'ei Hayahadut* 2 (1927) 98 (reprinted separately, Jerusalem 1927, p 36); *Kiryat Sefer* 5 (1928) 264-265; *Kitvei Yad Bekabbalah* (Jerusalem 1930), p. 147; *Leḥeker Kabbalat R. Yizḥak Hakohen* (Jerusalem 1934), p. 98, reprinted from *Tarbiz* 4 (1933) 263; *Kiryat Sefer* 5 (1928) 389.

[12]See "Levush Haneshamot Veḥalukka Derabbanan," *Tarbiz* 24 (1955) 294 and n.13. (Cf. his *Hakabbalah Bigeronah* [Jerusalem 1964], p. 80.) See also E. Gottlieb, *The Kabbalah in the Writings of R. Baḥya*, p. 214 n.1, who cites some discrepancies between the Derashot and the *Be'ur*, and S.Abramson in the introduction to the Derashot (p. 41), who tends to believe that ibn Sahula authored the *Be'ur*. Dr. Moshe Idel informs me that he is preparing a study on this topic.

[13]See, e.g., *Reshit Hakabbalah* (Jerusalem 1948), p. 189; *On the Kabbalah and its Symbolism* (New York 1965), p. 81; *Jewish Gnosticism Merkabah Mysticism and*

Many other scholars have utilized the Derashot. Among them were A. Berliner, who collected the comments of R. Hananel cited by ibn Shu'eib;[14] J. Lauterbach in his article on *Tashlikh*;[15] L. Silverman on customs of *Sefirat Ha'omer*;[16] S. Spiegel in his "Me'agadot Ha'akedah";[17] H. G. Enelow in his edition of *Menorat Hama'or*;[18] A. Shohat in his edition of *Shevet Yehudah*;[19] S. Lieberman in his essay on *Shir Hashirim*, in the *Tosefta ki-Feshutah* and in the second edition of *Sheki'in*;[20] A. Altmann in his comprehensive survey of the Delphic Maxim, where he introduced ibn Shu'eib's description of the body of man as created in the image of the Ten Sefirot;[21] I. Twersky, and others.[22]

The most important contemporary study of ibn Shu'eib's Derashot is S. Abramson's erudite introduction to the 1969 reprint of the Cracow edition of the Derashot. Abramson's study, which as he says was not intended to be exhaustive, is nonetheless a comprehensive and wide-ranging study of ibn Shu'eib's methodology and primarily of his sources and subsequent influence. Some of the important aspects of the Derashot to which Abramson points are the variety of sources ibn Shu'eib uses—Abramson identifies many obscure sources for passages in the Derashot, such as those from the Zohar, Ritva, R. Ezra, and various Midrashim—his integration of source material and commentary and his widespread influence; Abramson, wih his customary breadth, lists many citations of ibn Shu'eib in later literature. Abramson also includes a brief textual comparison between the Constantinople and the Cracow editions.

Talmudic Tradition (New York 1965), p. 68 n.12; "Hakarat Panim Vesidrei Sirtutin," *Sefer Hayovel Lesimḥah Assaf* (Jerusalem 1953) 468-469.

14 *Migdal Ḥananel* (Berlin 1876), pp. 25-42; see now C. Chavel, ed., *Perushei Rabbenu Ḥananel 'al Hatorah* (Jerusalem 1972).

15 Jacob Z. Lauterbach, *Rabbinical Essays* (Cincinnati 1951), pp. 351 and 369.

16 *HUCA* 22 (1949) 233.

17 *A. Marx Jubilee Volume* (New York 1950), pp. 473, 485, 495.

18 Israel Al-Nakawa, *Menorat Hama'or*, ed. H. G. Enelow (New York 1929-32), throughout the work.

19 Solomon ibn Verga, *Shevet Yehudah* (Jerusalem 1947), pp. 172-174. R. David G. Shapiro brought these references to my attention.

20 At the end of G. Scholem, *Jewish Gnosticism*; *Tosefta Kifshutah*, see discussion above, ch. V, n.54; S. Lieberman, *Sheki'in* (Jerusalem 1970), p. 102.

21 A. Altmann, ed., *Biblical and Other Studies* (Cambridge MA 1963), pp. 221-222.

22 E.g., *Rabad of Posquières* (Cambridge MA 1962), pp. 111 and 269 n.32. Some of the others are: A. Haberman in his edition of Falaqera's *Iggeret Hamusar, Koveẓ 'al Kad*, n.s. 1 (Jerusalem 1936), p. 59 n.11; I. Abrahams, *Hebrew Ethical Wills* (Philadelphia 1926), p. 76 n.67; A. Halkin, "The Medieval Attitude Toward Hebrew," *Biblical and Other Studies*, p. 241; D. Loewinger, *Sefunot* 7 (1963) 11; M. Halamish, *Sefer Hashanah Lebar Ilan* 13 (1976) 219.

A complete integrative treatment of ibn Shu'eib as a darshan, popularizer and thinker remains a desideratum which this study will, I hope, begin to fill.

GLOSSARY

aggadah—non-legal portions of Rabbinic literature
Aḥaronim—halakhic authorities after the fifteenth century
Berakah—blessing
darshan—preacher
derashah (pl. *derashot*)—sermon
devekut—cleaving to God
Din—strict justice; one of the ten *Sefirot*
halakhah(pl. *halakhot*)—Jewish law
ḥerem—an edict of excommunication
ḥesed—lovingkindness; one of the ten *Sefirot*
ḥukkim—statutes
kavannah—proper intention during prayer of fulfilling a *miẓvah*
Malkhut—kingdom; the last of the ten *Sefirot*
minhag (pl. *minhagim*)—custom
miẓvah (pl. *miẓvot*)—commandment
niddah—menstruant
parashah (pl. *parshiyot*)—pericopes of the Torah read in the weekly Sabbath service
Rishonim—halakhic authorities from the tenth to the fifteenth centuries
Sefirot—the ten aspects of the Divinity, according to the Kabbalah
Shekhinah—the indwelling presence of God, sometimes identified with *Malkhut*
sikhliot—rational
ta'amei hamiẓvot—reasons for the commandments
takkanah (pl. *takkanot*)—communal ordinances
tume'ah—ritual defilement
yeẓer, yeẓer hara'—man's evil inclination

BIBLIOGRAPHY

Primary Sources

Aaron Hakohen of Lunel. *Orḥot Ḥayyim* Jerusalem 1955.

Abarbanel, Isaac. *Commentary on the Torah*, 3 vols. Jerusalem 1964.

Abba Mari b. Moses of Lunel. *Minḥat Kena'ot*. Pressburg 1838.

Abraham b. David of Posquières (Rabad). *Ba'alei Hanefesh*, ed. Y. Kafaḥ. Jerusalem 1964.

-----. *Derashah Lerosh Hashanah*, ed A. Shishah Halevy. London 1955.

Abraham b. Moses Maimonides. "Ma'amar 'al odot Derashot Ḥazal" in R. Margaliyot, ed., *Milḥamot Hashem*. Jerusalem 1953.

Abraham b. Nathan Hayarḥi. *Sefer Hamanhig*, ed. Y. Raphael. Jerusalem 1978.

Abraham ibn Daud. *Emunah Ramah*. Frankfurt am Main 1853; repr. Jerusalem 1967.

-----. *Sefer Hakaballah*, ed. G. D. Cohen. Philadelphia 1967.

Abraham ibn Ezra. *Commentary on the Torah*, in standard editions of *Mikra'ot Gedolot.*

Abudraham, David b. Joseph. *Perush Haberakhot Vehatefilot Abudraham Hashalem.* Jerusalem 1963.

Abulafia, Abraham. "Letter to R. Judah Salmon" in A. Jellinek, ed., *Ginzei Ḥokhmat Hakabbalah*. Leipzig 1853.

Ahai Ga'on. *She'iltot Derav Aḥai Ga'on*, 3 vols. Jerusalem 1961.

Ahima'az b. Paltiel. *Megilat Ahima'aẓ*, ed. B. Klar. Jerusalem 1944.

Alami, Solomon. *Iggeret Hamusar*, ed. A. Haberman. Jerusalem 1946.

Aldabi, Meir. *Shevilei Emunah*. Warsaw 1887.

Alharizi, Judah. *Taḥkemoni.* Warsaw 1889.

Almosnino, Moses. *Me'ameẓ Koaḥ.* Venice 1588.

Anatoli, Jacob. *Malmad Hatalmidim.* Lyck 1866.

Aquinas, Thomas. *On the Governance of Rulers.* New York 1938.

Asher b. Yehiel. *Halakhot*, in standard editions of the Talmud.

Azriel b. Menaḥem. *Perush Ha'agadot Lerabi Azri'el*, ed. I. Tishby. Jerusalem 1945.

Baḥya b. Asher. *Be'ur 'al Hatorah*, 3 vols., ed. C. Chavel. Jerusalem 1966-1968.

-----. *Kad Hakemaḥ*, in *Kitvei Rabbenu Baḥya*, ed. C. Chavel. Jerusalem 1969.

-----. Commentary to *Pirkei Avot*, in *Kitvei Rabbenu Baḥya*, ed. C. Chavel. Jerusalem 1969.

-----. *Shulḥan Shel Arba'*, in *Kitvei Rabbenu Baḥya*, ed. C. Chavel. Jerusalem 1969.

Baḥya ibn Pakuda. *Ḥovot Halevavot*, trans. Judah ibn Tibbon, ed. A. Zifroni. Tel Aviv n.d. English trans. M. Hyamson. Jerusalem 1965.

Benjamin of Tudela. *Mas'ot Binyamin*. London 1907.

Be'ur Sodot Haramban. Reprint New York 1969.

Caspi, Joseph. "Guide to Knowledge" in I. Abrahams, *Hebrew Ethical Wills*, pp. 127-161. Philadelphia 1926.

-----. "Maẓref Lekesef" in *Mishneh Kessef*, vol. 2. Cracow 1906.

David b. Solomon ibn Abi Zimra. *Meẓudat David*. Israel 1964.

David Estillia. "Kiryat Sefer" in A. Neubauer, *Medieval Jewish Chronicles*. Oxford 1887; reprint Jerusalem 1967.

Ezra b. Solomon. "Commentary to Song of Songs" in C. Chavel, *Kitvei Haramban*, vol. 2, pp. 423-548. Jerusalem 1963.

Gikitilia, Joseph. *Sha'arei Orah*, 2 vols., ed. Y. Ben Shlomo. Jerusalem 1970.

Hame'iri, R. Menaḥem. *Beit Habeḥirah* on various tractates of Talmud.

Ḥananel, Rabbeinu. *Perushei Rabbenu Ḥananel 'al Hatorah*, ed. C. Chavel. Jerusalem 1972.

Ḥayyim b. Samuel b. David of Tudela. *Ẓeror Haḥayyim*, ed. Samuel Ḥagai Yerushalmi. Jerusalem 1966.

Hillel of Verona. *Sefer Tagmulei Hanefesh*, ed. J. B. Sermonetta. Jerusalem 1981.

"Iggeret Hakodesh" in C. Chavel, ed., *Kitvei Haramban*. Jerusalem 1963.

Isaac b. Sheshet (Rivash). *She'elot Uteshuvot Bar Sheshet.* Vilna 1878.

Isaac of Acco. *Me'irat 'Einayim*, ed. C. Erlanger. Jerusalem 1975.

Isaac ibn Sahula. *Meshal Hakadmoni*, ed. I. Zamora. Tel Aviv 1953.

Israel ibn al-Nakawa. *Menorat Hama'or*, 4 vols., ed. H. G. Enelow. New York 1929-1932.

Jacob b. Asher. *Arba' Turim*. Various editions.

Jacob b. Sheshet. *Sefer Meshiv Devarim Nekhoḥim*, ed. G. Vajda. Jerusalem 1968.

-----. "Sha'ar Hashamayim" in I. Blumenfeld, *Oẓar Neḥmad*, vol III. Vienna 1860.

Jehiel of Paris. "Vikuaḥ R. Yeḥi'el Mipariz" in J. Eisenstein, ed., *Oẓar Vikuḥim*. Repr. Israel 1964.

Joel ibn Shu'eib. *Commentary to Lamentations.* Venice 1611; photocopy Israel 1971.

-----. *'Olat Shabbat*. Venice 1577.

Jonah b. Abraham of Gerona. *Sha'arei Teshuvah.* Jerusalem 1967.

-----. Commentary on Proverbs. Tel Aviv 1963.

-----. *Sha'arei Ha'avodah*. Bnei Brak 1920.

Joseph ibn Shem Tov. *Ein Hakorei*. Small selection in A. Jellinek, *Kuntres Hamafte'aḥ*. Vienna 1881. Full text in Bodleian Hebrew ms. 350.

Joshua Halorki. "Iggeret Yehoshu'a Halorki" in J. Eisenstein, ed., *Oẓar Vikuḥim*. Israel 1969.

Joshua ibn Shu'eib. *Sefer Derashot 'al Hatorah*. Facsimile of Cracow edition of 1573 with introduction by Shraga Abramson, Jerusalem 1969. Constantinople 1523.

Judah of Barcelona. *Perush Sefer Yeẓirah*. Berlin 1885.

Judah b. Asher. *Zikhron Yehudah*, ed. J. Rosenberg. Berlin 1846; reprint Jerusalem 1968.

Judah Halevi. *Cuzari*. Hebrew trans. Judah ibn Tibbon, ed. A. Zifroni, Israel 1964. Hebrew trans. Yehuda Even Shmuel, Tel Aviv 1972.

Kalonymus b. Kalonymus. *Even Boḥan*, ed. A. Haberman. Tel Aviv 1956.

Kanfanton, Isaac. *Darkhei Hagemarah*. Petaḥ Tikvah n.d.

Karo, Isaac. *Toldot Yiẓhak*. Amsterdam, 1708.

Karo, Joseph. *Shulḥan Arukh*. Standard editions with commentaries.

-----. *Beit Yosef*. Standard editions of *Turim*.

Kimḥi, David. *Perush*. Various editions of the Hebrew Bible.

Levi b. Gershon (Ralbag, Gersonides). *Milḥamot Hashem*. Leipzig 1866.

Ma'arekhet Ha'elohut. Mantua 1558; photoprint Jerusalem 1963.

Maimonides (Moses b. Maimon, Rambam). *Iggeret Teiman*, ed. A. Halkin. New York 1952.

-----. *Iggerot Harambam*. Leipzig 1859.

-----. *Mishneh Torah*. Standard editions.

-----. *Moreh Nevukhim*. Standard editions with commentaries. Hebrew trans. Judah ibn Tibbon. English trans. S. Pines, Chicago 1963.

-----. *Shemonah Perakim*. Standard editions of the Talmud.

Meir ibn Gabbai. *'Avodat Hakodesh*. Venice 1612.

Mekhilta Derabi Yishma'el. Eds. H. Horovitz, I. Rabin. Jerusalem 1970.

Menaḥem b. Zeraḥ. *Ẓedah Laderekh*. Warsaw 1889.

Menaḥem Recanati. *Perush Rabbenu Menaḥem Recanati*. Jerusalem 1961.

-----. *Sefer Ta'amei Hamiẓvot*, ed. S. Lieberman. London 1962.

Midrash Rabbah. 2 vols., Vilna 1887. Ed. M. A. Mirkin, 10 vols., Tel Aviv 1961.

Moses b. Naḥman (Naḥmanides, Ramban). *Kitvei Haramban*, 2 vols., ed. C. Chavel. Jerusalem 1964.

-----. *Perushei Hatorah*, ed. C. Chavel. Jerusalem 1959.

-----. "Tashlum Derashat Haramban Torat Hashem Temimah," ed. E. Kupfer, *Tarbiz* 40 (1970) 64-83.

Moses de Leon. *Nefesh Haḥakhama*. Basle 1608; Jerusalem 1969.

-----. *Shekel Hakodesh*. London 1911; photoreprint Jerusalem 1969.

-----. "Shoshan 'Edut," ed. G. Scholem, *Koveẓ 'al Yad* 18 (1977) 330-370.

Moses Isserles (Rama). *Torot Ha'olah*. Tel Aviv n.d.

Moses Taku. "Ketav Tamim," ed. R. Kircheim, *Oẓar Neḥmad* 3 (1860) 54-99.
Nissim b. Reuben Gerondi. *Derashot Haran*, ed. L. Feldman. Jerusalem 1974.
Polikar, Isaac. "Viku'aḥ Hatorani 'im Hapilosoph" in *Ta'am Zekenim.* Frankfurt 1855.
-----. *'Ezer Hadat*, ed. G. Belasco. London n.d.; repr. Israel 1970.
Rashi (Solomon b. Isaac). Commentary to the Talmud. Standard editions of the Talmud.
Rieti, Moses. *Miḳdash Me'at.* Vienna 1851.
Samu'al Al-Maghribi. *Silencing the Jews*, ed. and trans. Moshe Pearlman. *Proceedings of the American Academy for Jewish Research*, vol. 32 (1964).
Seder Eliyahu Zuta, ed. M. Ish Shalom. Vienna 1904.
Sefer Habahir, ed. R. Margaliyot. Jerusalem 1951.
Sefer Haḥinukh, ed. C. Chavel. Jerusalem 1960.
Sefer Hapeliah. Korets 1784; repr. Israel n.d.
Sefer Ḥasidim, ed. J. Wistinetzky. Frankfurt 1924; photoprint Jerusalem 1969.
Sefer Yeẓirah. Jerusalem 1965.
Shem Tov ibn Ga'on. "Keter Shem Tov" in Judah Coriat, ed., *Ma'or Vashemesh.* Leghorn 1839.
Shem Tov ibn Shem Tov. *Sefer Ha'emunot.* Ferrara 1556; repr. Westmead, England 1969.
Sifra Devei Rav, with commentaries of Rabad and Samson of Sens. Jerusalem 1959.
Sifre on Deuteronomy, ed. L. Finkelstein. New York 1969.
Solomon b. Abraham ibn Adret (Rashba). *Ḥiddushei Aggadot*, ed. Sh. M. Weinberger. Jerusalem 1966.
-----. *Ḥiddushim.* Various tractates of the Talmud.
-----. "Ma'amar 'al Yishma'el," ed. J. Perles in *R. Salomo b. Abraham b. Adereth. Sein Leben und seine Schriften.* Breslau 1863.
-----. "Commentary to the Aggadot—Nedarim," ed. L. A. Feldman in A. Tarakower, ed., *Hagut 'Ivrit Ba'amerika*, vol. I. Tel Aviv 1972.
-----. "Letter Concerning Ta'amei Hamiẓvot," in A. Frumkin, ed., *Siddur R. Amram Ga'on.* Jerusalem 1912, pp. 78-80.
-----. *Responsa*, 7 vols. B'nei Brak, Tel Aviv, Jerusalem 1965-70.
Tikunei Zohar, ed. R. Margaliyot. Tel Aviv 1949.
Todros Abulafia. *Oẓar Hakavod.* Warsaw 1879.
-----. "Oẓar Hakavod to Ketubot," ed. L. Feldman in *Salo Baron Jubilee Volume*, Hebrew section, pp. 297-317. Jerusalem 1974.
Yeruḥam b. Meshullam. *Sefer Mesharim.* Venice 1553; reprint Israel 1975.
Yom Tov b. Abraham of Seville (Ritva). *Ḥiddushim—Sukah.* Tel Aviv 1958.
-----. "Hilkhot Berakhot" in M. Blau, ed., *Kitvei Haritva.* New York 1963.
-----. *Sefer Hazikaron*, ed. Kalman Kahana. Jerusalem 1956.
-----. *She'elot Uteshuvot*, ed. J. Kafah. Jerusalem 1959.

Zacuto, Abraham. *Sefer Yuḥasin Hashalem*, ed. Z. Filipowski. Frankfort 1857.

Zohar, 3 vols., ed. R. Margaliyot. Jerusalem 1964.

Secondary Works

Abramson, Shraga. Introduction to Facsimile of the Cracow 1573 edition of *Sefer Derashot 'al Hatorah* of Rabbi Joshua ibn Shu'eib. Jerusalem 1969.

-----. "Ma'amar Ḥazal Uferusho," *Molad* 27 (1971) 421-429.

-----. "Mafteḥot Litshuvot Hage'onim," *Wolfson Jubilee Volume*, Hebrew section, pp. 1-24. Jerusalem 1965.

Altmann, Alexander. "The Delphic Maxim in Medieval Islam and Judaism," in A. Altmann, ed., *Biblical and Other Studies* (Cambridge MA 1963), pp. 196-232.

-----. "Lishe'elat Ba'aluto shel Sefer Ta'amei Hamiẓvot," *Kiryat Sefer* 40 (1965) 256-276, 405-412.

Appel, Gersion. *A Philosophy of Miẓvot*. New York 1975.

Aptowitzer, A. "Beit Hamikdash Shel Ma'alah 'al pi Ha'agadah," *Tarbiz* 2 (1931) 137-153, 257-287.

Assis, Yom Tov. "The Jews of Aragon under James II." Unpublished Ph.D. thesis, Hebrew University, 1981.

Baer, Yizhak (Fritz). *Die Juden im Christlichen Spanien*, 2 vols. Berlin 1936.

-----. "Hareka' Hahistori shel Hara'ya Mehemna," *Zion* 5 (1940) 1-44.

-----. "Sefarim Umekorot Ḥadashim Letoldot Hayehudim Bisefarad," *Dvir* 2 (1923) 310-321.

-----. "Sefer Minḥat Kena'ot shel Avner Miburgos," *Tarbiz* 2 (1940) 188-206.

-----. "Seridim Mimeshorerei Kastilia Beme'ah Ha-14," *Minḥah Ledavid* (Jerusalem 1935), pp. 197-204.

-----. *Toldot Hayehudim Bisfarad Hanoẓrit*, 2nd ed. Tel Aviv 1959. English trans.: *A History of the Jews in Christian Spain*, 2 vols. Philadelphia 1961-65.

-----. "Torat Hakabbalah Bemishnato Hakristologit shel Avner Miburgos," in H. Schirmann, ed., *Sefer Hayovel Likhvod Gershom Scholem* (Jerusalem 1958), pp. 152-163.

Baron, Salo W. *Social and Religious History of the Jews*, 16 vols. 1952-1976.

-----. *The Jewish Community*, 3 vols. Philadelphia 1942.

Beinart, Haim. "Demutah Shel Haḥaẓranut Hayehudit Bisfarad Hanoẓrit," *Elites and Leading Groups* (Jerusalem 1966), pp. 55-71.

-----. "Hispano Jewish Society," *Journal of World History* 11 (1968) 226-237.

Ben-Sasson, Hayyim Hillel. "The Distribution of Wealth and Intellectual Abilities According to Ashkenazi Hasidim," (Hebrew), *Zion* 35 (1970) 61-79.

-----. "Galut Uge'ulah Be'einav Shel Dor Golei Sefarad," *Sefer Yovel Leyiẓḥak Baer* Jerusalem 1961), pp. 216-227.

-----. *Hakehillah Hayehudit Biyemei Habeinayim*. Jerusalem 1976.

-----. *Perakim Letoldot Hayehudim Biyemei Habeinayim*. Tel Aviv 1958.
-----. "Yiḥud 'Am Yisrael Livnei ha-Me'ah ha-12," *Perakim* 2 (1974) 145-218.
Bettan, Israel. *Studies in Jewish Preaching, Middle Ages*. Cincinnati 1939.
Blidstein, Gerald. "On Political Structures—Four Medieval Comments," *Journal of Jewish Sociology* 22 (1980) 47-58.
Bonebakker, S. A. "Aspects of the History of Literary Rhetoric and Poetics in Arabic Literature," *Viator* 1 (1970) 75-96.
Burke, Peter. *Popular Culture in Early Modern Europe.* New York 1978.
Carlyle, A. J. *Medieval Political Theory*, vol. 3. New York 1950.
Curtius, E. R. *European Literature in the Latin Middle Ages.* New York 1953.
Dan, Yosef. *Sifrut Hamussar Vehadrush.* Jerusalem 1975.
-----. Review of *Recherches sur la philosophie et la Kabbale* by G. Vajda, *Kiryat Sefer* 39 (1963) 341-344.
----- and Tishby, I. *Mivḥar Sifrut Hamussar*. Jerusalem 1970.
Deyermond, A. D. *A Literary History of Spain: The Middle Ages.* London 1971.
Dinur, Ben Zion. *Yisrael Bagolah*, 10 vols., 2nd ed. Tel Aviv-Jerusalem 1958-72.
Elbaum, Jacob. "Shalosh Derashot Ashkenaziyot Kedumot," *Kiryat Sefer* 48 (1973) 340-347.
Epstein, I. *The Responsa of Rabbi Solomon ben Adereth of Barcelona.* Reprinted New York 1968.
Erb, Peter C. "Vernacular Material for Preaching in MS Cambridge Univ. Library Ii. III. i," *Medieval Studies* 33 (1971) 63ff.
Fox, Marvin. "Hatefilah Bemaḥshavto Shel Harambam" in G. H. Cohn, ed., *Prayer in Judaism: Continuity and Change* (Jerusalem 1978), pp. 142-167.
Freimann, Alfredo. "Menaḥem b. Zeraḥ," *Annuario Di Studi Ebraici* I (1934) 147-167.
Gilat, Y. D. "Shtei Bakashot Lerabi Mosheh Mikuẓi," *Tarbiz* 28 (1959) 55.
Ginzberg, Louis. *Legends of the Jews*, 7 vols. Philadelphia 1913-1938.
Glicksberg, S. *Haderashah Beyisra'el.* Tel Aviv 1944.
Goitein, Shelomo. *A Mediterranean Society*, vol. 2. Los Angeles 1971.
Gottlieb, Efraim. *The Kabbalah in the Writings of R. Baḥya Ben Asher* (Hebrew). Tel Aviv 1970.
-----. *Meḥkarim Besifrut Hakabbalah*, ed. J. Hacker. Tel Aviv 1976.
Guttman, Julius. *Philosophies of Judaism*, trans. R. Z. Werblowsky. New York 1963.
Hakohen, Naftali. *Shem Hagedolim Alufei Ya'akov*. Haifa 1967.
Halkin, A. S. "Haḥerem 'al Limud Hapilosofiya," *Perakim* 1 (1967) 35-53.
-----. "The Medieval Attitude Toward Hebrew" in A. Altmann, ed., *Biblical and Other Studies* (Cambridge MA 1963), pp. 232-248.
-----. "Yedaia Bedershi's Apology" in A. Altmann, ed., *Jewish Medieval and Renaissance Studies* (Cambridge MA 1967), pp. 165-184.

Heinemann, Isaak. *Darkhei Ha'aggadah.* Jerusalem 1954.
-----. *Ta'amei Hamiẓvot Besifrut Yisra'el*, 2 vols. Jerusalem 1959.
-----. "Temunat Hahistorya shel RYHL," *Zion* 9 (1943) 147-177.
Heinemann, Joseph, *Aggadot Vetoldoteihem*, Jerusalem 1974.
-----. *Derashot Beẓibbur Bitkufat Hatalmud.* Jerusalem 1970.
Henoch, C. *Haramban Keḥoker Umekubal.* Jerusalem 1978.
Hirsch, W. *Rabbinic Psychology.* London 1947.
Horowitz, Carmi. "An Unpublished Derashah to *Teẓaveh*" in I. Twersky, ed., *Studies in Medieval History and Literature* (Cambridge MA 1979), pp. 261-282.
-----. "Rashba's Commentary to the Aggadot—Philosophic and Kabbalistic Aspects" (Hebrew), *Da'at* 18 (1987-8) 15-25.
Huna, Hayyim. "Sod Hadevekut Eẓel Haramban," *Sinai* 11 (1943) 86-99.
Huyser, Henkje. "The Medium is the Message." Unpublished Ph.D. thesis, Katholische Theologische Hogeschoul Te Utrecht, 1980.
Idel, Moshe. "The Concept of the Torah in Heikhalot Literature and Kabbalah," *Jerusalem Studies in Jewish Thought* (Hebrew) 1 (1981) 49-58.
-----. "An Unknown Commentary on Nahmanides' Mystic Doctrines" (Hebrew), *Da'at* 2-3 (1978-1979) 121-122.
-----. "Hasefirot Sheme'al Hasefirot," *Tarbiz* 51 (1982) 239-280.
Katz, Jacob. "Halakhah and Kabbalah—First Contacts," *Yizhak Baer Memorial Volume* (Jerusalem 1980) pp. 148-172.
-----. "Halakhah Vekabbalah Kenos'ei Limud Mitḥarim," *Da'at* 7 (1981) 37-68.
Kayserling, M. *Die Juden in Navarra.* Berlin 1861.
Klein-Braslavy, Sarah. "The Influence of R. Nissim Girondi in Crescas' and Albo's Principles," *Eshel Beersheva* 2 (1980) 177-198.
Lauterbach, Jacob Z. *Rabbinical Essays.* Cincinnati 1951.
Lieberman, Saul. "Mishnat Shir Hashirim" in G. Scholem, *Jewish Gnosticism Merkabah Mysticism and Talmudic Tradition* (New York 1965), pp. 118-126.
-----. *Sheki'in.* Jerusalem 1970.
-----. *Tosefta Kifshutah*, 14 vols. New York 1955--.
Loewinger, D. S. "R. Shem Tov b. Abraham b. Gaon," *Sefunot* 7 (1963) 9-29.
Lovejoy, A. D. *The Great Chain of Being.* New York 1960.
Meier, Menahem. "A Critical Edition of Sefer Ta'amey Hamizvot." Unpublished Ph.D. thesis, Brandeis University 1974.
Murphy, James J. *Medieval Rhetoric: A Select Bibliography.* Toronto 1971.
-----. *Rhetoric in the Middle Ages.* Berkeley 1974.
Netanyahu, Benzion. *Abravanel*, 2nd ed. Philadelphia 1968.
-----. "Zeman Ḥiburam Shel Hakanah Vehapliah," *Salo Baron Jubilee Volume* (Jerusalem 1974), Hebrew section, pp. 247-268.
Neuman, A. A. *The Jews in Spain*, 2 vols. Philadelphia 1942.
O'Callaghan, Joseph F. *A History of Medieval Spain.* Ithaca 1975.

Oust, G. R. "Literature and Pulpit in Medieval England," *Estudios Lulianos* 7 (1963) 234-235.
Pedersen, J. "The Islamic Preacher" in S. Lowinger, J. Somogyi, eds., *Ignace Goldziher Memorial Volume* I (Budapest 1948), pp. 220-250.
Perles, J. *R. Salomo b. Abraham b. Adereth, Sein Leben und seine Schriften.* Breslau 1863.
Rabinowitz, H. R. *Diyokna'ot shel Darshanim*. Jerusalem 1967.
Roth, Cecil. *Gleanings.* New York 1967.
Sandler, Perez. "Live'ayat Pardes Vehashitah Hameruba'at," *Sefer Urbach Haḥevrah Leḥeker Hamikra* (1955), pp. 222-235.
Saperstein, Marc. *Decoding the Rabbis.* Cambridge MA 1980.
Scholem, Gershom. "Der Begriff der Kavvanah in dem alten Kabbalah," *Monatschrift für Geschichte und Wissenschaft des Judenthums* 78 (1934) 492-518.
-----. *Hakabbalah Begeronah.* Jerusalem 1964.
-----. *Hakabbalah shel Sefer Hatemunah*, ed. Y. Ben Shlomo. Jerusalem 1969.
-----. "Hakarat Panim Vesidrei Sirtutin," *Sefer Hayovel Lesimḥah Assaf* (Jerusalem 1953) pp. 459-495.
-----.*Jewish Gnosticism, Merkabah Mysticism and Talmudic Tradition.* New York 1965.
-----. *Kabbalah.* Jerusalem 1974.
-----. *Kabbalat R. Ya'akov Verabi Yiẓḥak.* Jerusalem 1927. (Offprint of *Mada'ei Hayahadut* 2 [1927] 165-293).
-----. *Kitvei Yad Bekabbalah.* Jerusalem 1930.
-----. *Leḥeker Kabbalat R. Yiẓḥak Hakohen* Jerusalem 1934.
-----. "Levush Haneshamot Veḥalukka Derabanan," *Tarbiz* 24 (1955) 290-306.
-----. *Major Trends in Jewish Mysticism*, 3rd rev. ed. New York 1961.
-----. *On the Kabbalah and Its Symbolism.* New York 1965.
-----. *Perakim Letoldot Sifrut Hakabbalah.* Jerusalem 1931.
-----. *Reshit Hakabbalah.* Jerusalem 1948.
-----. "Seridei Sifro shel R. Shem Tov ibn Ga'on 'al Yesodot Torat Hasefirot," *Kiryat Sefer* 8 (1931) 397-408, 534-542; 9 (1932) 126-133.
-----. "Te'udah Ḥadashah Letoldot Reshit Hakabbalah" in Y. Fikhman, ed., *Sefer Bialik* (Tel Aviv 1934), pp. 141-162.
Schwarz, Leo. *Memoirs of My People.* New York 1963.
Schweid, Eliezer. *Harambam Veḥug Hashpa'ato*, ed. D. Oriyon. Jerusalem 1968.
Septimus, Bernard (Dov). "Ma'avak 'al shilton ẓiburi bevarẓelona bitkufat napulmus 'al sifrei harambam," *Tarbiz* 42 (1973) 389-400.
-----. "Piety and Power in 13th Century Catalonia" in I. Twersky, ed., *Studies in Medieval Jewish History and Literature* (Cambridge MA 1979), pp. 195-230.

Shalem, Shim'on. *Rabbi Moshe Alsheikh.* Jerusalem 1966.

Shilo, Samuel. *Dina Demalkhuta Dina.* Jerusalem 1975.

Spiegel, Shalom. "Me'aggadot Ha'akedah," *A. Marx Jubilee Volume* (New York 1950), pp. 471-547.

Stein, S. M. "Rationalists and Kabbalists in Medieval Allegory," *Journal of Jewish Studies* 6 (1955) 73-86.

Talmage, Frank. "David Kimḥi and the Rationalist Tradition," *HUCA* 39 (1968) 177-218.

-----. *David Kimḥi, The Man and the Commentaries.* Cambridge MA 1975.

Tishby, I. "Aggadah Vekabbalah Beferushei Ha'agadot shel R. Ezra Ve-R. Azriel Migeronah," *Minḥah Liyehudah* (Jerusalem 1950), pp. 170-174.

-----. *Mishnat Hazohar*, 2 vols. Jerusalem 1957-61.

Twersky, Isadore. "Aspects of the Social and Cultural History of Provencal Jewry," *Journal of World History* 11 (1968) 196-207.

-----. *Introduction to the Code of Maimonides (Mishneh Torah).* New Haven 1980.

-----. *A Maimonides Reader*. New York 1972.

-----. "Mishneh Torah, Megamato Vetafkido," *Proceedings of the Israel Academy of Science and Humnities* 5 (1972) 1-22.

-----. *Rabad of Posquières: A Twelfth Century Talmudist* Cambridge MA 1962.

-----. Review of *Derashah Lerosh Hashanah* of Rabad, ed. Avraham S. Halevy, *Kiryat Sefer* 32 (1957) 440-443.

-----. "The Shulḥan 'Aruk: Enduring Code of Jewish Law," *Judaism* 16 (1967) 141-159. Reprinted in J. Goldin, ed., *The Jewish Expression* (New York 1970), pp. 322-343.

-----, ed. *Rabbi Moses Nahmanides (Ramban): Explorations in his Religious and Literary Virtuosity.* Cambridge MA 1983.

-----. "R. Yedaiah Hapenini Uferusho La'agadah" in S. Stein and R. Loewe, eds., *Studies in Jewish Religious and Intellectual History Presented to Alexander Altman* (Alabama 1980), Hebrew section, pp. 63-92.

Urbach, E. E. *Ḥazal, Emunot Vede'ot.* Jerusalem 1969.

Vajda, G. "Un chapitre de l'histoire du conflit, entre la Kabbale et la Philosophie," *Archives d'Histoire Doctrinal et Littéraire du Moyen Age* (1956) 45-144.

Werblowsky, R. J. Z. "Faith, Hope and Trust: A Study in the Concept of Bitaḥon," *Papers of the Institute of Jewish Studies* 1 (1964) 95-139.

Wilensky, S. O. Heller. "Isaac ibn Latif—Philosopher or Kabbalist?" in A. Altmann, ed., *Jewish Medieval and Renaissance Studies* (Cambridge MA 1967), pp. 185-223.

Wolfson, Harry A. "Judah Hallevi on Causality and Miracles," *Mayer Waxman Jubilee Volume* (Jerusalem 1966), pp. 137-153. Reprinted in I. Twersky and G. Williams, eds., *Studies in the History of Philosophy and Religion*, vol. II (Cambridge MA 1977).

-----. "Maimonides and Hallevi in Design Chance and Necessity," *PAAJR* 11 (1941) 105-163. Reprinted in *Studies in the History of Philosophy and Religion*, vol. II, pp. 1-59.

-----. "Maimonides and Hallevy on Prophecy," *JQR* n.s. 32 (1942) 345-370; 33 (1942) 49-82. Reprinted in *Studies in the History of Philosophy and Religion*, vol. II, pp. 60-119.

-----. *Philo: Foundations of Religious Philosophy in Judaism, Christianity and Islam*, 2 vols. Cambridge MA 1962.

-----. *The Philosophy of the Kalam.* Cambridge MA 1976.

Yerushalmi, Yosef H. "The Lisbon Massacre of 1506 and the Royal Image in the Shevet Yehuda," *HUCA Supplements* 1 (1976).

Zinberg, I. *A History of Jewish Literature*, vols. II-III, trans. B. Martin. Cleveland 1972-73.

Zunz, L. *Haderashot Beyisr'ael*, ed. H. Albeck. Jerusalem 1954.

Index of Manuscript Citations

Subject Index

Index of Names

Index of Citations from Derashot al Hatorah

On the left is the page and column cited from the 1575 Cracow edition of the Derashot.

CENTER FOR JEWISH STUDIES

HARVARD JUDAIC MONOGRAPHS

1. *David Kimhi: The Man and the Commentaries*, by Frank Talmage
2. *Studies in Medieval Jewish History and Literature*, edited by Isadore Twersky
3. *Decoding the Rabbis: A Thirteenth-Century Commentary on the Aggadah*, by Marc Saperstein
4. *Hispano-Jewish Culture in Transition: The Career and Controversies of Ramah*, by Bernard Septimus
5. *Studies in Medieval Jewish History and Literature, Volume II*, edited by Isadore Twersky
6. *The Jewish Sermon in 14th Century Spain: The Derashot of R. Joshua ibn Shu'eib*, by Carmi Horowitz

HARVARD JUDAIC TEXTS AND STUDIES

I. *Rabbi Moses Naḥmanides (Ramban): Explorations in His Religious and Literary Virtuosity*, edited by Isadore Twersky

II. *Jewish Thought in the Sixteenth Century*, edited by Bernard Dov Cooperman

III. *Christian Hebraists and Dutch Rabbis: Seventeenth Century Apologetics and the Study of Maimonides' "Mishneh Torah,"* by Aaron Katchen

IV. *Danzig: Between East and West*, edited by Isadore Twersky

V. *Hasidism: Continuity or Innovation*, edited by Bezalel Safran

VI. *Jewish Thought in the Seventeenth Century*, edited by Isadore Twersky and Bernard Septimus